Nineteenth-century adventure fiction relating to the British empire usually served to promote, celebrate, and justify the imperial project, asserting the essential and privileging difference between 'us' and 'them', colonizing and colonized. Andrea White's study opens with an examination of popular exploration literature in relation to later adventure stories, showing how a shared view of the white man in the tropics authorized the European intrusion into other lands. She then sets the fiction of Joseph Conrad in this context, showing how Conrad in fact demythologized and disrupted the imperial subject constructed in earlier writing, by simultaneously – with the modernist's double vision – admiring man's capacity to dream but applauding the desire to condemn many of its consequences. She argues that the very complexity of Conrad's work provided an alternative, and more critical, means of evaluating the experience of empire.

# JOSEPH CONRAD AND THE ADVENTURE TRADITION

# JOSEPH CONRAD AND THE ADVENTURE TRADITION

Constructing and deconstructing the imperial subject

ANDREA WHITE

Department of English, California State University at Northridge

CAMBRIDGE
UNIVERSITY PRESS

Published by the Press Syndicate of the University of Cambridge
The Pitt Building, Trumpington Street, Cambridge CB2 1RP
40 West 20th Street, New York, NY 10011–4211, USA
10 Stamford Road, Oakleigh, Melbourne 3166, Australia

First published 1993
Reprinted 1995

Printed in Great Britain at Antony Rowe Ltd, Chippenham, Wiltshire

*A catalogue record for this book is available from the British Library*

*Library of Congress cataloguing in publication data*

White, Andrea.
Joseph Conrad and the adventure tradition: constructing and
deconstructing the imperial subject / by Andrea White.
p.   cm.
Includes bibliographical references and index.
ISBN 0–521–41606–x (hardback)
1. Conrad, Joseph, 1857–1924 – Criticism and interpretation. 2. Adventure stories, English
– History and criticism. 3. Imperialism in literature. 4. Colonies in literature.
I. Title.
PR6005.04Z928   1993
823'.912—dc20        92–15469        CIP

ISBN 0 521 41606 x hardback

*To my Parents,*
*Gretchen and Douglas Stapel*

In the next land we found were Kyklopês,
giants, louts, without a law to bless them.
In ignorance leaving the fruitage of the earth in mystery
to the immortal gods, they neither plow
nor sow by hand, nor till the ground, though grain –
wild wheat and barley – grows untended, and
wine-grapes, in clusters, ripen in heaven's rain.

The Odyssey

Either [Columbus] conceives the Indians (though without using
these words) as human beings altogether, having the same rights
as himself; but then he sees them not only as equals but also as
identical, and this behavior leads to assimiliationism, the
projection of his own values on the others. Or else he starts from
the difference, but the latter is immediately translated into terms
of superiority and inferiority (in his case, obviously, it is the
Indians who are inferior). What is denied is the existence of a
human substance truly other, something capable of being not
merely an imperfect state of oneself. These two elementary
figures of the experience of alterity are both grounded in
egocentrism, in the identification of our own values with values
in general, of our *I* with the universe – in the conviction that the
world is one.

Tzvetan Todorov, The Conquest of America

Surely, an idiom should never incline toward racism. It often
does, however, and this is not altogether fortuitous: there's no
racism without a language. The point is not that acts of racial
violence are only words but rather that they have to have a
word. Even though it offers the excuse of blood, color, birth – or,
rather *because* it uses this naturalist and sometimes creationist
discourse – racism always betrays the perversion of a man, the
"talking animal." It institutes, declares, writes, inscribes,
prescribes. A system of marks, it outlines space in order to assign
forced residence or to close off borders. It does not discern, it
discriminates.

Jacques Derrida, "Racism's Last Word"

"Mr. Baldwin, I presume!"

<blockquote>Chinua Achebe's greeting to James Baldwin upon finally
meeting him "in the jungles of Florida in 1988..."</blockquote>

Chinua Achebe, Hopes and Impediments

# Contents

# Acknowledgments

My special thanks go to Vincent J. Cheng at the University of Southern California, under whose direction I began this work. Without his time – which he gave abundantly – his good counsel, his generous support and enthusiasm, this project would have been daunting, indeed. The entire generative process was made even more productive through the pertinent and helpful suggestions and observations of Professors David Eggenschwiler and John Wills, Jr., also of the University of Southern California.

I am also mindful of the extent to which the work that preceded my own enabled it. Certainly one of the great contributions to recent Conrad scholarship has been the multi-volume collection of Conrad's letters edited by Frederick R. Karl and Laurence Davies. I do not know which facilitated my project more, those volumes or my word-processor; both were indispensable. Another prior discourse whose influence, both direct and indirect, has had a profound effect on my own thinking is the work of Michel Foucault and other major theorists writing today about literary representations of the Other. Like the works of those writers, this study considers discourse to be a form of power; words matter. My hope for such a focus, an admittedly immodest one, is that the xenophobia and racism that still plague our private thinking and public lives might be affected – even reversed – by such a willingness to understand the powerful ideological content of our discourse and to make visible the often tragic relationship that exists between those words and the patterns of domination they authorize.

I would also like to acknowledge the helpfulness, at various stages of the writing, of my colleagues, Barbara Gleason, Thomas Wolfe, and Kim Gillespie, all of whom offered insights and arguments that challenged and enriched my own. Finally, it has been Bernard, Naomi, and Molly White who have provided the community of support and confidence necessary for such an undertaking.

# Introduction

When F. R. Leavis, one of the early rescuers of Joseph Conrad's then uncertain literary reputation, included that writer in his "Great Tradition" in 1948, he saved Conrad from the "infernal tail of ships" Conrad claimed followed him (Jean-Aubrey, *Conrad*, II, p. 316). In doing so, he privileged Conrad's more obviously modernist productions, thus securing for the Polish sailor a place in the academy. As a result, Leavis, the academy, and the anthologies gave short shrift to the early works and consigned them to an easily forgotten shelf marked "apprentice fiction," as though they were maverick, somehow, and therefore of little significance. However, ideas intrinsic to those early works pertain throughout Conrad's work. The books are especially significant in their pivotal attitudes towards the subject of empire.

Reading Conrad only in Leavis' "great" tradition would not only silence the early work, but also necessitate a particular point of view, one that places Conrad in the established mainstream of English novelists. Leavis admits that Conrad "brought a great deal from outside", and goes on to assert, rather vaguely, that, nonetheless,

it was of the utmost importance to him that he found a serious art of fiction there in English, and that there *were*, in English, great novelists to study. He drew from English literature what he needed, and learnt in that peculiar way of genius which is so different from imitation. And for us, who have *him* as well as the others, there he is, unquestionably a constitutive part of the tradition, belonging in the full sense. (*The Great Tradition*, p. 18)

But I would like to suggest that what Conrad brought from "outside," were not only the works of "the French masters," whose influence Leavis admits, but also the very "minor" English works that Leavis would omit from his canon as representing merely the "present vogue of the Victorian age," and here he instances, among

I

others, Anthony Trollope and Frederick Marryat (p. 1). These writers and others definitely outside Leavis' "great" tradition shaped Conrad's thinking fundamentally. In fact, as Ford Madox Ford so irreverently phrased it, as a mariner, it "was Conrad's great good luck to be spared the usual literature that attends the upbringing of the British writer," picking up instead "such dogeared books as are found in the professional quarters of ships' crews" (Ford, *Conrad*, p. 96). But of course, Ford also occupies only the extreme margins of Leavis' study.

It was this largely non-canonical reading, his particular Polish past, and his actual participation as a proud member of the British Merchant Marine in the business of empire that led to his particular interest in the imperial subject. He was influenced from an early age by the legends about and writings by the heroic figure of the day, the explorer-adventurer, and he wrote appreciatively about the civilizing work of Captain James Cook, Sir John Franklin, Francis Leopold McClintock, R.N., Rajah James Brooke, and David Livingstone – all English explorers. And the realization he arrived at, which in so many ways precipitated his writing in the first place, resulted from the great disparity he himself witnessed between the aspirations and reported achievements of these figures, on the one hand, and the actual conditions at the outposts themselves, on the other. It was this degeneration he was moved to record, cherishing the disinterested ideals associated with these early adventurers while marking the sordid realities those dreams had in fact engendered.

Ironically, perhaps Ford was attempting a similar rescue maneuver in maintaining that *Almayer's Folly* was begun on the flyleaf of Conrad's copy of *Madame Bovary* (Ford, *Conrad*, p. 107). Even though Conrad himself never made such a concrete and direct connection between Flaubert's work and his own first novel, Ford's contention, apocryphal or not, does provide Conrad with a more respectable lineage than the one he provides for himself with his references to Captain Cook and Captain Marryat. Much can be gained, I believe, by contextualizing the "apprentice work" differently, neither in the "great" tradition nor in the Flaubertian tradition, thus enabling another way of looking at and valuing it and the work that immediately follows. This study will attempt to provide a context for the reading of Conrad's early work as it contributed to the on-going imperial conversation, and to understand the historical, biographical, and literary forces at work at the time, the horizontal influences working upon him as well as the traditions he inherited as he first started to write.

Attitudes towards empire can be tracked throughout the late nineteenth century in the enormously popular travel writing, the adventure fiction, and in the periodical literature of the day. As part of such a pursuit, an understanding of Conrad's early work is essential, and while illuminating that pursuit, such a view illuminates the work itself. However, in 1924, the year of Conrad's death, in an attempt made to assess the influence of literature on imperial outlooks, a multi-volume work, called *The British Empire*, included as one of its volumes *The Literature and the Art of the Empire* which failed to mention the name of Joseph Conrad. The work was inspired by the British Empire Exhibition which was taking place in London that year in order to "bring vividly before the public... the vast material resources and industries of the Empire ..." As the work's editor, Hugh Gunn, explained in the preface, the "time seemed appropriate for such a survey," since the Empire, whose "Dominions had contributed so magnificently to the victory," had so recently "emerged victorious from the greatest of wars." Given the date and the occasion, in the flush of perceived imperial strength – never mind that 1924 was also the year Gandhi was released from prison and demands for Indian Independence were vehemently renewed – the assumptions and coverage of the "survey" were foregone. Literature, according to Gunn and the volume's author, Edward Salmon, could be divided into works that treated the imperial subject and those that did not, a division that seems to have pertained throughout the later part of the nineteenth century also. Little interest in the "domestic" fiction is displayed here, while of the former, much is written, but rather selectively, about those with attitudes conducive to imperial unity. Kingsley, Ballantyne, Marryat, Kipling, Henty, and Haggard are heralded as having done their share to "inculcate knowledge of, and pride in, the Empire" (Salmon, *Literature and Art of the Empire*, p. 116) and having provided a counter influence to the provincial thinking of such a "Little Englander" as Thomas Hardy (p. 158). Of Stevenson's fiction, Salmon mentions only *Treasure Island* and can thus happily pronounce him an imperialist, describing him as having the "very qualities of the Empire-builder" (p. 149). And even though Hugh Clifford is congratulated here for making "Malaya and North Borneo in sketch and story peculiarly his own" (p. 117), no mention at all is made of Joseph Conrad, not for failing to treat the imperial subject, but, we can only suppose, for not depicting it in the spirit of the current exhibition.

And his exclusion is not only strange but ironic. Conrad would have shared Gunn's admiration for the books he describes as "entrancing reminiscences or records of men who went forth from these islands as Pioneers to brave the perils of uncharted seas and the dangers of unknown lands, inspired more by the spirit of adventure inherent in the race than by any calculated design for personal gain or lust for the acquisition of new territories" (p. iii). It was those "books of travel and discovery" which made the sea for Conrad a "hallowed" ground, he confessed, written by or about "men great in their endeavour and in hard-won successes of militant geography...each bearing in his breast a spark of the sacred fire," among them Mungo Park, James Cook, and David Livingstone (*Last Essays*, p. 21). But for Conrad, adventuring and pioneering, while often admirable endeavors, were not synonomous with empire-building; they were, in fact, antithetical.

As many recent readers of Conrad have noticed and discussed, his works certainly addressed the imperial subject. Irving Howe's *Politics and the Novel*, written in the centenary year, 1957, Eloise Knapp Hay's *The Political Novels of Joseph Conrad* (1963), and Avrom Fleishman's *Conrad's Politics* (1967) all argue for both the importance to his work and the complexity of Conrad's political views. In doing so, they qualify on the one hand such influential works as Thomas Moser's *Joseph Conrad: Achievement and Decline* (1957), Albert J. Guerard's *Conrad the Novelist* (1958), and Ian Watt's *Conrad in the Nineteenth Century* (1979) which all appraise Conrad's significance in other than political terms, and refute on the other hand those simplistic cold war views then current of Conrad as a kind of spokesman against "Communist tyranny and revolutionary brutality" (Fleishman, *Conrad's Politics*, p. vii). That Conrad was politically conservative, all these writers readily admit; that he was the "aristo-royalist apologist" Ford and Conrad's early biographer, Leo Gurko, suggested is a view they resist (Fleishman, *Conrad's Politics*, p. vii). That he was also an anti-imperialist, they all argue too but for different reasons and with varying qualifications. However, their interest in Conrad's understanding of people as members of social/political communities leads them to study primarily the vast political canvases of *Nostromo*, *The Secret Agent*, and *Under Western Eyes* rather than the early work. Nor does their scrutiny allow them to consider the genre in which

Conrad's pre-1900 work belonged and the role played by that particular "form of disclosure" (Todorov, *Conquest*, p. 253), which is the aim of this study.

As a function of his particular conservatism, Conrad saw that rapacious expansionism was as undesirable as revolution, and the intent of his fiction was to unmask the benevolent pretensions of either cause, suspecting all causes to be tainted, as he confided to his socialist friend R. B. Cunninghame Graham (Watts, *Letters*, p. 68). From within the genre that had constructed the imperial subject, then, he wrote a fiction at odds with the traditional assumptions of the genre that was being used increasingly in the service of imperial expansion. For many contemporary readers, the familiarity of the discourse masked the subversion; for them Conrad's early writing was simply adventure fiction *manqué*. Conrad was aware that his choice of genres might predispose an audience long accustomed to adventure fiction and its assertions to read his fiction similarly. He admitted to Richard Curle in a letter written not many months before his death that

the nature of my writing runs the risk of being obscured by the nature of my material. I admit it is natural; but only the appreciation of a special personal intelligence can counteract the superficial appreciation of the inferior intelligence of the mass of readers and critics. (Jean-Aubry, *Conrad*, II, p. 316)

Even though the subversion of Conrad's island world, the Borneo of his early fiction, had been anticipated by Robert Louis Stevenson's South Sea fictions whose unheroic depictions of dissolute white men in empire's outposts helped create an audience for Conrad's writing, the audience was indeed a limited one who saw that Conrad was using adventure as a lever against the traditional framework (Zweig, *The Adventurer*, p. 189) and who applauded his effort to do so. Choosing to write from within the fiction that had traditionally celebrated an unqualified kind of heroism, Conrad achieved a critical irony but also announced his own regret that the dream of pure, disinterested adventure was no longer possible.

What, then, characterized this genre so familiar to Conrad and to his readers? Over the course of the nineteenth century, when nationalism and expansionism were major themes of European life and thought, adventure fiction evolved into a genre that demanded of its audience particular responses, and in doing so obeyed particular conventions. Most genre studies assume, along with Tzvetan Todorov, that "the form of disclosure is connected to the ideologies in force," that any genre affords, even necessitates, a special way of seeing, one that responds to current concerns in a culture (Todorov, *Conquest*, p. 253). Certainly, then, the concurrence of the English adventure novel's great popularity in the nineteenth century with the growth of Britain's empire into an extensive and formidable world power was not an accidental one. Like any other genre, adventure fiction reflected and constructed a social reality. This adventure fiction and much of the travel writing of the time also purported to chronicle the English adventure in the lands beyond Europe then being explored and colonized, but they did so in such a manner that they formed the energizing myth of English imperialism. While seeming to inform the stay-at-homes, this writing shaped a particular outlook. In fact, as these discourses engaged in narrating the story of the white man in the tropics, sorting out who those Others were who inhabited the foreign lands, who the tellers and readers of the story were, what their relationships were, what was civilization and what was savagery, the overall stance was largely interpretive and as such served as the culture's dominant fiction, arguing that the benefits of civilization justified the white man's – especially the Englishman's – incursions into other lands.

In thus constituting the imperial subject, the genre of adventure fiction was extremely powerful, but by the early years of the twentieth century, its evolved interpretation was not only challenged from without – the Boer War turned many staunch supporters of imperialism into skeptics – but it was also subverted from within. The fiction underwent a change from that of Marryat, Ballantyne, Henty, and Haggard, which expressed an intoxication with the imperial subject, to a fiction that reflected changing and often complex attitudes towards imperialism. Conrad's early work, anticipated in some respects by Haggard and, as already mentioned, by Stevenson, demythologized the basic assumptions of the very genre it appeared to derive from. *Almayer's Folly* (1895), *An Outcast of the Islands* (1896), "An Outpost of Progress" (1897) and "Heart of Darkness" (1899) were all written out of the tradition of adventure fiction and showed profound influences of that form. As an early reviewer of *Youth* noted, the volume that included "Heart of Darkness," "in no one is the essence of the adventurous spirit more instinctive" than in Conrad (Sherry, *Conrad*, p. 135). Like many Victorians before him, Conrad admired man's capacity to dream, to reach, but he had the modernist's double vision which demanded that he applaud the desire but condemn its disastrous consequences, both at once. And as the maps filled up, the dreams gave way to facts, often unpalatable ones, and the adventure turned inward.

Conrad's works, then, were initially read within or against that tradition also, but they challenged to greater or lesser extents the ways in which that form had constituted the imperial subject. In his fiction, the nature of the telling itself made the tale suspect; it lent instability rather than authority. The method involved the reader in moral judgments that were no longer simple and depicted situations without offering conclusive interpretations. This study will explore the ways in which nineteenth-century adventure fiction reinscribed the imperial subject already constructed by the currently popular travel writing; the great power of both genres on several generations of British readers; and Conrad's subsequent demythologizing of that subject in his early fiction, thus providing a different, more illuminating context for the early works.

# CHAPTER I

# Constructing the imperial subject : nineteenth-century travel writing

In 1891, the year after Kipling returned from India to London, Joseph Conrad spent most of his time in hospital recovering from the Congo. Stevenson's works *The Wrecker* and *In the South Seas* were published that year, as was "Mr. Kipling's Stories," an essay by Andrew Lang, himself a prominent writer/critic and one-time collaborator with H. Rider Haggard. In this essay, Lang wrote appreciatively of the new adventure literature:

There has, indeed, arisen a taste for exotic literature: people have become alive to the strangeness and fascination of the world beyond the bounds of Europe and the United States. But that is only because men of imagination and literary skill have been the new conquerors – the Corteses and Balboas of India, Africa, Australia, Japan, and the isles of the Southern Seas. All such conquerors, whether they write with the polish of M. Pierre Loti, or with the carelessness of Mr. Boldrewood, have, at least, seen new worlds for themselves; have gone out of the streets of the over-populated lands into the open air; have sailed and ridden, walked and hunted; have escaped from the fog and smoke of towns. New strength has come from fresher air into their brains and blood, hence the novelty and buoyancy of the stories which they tell. (Lang, *Essays*, p. 200)

Lang's impression is borne out by the commercial success of adventure stories. Captain Mayne Reid's *The Scalp Hunters* (1851), a romance of northern Mexico, sold over a million copies in Great Britain alone by 1890. Charles Kingsley's *Westward Ho!* (1855) sold 8,000 in two years and in an 1889 sixpence reprint, it sold over 500,000 copies. Robert Louis Stevenson's works were re-issued, collected and translated into at least twenty different languages; and three different novels by H. Rider Haggard ran concurrently in various periodicals in one year, 1887. His *Allan Quatermain* sold 10,000 copies in one year alone, 1888. Of G. A. Henty's sales, his publisher W. G. Blackie claimed "that with our figure [some 3,514,000 printed and presumably sold], Scribner's and Donohue's plus an unknown quantity for other pirated editions, it looks as if 25,000,000 is not impossible" (Arnold, *Held Fast*, p. 17). R. M. Ballantyne wrote over 100 books, all of them extremely popular throughout the century, especially *The Coral Island* (1857) and *Black Ivory* (1873).

Of course, the "exotic literature" that Lang describes here did not simply "arise," and readers did not magically "become alive" to the attractions of foreign climes. Those interests had been created, in great part, by the travel narratives that were also immensely popular, a genre whose initial construction of the imperial subject greatly influenced adventure fiction. At least since Richard Hakluyt's *The Principall Navigations, Voiages and Discoveries of the English Nation* first appeared in 1589, travel writing about lands newly discovered by England promised to inform an increasingly interested readership at home while it also sought to encourage continued exploration, colonization, and the development of trade. By 1772, the publications of volumes about such sensational journeys of discovery as James Cook's second voyage to the South Seas were eagerly awaited; consequently, the acquisition of officers' journals and log-books was the subject of great competition among the publishers of the day. According to a note in an 1860 edition of Cook's voyages, Cook had collected his officers' journals and log-books on the homeward leg of their journey to seal and turn over to the Admiralty. Unknown to him, his coxswain and boatswain's mate had each kept journals which they had offered to booksellers, who, eager for any advance copy, would have published them. However, as Cook explained in a letter to the Admiralty, "they were so badly written that no one could read them" (Barrow (ed.), *Voyages*, n. 212). Semi-literate or not, the coxswain's and boatswain's accounts might have told a story the Admiralty was not anxious to have published, an account at variance with the official view of empire-expanding travel and its hero, the navigator-explorer-traveller.

That this figure was an influential nineteenth-century hero can be seen in the actual listings of contemporary publications which chronicle the growth of and changes in this literature about other lands. According to *The New Cambridge Bibliography of English Literature* (*NCBEL*), 1800–1900, travel writing had been a prominent genre for over two centuries, and while books about America and Europe remained popular, the emphasis had shifted from books in the eighteenth century about Asia and the coasts of Africa to those in the nineteenth century about Australia and the Pacific and the African interior. With the expansion of empire, books about those newly acquired countries multiplied; the travel writing, both non-fiction and fiction, followed the explorers and travellers, and an increasing market for their accounts flourished back home in England's urban centers. Under "Africa" alone, *NCBEL* lists seventy-five books, among them titles such as Sir Richard Francis Burton's *The Lake Regions of Central Equatorial Africa* (1860), the Rev. James Stewart's *Zambesi Journal* (1862–3), John Hanning Speke's *Journal of Discovery of the Source of the Nile* (1863) and Sir Henry Morton Stanley's *Through the Dark Continent* (1878). And one such work even appears on Richard Altick's "best seller" list of nineteenth-century books, David Livingstone's *Missionary Travels and Researches in South Africa* (1857) which sold over 70,000 copies such was the interest at home in the English experience in Africa (Altick, *Common Reader*, p. 388 and Jeal, *Livingstone*, p. 163). According to one of Livingstone's biographers, the first edition of 12,000 copies was over-subscribed before it was even published (Simmons, *Livingstone and Africa*, p. 73). Arctic exploration also commanded popular attention, for another nineteenth-century best seller was Sir Leopold McClintock's *The Voyage of the Fox in the Arctic Seas* (1859) which sold 12,000 copies by 1863 (Altick, *Common Reader*, p. 388). Among this book's enthusiasts was Conrad who wrote of it in "Geography and Some Explorers" that although a little book, "it records with manly simplicity the tragic ending of a great tale," i.e. Sir John Franklin's polar expedition. Conrad explains its "falling into [his] hands by the fact that the fate of Sir John Franklin was a matter of European interest, and that Sir Leopold McClintock's book was translated, I believe, into every language of the white races" (*Last Essays*, p. 11). His copy, which he claims to have read when he and it were ten years old, "was in French." Other books he referred to, Sir James Brooke's *A Letter from Borneo* (1842) and Alfred Wallace's *The Malay Archipelago* (1869) are also among *NCBEL*'s abundant listings for "Australia and the Pacific."[1] Charles Doughty's *Travels in Arabia Deserta* (1880) and Isabella Bird Bishop's *Journeys in Persia and Kurdistan* (1891) are characteristic of the numerous entries under "Asia."

Eagerly awaited and widely read, these "travels," "researches," "journals," and "voyages," then, suggested a certain disinterested objectivity and promised to inform. With accompanying maps, appendices, charts, "views" sketched by on-the-spot draftsmen, and, as the nineteenth century wore on, photographs, the genre represented itself as non-fiction. The prefaces to these works abounded with the journal writer's declarations of intent to inform and professions of ineptitude as to being anything other than a straightforward, plain writer of unembellished facts. The discourse repeated these intentions, and appended were data-filled footnotes about flora and fauna, technical accounts of bearings, and apparently disinterested details of native life. In spite of this non-fictional stance, however, these works were, in actuality, shaped in large part by official thought and prevailing ideologies and in turn shaped the attitudes of readers towards the English presence in the outposts of empire. Distinguished knights, devoted officers in Her Majesty's Royal Navy, or intrepid missionaries, most of these travellers were on official business, and whether the official project involved scientific explorations, the opening of trade routes, and/or the establishment of missions, as representatives of church and state, their "notes" and "journals of discoveries" were ideologically charged. While it is true that the views of individual travellers on the imperial endeavor, race, civilization, and progress were not identical and that significant differences of opinion mark their writings, the depiction of the white man and the Other, in the travel writing of such disparate figures as Cook, McClintock, Brooke, Speke, and Livingstone, generally served imperial concerns well.

## CAPTAIN JAMES COOK

So valorized was this genre and its hero, the explorer, that even perceptive readers were unwilling to consider the discourse as subjective or tendentious. Although Conrad claimed that the aims of many early explorers were "prompted by an acquisitive spirit, the idea of lucre in some form, the desire of trade or the desire of loot, disguised in more or less fine words" (*Last Essays*, p. 10), he praised Captain James Cook's three voyages as being free from that taint of acquisitiveness. But something – albeit less palpable than loot – drove Cook repeatedly to abandon London, a growing family, and the congenial company at the Mitre Inn. Did Conrad claim a kinship with Cook who also, after several years of plying the coal route from Newcastle to London, signed on for deep-water sailing, preferring, as Jacques Darras noticed, "raw life to cooked"? (Darras, *Empire*, p. 146 n).

Cook's voyages, of course, like those of most explorer-travellers of the time, were being officially financed for commercial and political as well as for scientific purposes. Even this most admirable of eighteenth-century geographer/navigators set the pattern in many ways for the explorations to follow in the nineteenth century and looked with the same possessive eye on the lands he "discovered" as had explorers at least since Columbus. The sense of opportunity and possession as God-given and unopposed informs the writings of Cook and expresses an attitude the European continued to have and to express toward lands newly discovered by him. Although Edward Said is speaking here of an outlook characteristic of the nineteenth century, both early and late, he is accurately describing Cook's ideological baggage also: "[The] distant hegemony over nonwhite peoples seemed inscribed by right in the very fabric of European and Western Christian society, whether that society was liberal, monarchical, or revolutionary" (Deane (ed.), *Nationalism*, p. 71). In expressing such attitudes, these narratives projected the image of the benevolent white man bearing the light of civilization to the dark, "undiscovered" places of the earth. Although Cook's first voyage in 1768 was not expressly expansionist but a primarily scientific expedition under the sponsorship of both the Admiralty and the Royal Society, his journal from that first voyage records that upon completion of the scientific observation of the transit of Venus across the sun's disc, Cook continued his exploration of the Pacific, under orders to chart those seas and make further discoveries. In so doing, he claimed many islands in the South Seas for England. His journal entry for Tuesday, August 21, 1770 records such a landing on the southwest coast of Australia:

I now once More hoisted English Colours, and in the Name of His Majesty King George the Third took possession of the whole Eastern coast from the above Lat. down to this place by the Name of New Wales, together with all the Bays, Harbours, Rivers, and Islands, situated upon the said Coast; after which we fired 3 Volleys of small Arms, which were answer'd by the like number from the Ship. (Wharton, *Cook's Journal*, p. 312)

Cook had aptly named the island on which he performed this ceremony Possession Island. Like Adam naming the animals, Cook thus enacts his dominion over the "undiscovered" part of creation; naming whatever he "finds," as he does throughout these voyages, he announces and confirms the white man's God-given sovereignty in an apparently transparent prose.

And, indeed, based on his recommendations of the lands he then discovered, charted, named, and claimed for trade and colonization, he was sent on two more voyages to the South Seas well supplied with garden seeds, domestic animals "and such articles of commerce as were most likely to promote a friendly intercourse with the natives and to induce them to open a traffic with the English" (Barrow (ed.), *Voyages*, p. 231). By the third voyage, the telling of which had to be taken over by Captain King upon Cook's death, he is not only possessing "virgin" lands in the name of the English king, but he is also dispossessing "interlopers." Arriving at "Otaheite" Cook learns that Spanish ships, in his absence, have arrived from Lima about eight months before and that they have "taken possession of the island, in the name of his Catholic Majesty," and have inscribed a cross with the Spanish King's name, and date of the year 1777. Feeling that "these erections" indicated "a deeper design than the natives were aware," Cook "took the liberty to pull down and carry away [the cross], telling them at the same time to beware of their Spanish visitors, and not to be over-fond of them." A few days later, Cook "caused the Spanish inscription to be erased, the cross to be effaced, and a new inscription to be cut, with the name of the English ships that had discovered the island, the date 1772 when first discovered, and the name of his Majesty, King George, to take place of that of the Spanish King Carlos" (Rickman, *Journal*, pp. 132–133). The image projected here is of the Englishman's claims to the land as a rightful privilege and even as a duty. While the Spanish have deep "designs" on the unsophisticated natives, the moral intentions of England's enterprise are placed beyond questioning by Cook's implied desire to protect these people against Catholic Spain's machinations and his decisiveness in doing so. This "othering" will become a familiar note in the travel writing of the next century also. Next to the diabolical Spanish, Cook places the "hearty English tars" and congratulates them on their cheerfulness and alertness (Barrow (ed.), *Voyages*, pp. 96, 99).

But it is the native as Other that pervades this discourse even more consistently. The actions described above would seem even more magnanimous to readers when they remember who these natives are Cook is so dutiful in protecting, depicted as they have been, as undeserving of Cook's generosity. Throughout these voyages he complains of what he refers to as the people's thievery, although Cook's most recent biographer suggests an alternate construction:

"visiting canoes tended to disregard European ethics of trade, paddling off without return for what they were given" (Beaglehole, *Life*, p. 204). But Beaglehole's description admits of a cultural relativism apparently unavailable to Cook who makes one of his few philosophical observations on the subject, that the more "natural" man's state, the more he is given to thievery. And when he makes the even more bald statement that the lighter skinned people are less addicted to thievery (*Captain Cook's Journals*, p. 118), the racist implications are masked, coming as these remarks do from a man of science, valued by Dr. Johnson, among others, for his "accuracy" (Boswell, *Life*, p. 722). Natural or not, Cook hopes to teach the natives that theft is a crime and, as such, punishable. Always fair, Cook tries accused thieves before judging them. But just as firmly, he then sentences the guilty ones to the loss of one or both ears "to intimidate the people from meddling with what was not their own; at the same time they were given to understand that theft, among us, was considered as a capital crime" (Rickman, *Journal*, p. 174). In other words, this writing informs us, the natives, a rather undeserving lot, got off easy, and the white man emerges as firm and decisive but extremely judicious in representing and enforcing civilized order. Somehow the contradiction between the reports of victorious deeds of "possession" – "inscribed by right," after all – and those punishable acts of thievery is made invisible. Apparently, claiming for one's own country the lands of another does not constitute theft or "meddling."

That evils such as thievery are "natural" is at some variance with the prevailing admiration, since at least Rousseau's *Discours sur les Arts et Sciences* in 1749, for the Noble Savage. But while he tried to resist already formulated attitudes and "see new worlds for himself," Cook was not immune to the ideological forces of his age, paradoxical as they were. In fact the "double movement" Todorov attributes to Columbus, who saw the native as both Noble Savage and Dirty Dog and thus potential slave, also characterizes Cook's reflections. On the one hand he often writes that contact with Englishmen could improve native life – the native is in need of improving, if not enslaving – but he also questions the rightness of that endeavor. About "the natives of New Holland," he writes in his journal for August, 1771, and later, upon his return home to London, he repeats in a letter to a friend the following thought: "They are far more happier than we Europeans; being wholy [sic] unacquainted not only with the superfluous but the necessary Conveniences so much sought after in Europe, they are happy in not knowing the use of them. They live in a Tranquillity which is not disturb'd by the Inequality of Condition..." (Beaglehole, *Life*, p. 252 and Megaw (ed.), *Discoverer*, p. 56).[2]

But this stance, that the native's life is an attractive and even enviable one, somehow does not prevent Cook from repeating the view that these primitive people will benefit from their encounter with the English. His predominant view, after all, is of the native as naked – "they haven't the invention to clothe themselves" (Rickman, *Journal*, p. 240) – and here he echoes Columbus. For both men, and particularly for Victorian explorers to follow, the observation carried with it a kind of license to intrude. To these Europeans, clothes signified culture. Thus, the absence of clothing/culture invited "us" to view "them" as an inhuman part of nature, whose assets and defects could be catalogued as though they were useful, or miserable, animals. And of course, if the native was culturally virgin, he was "a blank page awaiting [European] inscription" (Todorov, *Conquest*, p. 36).

But the claims of this discourse to straightforward truth telling precluded disbelief, and the ethos of the non-fictional narrator invited approval. Cook understood this equation and was, in fact, outraged to find upon returning home from his second voyage his first journal transformed by a professional writer who had been paid £6,000 to add classical flourishes to Cook's plain prose. Thus, instead of "I walked about with the king of the island," the inflated version read "the commander pursued his journey under the auspices of the potentate" (Barrow (ed.), *Voyages*, p. xiii). Instead of "birds," we get "feathered choristers" and so on. Cook forbade its publication but wrote a preface to an account of his second voyage in which he defended his own plain style and hoped the reader would remember that since he had been "constantly at sea from his youth" he had not had "the opportunity of cultivating letters." Furthermore, he argued, a plain style suited the non-fictional nature of the work:

as I am on the point of sailing on a third expedition, I leave this account of my last voyage in the hands of some friends, who are pleased to think that what I have here to relate is better given in my own words, than in the words by another person, especially as it is a work designed for information, and not merely for amusement; in which it is their opinion that candour and fidelity will counterbalance the want of ornament. (Barrow (ed.), *Voyages*, pp. xiii, xiv)

As we shall see, this image of the adventurer as a non-bookish, practical man becomes a familiar one throughout travel narratives and adventure fiction. H. Rider Haggard's Allan Quatermain, for example, prides himself on being an unlettered, plain-spoken, old elephant hunter. G. A. Henty's heroes and Ballantyne's narrators similarly assert their authority to write on the basis of actual experience rather than scholarly knowledge, and the assertion serves to win the reader's confidence in the teller's credibility. Unschooled as he might have been, Cook knew that as non-fiction, this writing made its greatest appeal as referential, not expressive or persuasive, prose; thus genre expectations constrained him to assert his authority to write on the basis of actual experience, and the assertion served to win the reader's confidence in the teller's credibility. And the travel writer not only had first-hand knowledge of his subject, but also the aims of the travel adventure itself were so thoroughly revealed – in prefaces, footnotes and the discourse itself – that readers viewed the enterprise as innocent.[3] But the assumption that remained unexamined here was that one's "own words" are somehow neutral and not already saturated with dominant ideologies, that "candour" and "fidelity" are somehow synonymous.

For the purpose of the nineteenth century's intensified empire-building, however, and the Victorian propensity for "fine words," Cook's style was a bit too plain and lacked the moral tone necessary to such a heroic endeavor. Victorian biographers wanted to produce a grander figure than Cook's plain words suggested, and one such myth-maker, Captain Albert Markham, R.N., wrapped Cook's first voyage in fine words indeed. In his 1891 biography of Sir John Franklin, Markham spoke of Cook and the long sought southern continent, parts of it already sighted by the Dutch:

All was vagueness, uncertainty, and conjecture. It remained for our great navigator Cook to lift the veil of doubt and uncertainty which still enshrouded the great southern land, and by his ability and energy to give to his country a continent that in riches and importance is now second to no empire in the world. (Markham, *Franklin*, p. 23)

The image of the white man, particularly the Englishman, as "one of us," "our great navigator Cook," opposes him to an implied and inferior Other who inhabits that dark world the white man illuminates and enlivens as he "lifts the veil" and removes the shroud in the service of empire. The fine words here betray the moral stance.

As certain as light and life are preferable to darkness and death is the unquestionable good of this expedition. The formulation as such places the endeavor beyond scrutiny.

Markham and other Victorian biographers, then, tried to shape the legend by interjecting the moral tone absent in Cook's own writing. Occasionally a smoothing out of the too revealing rough edges of Cook's matter-of-factness was also demanded. For example, Cook's journal entry for Tuesday, October 10, 1769 narrates a scuffle that ensued in which several Maoris were killed upon his crew's attempt to land off New Zealand's North Island coast. Not complying with Cook's commands to aid them, a canoe full of Maoris began to attack the Englishmen instead, thus "obliging" Cook

to fire upon them, and unfortunately either 2 or 3 were kill'd and one wounded, and 3 jumped overboard. These last we took up and brought on board, where they was [sic] Cloathed and Treated with all imaginable kindness. . . . I am aware that most Humane men who have not experienced things of this nature will Censure my Conduct in firing upon the People in their Boat, nor do I myself think that the reason I had for seizing upon her will at all justify me; and had I thought that they would have made the Least Resistance I would not have come near them; but as they did, I was not to stand still and suffer either myself or those that were with me to be knocked on the head. (Barrow (ed.), *Cook's Voyages*, p. 49)

The writing appeals to "humane men," presumably in and out of the Admiralty who have stayed at home, the very audience he seeks to inform, and it attempts to defend itself against their blame, inclining the reader to view the Indian as unreasonably hostile and the white man as necessarily defensive and thus innocent. Cook subsequently adds that they named this bay "Poverty Bay, because it afforded us no one thing we wanted." Markham collapses this experience into an account of Cook's naming of the bay Poverty Bay "on account of the inhospitable, not to say hostile, reception the expedition met with at the hands of the natives" (Markham, *Franklin*, p. 24). In itself, it seems an inadequate explanation, but in comparing it to Cook's journal, we understand what facts it tries to mute or dodge. The image projected here is of a beneficent expedition, bent on the admirable goal of lifting "the veil of doubt and uncertainty," rejected by the obviously unenlightened native population whose lack of gracious courtesy and hospitality impedes the natural course of progress.

Conrad had hoped that "a part of the Elysian Fields" had been set apart for great navigators such as Cook (*Last Essays*, p. 9). He must have appreciated the refreshing absence of "fine words" in Cook's writing, that moralizing language of so many Victorians in various imperial outposts. Registering his "abhorrance of the brutal custom of eating men," for example, naming the place he finds evidence of it Cannibal Bay (Barrow (ed.), *Voyages*, p. 65), Cook nonetheless does not invoke Christian morality. As a Fellow of the Royal Society, the moral obligation he felt was that of a discoverer, to fill in the maps (Barrow (ed.), *Voyages*, p. 77). But as we have seen, the scientist was not altogether immune to current representations of primitive people and of the imperial endeavor that Cook's writings in many ways continued.

## Sir Francis Leopold McClintock

But Cook's attempt to report what he sees honestly and to admit and record his ambivalent thoughts without imposing the ready-made explanations that would reconcile the apparent contradictions does not characterize most later official explorer/adventurers. As Edward Said has noticed, "the simple fact is that between 1815, when European powers were in occupation of approximately 35 percent of the earth's surface, and 1918, when that occupation had extended to 85 percent of the earth's surface, discursive power increased accordingly" (*World*, p. 222). Echoing Foucault, Said postulates "discourse" here as a kind of machine for manufacturing attitudes, one that is rendered invisible in various ways. The interpretive bent of nineteenth-century imperial discourse was often made to seem natural and inevitable by an appeal to progress, a phenomenon that most Victorians saw as inevitable and unquestionably good. Thus to block such progress, including the waxing, expanding, maintaining and occasionally even the waning of empires, was to oppose the natural order of things. This assumption operates so naturally that we tend to consume the judgment as fact. But to read about McClintock's voyage of the *Fox* is to notice more clearly how the fine words do operate and how Victorian travel accounts illustrate so effectively the Foucauldian idea of discourse as power. That the quest romance precedes and informs both the non-fictional and fictional accounts of empire-expanding travel and exploration, casting as it does the adventurer/explorer as a quest hero, effectively silences any doubts we might have about the rightness of this enterprise (see chapter 2, below). Struggling through the darkness like St. George towards divinely sanctioned goals and then returning home to the regions of light, legitimates the endeavor. It was McClintock's book, we should remember, that let in, for Conrad, "the breath of the stern romance of polar exploration into the existence of a boy whose knowledge of the poles of the earth had been till then of an abstract formal kind" (*Last Essays*, p. 12).

McClintock himself was indeed a kind of knight errant who answered his lady's call for help with no promise of gain, carried her colors into battle, and upon his successful return home dedicated the record of his voyage to her. This account must have appealed to Conrad greatly, for it chronicles a community of men bent on a rescue mission the only reward for which would be a woman's gratitude. In fact, the aims of this voyage were so pure and disinterested – that is, so devoid of interest to the centers of power – that it almost did not occur. Since 1845 when her husband Sir John Franklin and his crew had failed to return home from their voyage of exploration to the Arctic, Lady Jane Franklin had written letters and urged rescue expeditions. Several had been sent out but none had succeeded in discovering the fate of the missing men. In 1854 the outbreak of war in the Crimea provided stiff competition, and the British government ended official search expeditions, crossing off the Navy List the names of Sir John Franklin, his officers and men, according to William Wonders' introduction to McClintock's *Voyage* (p. xvi). Crimea demanded the government's interest as did the Indian mutiny of 1857. African exploration was continuing apace, and few gains were seen for the Arctic. But Lady Franklin persisted, and she did so using the fine words she knew were necessary. Writing to Palmerston on 2 December 1856, she accused the government of looking on "as unconcerned spectators" and as having "prematurely cast off... their responsibility." She argues most persuasively:

It would be a waste of words to attempt to refute again the main objections that have been urged against a renewed search, as involving extraordinary danger and risking life. The safe return of our officers and men cannot be denied, neither will it be disputed that each succeeding year diminishes the risk of casualty; and indeed, I feel it would be especially superfluous and unseasonable to argue against this particular objection, or against the financial one which generally accompanies it, at a moment when new expeditions for the glorious interests of science, and which every true lover of science and of his country must rejoice in, are contemplated for the interior of Africa and other parts which are far less favorable to human life than the icy regions of the north. (McClintock, *Voyage*, Appendix pp. 324–325)

The reasonableness and readiness to agree in the opening lines bespeak a woman who has learned to keep her place, but the subtle sarcasm of "glorious" and "true lover of science and of his country" evince an angry but perceptive woman. She realizes the Arctic project is now low priority, even though she believes it is of far greater value in purely human terms than some of the government's more pressing projects in Africa, and thus she attempts to place Franklin's endeavor in the same patriotic light as other more privileged government concerns. She goes on to argue that these men should be seen as worthy and as heroic as soldiers on a battlefield, that they have died

in the service of their country as truly as if they had perished by the rifle, the cannon-ball, or the bayonet. Nay more, by attaining the northern and already-surveyed coast of America, it is clear that they solved the problem which was the object of their labors, or, in the beautiful words of Sir John Richardson, that "they forged the last link of the North-West passage with their lives." (p. 325)

That their discovery is as important to England's national interests as African exploration or victory in the Crimea, she argues, entitles them to an equal claim on their country's conscience and treasury.

Not only is the patriotic merit of their labors beyond reproach, but saving any remains or records is a "sacred" duty, Lady Franklin argues. "A mission so sacred is worthy of a government which has grudged and spared nothing for its heroic soldiers and sailors in other fields of warfare, and will surely be approved by our gracious queen, who overlooks none of Her loyal subjects suffering and dying for their country's honor." But the Crimea absorbed the Queen's attention during these years, and although the Prince Consort was helpful and obtained McClintock's appointment from the Admiralty after he and all the officers volunteered their services free, Lady Franklin herself bought and outfitted the *Fox* and financed the expedition. By 1861 the Queen herself was a widow, but by then McClintock had returned, successfully.

While *The Voyage of the Fox* was dedicated to Jane Franklin, it was addressed to several audiences, among them "the uninitiated" to whom McClintock explains certain Arctic commonplaces as are necessary to his narrative, to possible "future voyagers," to readers "interested in the popular descriptions of the native Esquimaux, as well as of the lower animals," to the families of the lost men, to "men of science," and to the great English public generally to whom he poses various philosophical inquiries on Time and Eternity as well as such thoughts as "Have we English done more, or as much, for the aborigines in any of our numerous colonies, and especially for the Esquimaux within our own territories of Labrador and Hudson's Bay?" when describing Danish benevolence toward the native population of Greenland whose trade that government monopolized (McClintock, *Voyage*, p. 17). That "All [the Eskimos] have become Christians, and many can read and write," under the Danes' tutelage, is a goal the accomplishment of which is never questioned by McClintock; in fact, the writing implies that such should be the goal of all compassionate, civilized people. That it is Britain's moral duty to do likewise seems the point of the question posed above, and is an idea echoed in the adventure fiction, especially in that of Ballantyne, as we shall see. Yet in his Preface to the 1860 edition of McClintock's *Voyage*, Roderick Murchison of the Royal Geographic Society wrote "the gallant McClintock, when he penned his journal amid the Arctic ices, had no idea whatever of publishing it" (McClintock, *Voyage*, p. xxvii). That claim may or may not be true, but the book certainly speaks out to various audiences, with specific intentions, sometimes quite directly. However, Murchison's claim does argue for a kind of innocence, an argument further buttressed by his promise to the readers that the work will "gratify every lover of truthful and ardent research" (McClintock, *Voyage*, p. xxxix). Again, the validating claim is that the work can be trusted as a factual, disinterested account intent only on informing a curious public and revealing truths. But such a claim encourages readers to consume judgments, for example the one discussed above, as facts.

But of course *The Voyage of the Fox* is not simply an impersonal log book in which factual observations have been entered; rather it is an absorbing narrative bent on telling the story – an interpretive act in itself – that, as Conrad noted, the "white races" of Europe were caught up in. In fact, much of it reads like a compelling mystery in which McClintock and his crew are the hero/detectives, piecing together such fragments of evidence as they can uncover. And the great discovery which they literally do uncover from underneath a cairn – the last words from Franklin's expedition – is dealt with in flashback. The chronological sequence is interrupted, the suspense is intensified, and the revelation of the recovered note's contents is postponed until late in the book, long after the discovery is actually made. McClintock's journal leaps from March to June 24 at which point, while summarizing in a few brief paragraphs what has passed in the interim, he concludes: "but all this is as nothing to the interest attached to the Franklin records picked up by Hobson, and now safe in my possession! We now know the fate of the 'Erebus' and 'Terror'" (McClintock, *Voyage*, p. 222). He then goes back to April 2 and creates entries for the missing time, reconstructing them from notes, entries that will narrate the events leading up to the great discovery thirty-three pages later, in May, a message left from the Franklin Expedition dated 28 May 1847 that "all [was] well." The tragic news had been inscribed on the margins, almost a year later, that Franklin had died in June and that nine officers and fifteen men had also died. No trace of the remaining 105 men was found apart from some clothing and small possessions. In fact, the non-fictional demands of journal writing, enabled an honesty that worked in an interestingly novelistic manner. Of necessity, he had stopped writing at any length during the winter, noting only "dry facts" and "the most trivial notes," and when he came back to his diary, as he called it, in late June, he regretted that his present life rendered him "unfit" for "writing up a journal," for "with such ample materials what a deeply interesting volume might be written!" (McClintock, *Voyage*, p. 222). And yet, he does work up his material in a manner that is certainly not dry and manipulates the time sequence in such a way that the reader is compelled to view the endeavor as worthy and the men as heroic.

At the same time, the ideals espoused along the way become naturalized also, and the view of the Other is absorbed and accepted. Glimpses provided of natives are scanty in this narrative. When we do see them, to their credit, they are "goodhumored and friendly." But they are also variously described as "improvident," "untaught savages," often thievish – especially the women – and generally dirty. In early August of 1857, McClintock records that the men washed and "cropped" their young Eskimo dog-driver and then dressed him in sailor's clothes, and while "he was evidently not at home in them, [he] was not the less proud of his improved appearance, as reflected in the admiring glances of his countrymen"

(McClintock, *Voyage*, p. 25). The view is of an infinitely "improvable" people who can be bettered through the white man's superior practices and ideologies. Patrick Brantlinger's description of Foucauld's theory of discourse as "strategies of power and subjection, inclusion and exclusion, the voiced and the silenced" is evidenced here. (Brantlinger, "Victorians," p. 166). Not only is the white man's right to "civilize" never questioned by this discourse, in which the Other is rendered silent, but his need to do so is a necessary good and a moral duty.

But no matter how improved the native is after his encounter with civilization and its representatives, the civilizers remain strangely untouched. In this discourse, both of travel writing and adventure fiction, one of the claims is that the hero/adventurer affects and even changes those he encounters, but remains stolidly unaffected by his experiences himself. In fact, in many ways, he seems hardly to have left England but to have taken its amenities, attitudes, and moral orders along with him. The narration is always structured – in the three-fold manner of the quest romance – by the hero's setting out, for some ennobling cause, his adventures and encounters with the Other, and his successful return home. He then retires to his country estate and writes up his adventures as though nothing had really happened to him. McClintock's story too, then, concludes when he returns home, is in fact paid £5,000 by the Admiralty, is knighted, and retires.

Not until Conrad will the effects of the travels on the traveller be recounted in the writing, but in fact travellers such as Mungo Park, Cook, and Livingstone returned home after each trip restless enough to want to go back again, each time knowing the risks they were taking. And they certainly were not the only Englishmen to die in Empire's Outposts. Even though McClintock did not, he was drawn back repeatedly to known and unknown Arctic dangers. That these other lands presented enticing alternatives to life at home to crews as well as to captains is seen from the ships' records of deserters who all must have found the thought of life-as-usual at home a dull, unappealing grind for various reasons; perhaps, they were even disturbed and fascinated by worlds so different from their own. As Peter Knox-Shaw suggests in *The Explorer in English Fiction*, part of the attraction for many travellers was the "imagined encounter with origins," their narratives often enacting "the story of Genesis in a pristine, often Edenic setting" (see also Marianna Torgovnick's discussion in *Gone Primitive* of "transcendental homelessness"). The number of synonyms alone in several European languages for "going/gone native" – gone bush, gone fantee, gone primitive – reveals the extent of the phenomenon; that they all carry derogatory connotations also indicates that such an action constituted a betrayal, one that threatened the "civilized" tenets of "superior" cultures. In any case, these travellers certainly were not as unaffected as the writing would have us believe. By 1887, H. Rider Haggard's heroes repeatedly assert their desire to return to Africa, attributing that desire to their dissatisfaction with the greyness of modern urban life at home and the impossibility there of any heroic action. His Allan Quatermain and Sir Henry Curtis object to the inadequacies and paleness of life in modern England and head back to Africa once again, and in doing so sound a subversive note. To endow the wilderness with such appeal in narratives that defend the imperial enterprise is to question the assumed superiority of civilized English life. Of course Conrad's Marlow makes no secret of the changes wrought on him by the wilderness, and such transformations openly challenge the assumptions of imperialism. Perhaps it is no accident that Sir John Franklin's nephew, Victorian England's poet laureate, spoke for many of his contemporaries through the voice of that archetypal hero/wanderer, Ulysses:

> Yet all experience is an arch wherethrough
> Gleams that untravelled world whose margin fades
> Forever and forever when I move.
> How dull it is to pause...

The desire Tennyson here evinces of flying from the grey, commonplaces of the modern world can be glimpsed throughout the travel narratives and adventure fiction of the age, even though the writing works to present an unmoved, unruffled representative of a superior, progressive culture whose attitudes and ideologies are firmly in place.

## RAJAH JAMES BROOKE OF SARAWAK

The "fine words" that masked self-interest in defending the imperial project took many forms. The simple benevolence of conferring civilization on the backward peoples of the earth was usually offered. Material progress, education, the suppression of the slave trade were some of the fruits, this argument went, of the establishment of trading centers and also of colonies. But religious assumptions also came to inform these aims powerfully. As Christine Bolt has noticed, religion was the most crucial aspect of African culture for Victorian writers (Bolt, *Victorian Attitudes*, p. 110), and it played a fundamental role in the development of empire generally. As T. Walter Herbert shows in his *Marquesan Encounters*, nineteenth-century thought as it informed colonial expansion, grew in large part out of the doctrine of the millennium, expounded by Scottish commonsense philosophers, which held that "God progressively unfolds his plans for the human race by way of a series of encounters in which those who are bearers of his truth come into conflict with the forces of darkness" (p. 57).

According to Herbert, they had found that Christianity alone supplies "the most powerful motives and the most effective machinery for originating and accomplishing the processes of civilization" (p. 55). James Brooke, for whose character Conrad and Charles Kingsley both professed great admiration, might not have viewed Christianity as "machinery," but "adding knowledge, increasing trade, and spreading Christianity" were his professed goals in quitting England in 1838 for Borneo and becoming the British government agent there. Like Kipling, Brooke was born in India and considered the obligatory years of education in England a kind of punishment. Although those years were not the actual purgatory Kipling's seem to have been, Brooke found it dull to pause in England either to go to school or later, having returned at sixteen to enlist in the infantry in Bengal, to recover from wounds sustained at Rangpur. Thus the opportunity to leave England once more gratified personal desires while at the same time it allowed him to perform a public service. "I go to awake the spirit of slumbering philanthropy with regard to these islands," he writes in his journal, sounding the note of disinterested knight-errantry. "Fortune and life I give freely, and if I fail in the attempt, I shall not have lived wholly in vain" (Keppel, *Expedition*, 1, p. 4).

These are fine words, indeed, and his admirers read the high-mindedness as sincere. When Captain The Honourable Henry Keppel, R.N., wrote of Brooke, he points, unwittingly, to less purely altruistic motives: "to carry to the Malay races, so long the terror of the European merchant vessel, the blessings of civilization, to suppress piracy and extirpate the slave trade, became his humane and generous objects" (Keppel, *Expedition*, 1, p. 3). This writing somewhat obscures the official nature of Keppel's relationship to

Brooke. Brooke, in fact, had enlisted the Royal Navy's help in wiping out pirate strongholds, whose presence endangered Brooke's political position in Sarawak (see Singh, *Brunei*). However, the "blessings of civilization," Christianity and trade among them, would result from safe, pirate-less seas. Not that Brooke saw these intentions as incompatible; promoting progress was a Christian duty even if it also benefited English trade. In his journal for Sunday, August 4, 1838, after performing "divine service myself! manfully overcoming that horror which I have to the sound of my own voice before an audience," he walks off alone into the forest:

But here and there the touch of time has cast his withering hand upon their leafy brow, and decay has begun his work upon the gigantic and unbending trunk. How trite, and how true! It was thus I meditated in my walk. The foot of European, I said, has never touched where my foot now presses – seldom the native wanders here... The Creator's gift, as yet neglected by the creature; and yet the time may be confidently looked for, when the axe shall level the forest, and the plough turn the ground. (Brooke, *Narrative*, p. 19)

The faith in progress expressed here admits of neither irony nor ambivalence, and the sense of opportunity and possession as God-given informs these words as it did Columbus' and Cook's before him. But the thoughtful, philosophical tone helps the reader assume that Brooke indeed is the bearer of God's truths, and that this vision of progress has been divinely ordained. Thus, most readers, accepting the genre at face value, responded to the "fine words" as noble, not ulterior or to be questioned, but as morally irreproachable.

In a letter he sent through a friend in 1841 to Her Majesty's Secretary of State for the Colonies, Brooke argues persuasively for increased English involvement in Malaya and eventual colonization. He appeals to humane Englishmen to help him in the work he has heretofore carried on alone, "to suppress piracy and the slave trade which are openly carried on" (Brooke, *Letter*, p. 6), and to help the oppressed Dyaks who have suffered at the hands of rapacious Malay chiefs. Certainly the Dyaks, recommended as "virtuous and most unhappy," deserve the attention given now to the Africans and without the "vast expenditure of lives and money which exertions on the African coast yearly cost" (p. 17). Unlike that "white man's grave," Borneo's climate is healthy, her rivers are navigable, and the soil of her plains is moist and rich (p. 14). Although Conrad's debt to Brooke was great, as already mentioned, Brooke's view of progress was certainly not Conrad's who considered steam and all contrivances contributing to haste the work of the devil. Consequently, the same Bornean jungles described by Brooke are unfamiliar to readers of Conrad. Inviting colonization, Brooke describes the "verdant canopies" of forest, the "long vistas of noble trees," and the "rich foliage" which "kisses the tide as it flows by," a veritable paradise unknown to Almayer.

Many at home accused Brooke of using excessive force in quelling native rebellions and suppressing the pirates, and perhaps such an appeal as he made here was meant to forestall this domestic criticism. But his trump card, a warning that if Britain hung back the Dutch would step in, was not lost, and British support and sympathy for Brooke won the day. Charles Kingsley, among others, defended him and dedicated his *Westward Ho!* to Brooke. Something of his admiration can be seen in his central character Amayas Leigh described as representative of that strain of Victorian thought that celebrated strength and deeds over words, practical force and virtuous (British) manhood (Houghton, *Victorian Frame of Mind*, p. 122). Queen Victoria accorded him a hero's welcome in 1857, conferring a knighthood upon him and entertaining him at Windsor.

However, Brooke, like Cook, was also uneasy about the consequences for the native Dyak of cultural contact with Europe. Others also would worry about the possible contaminating influence of the West on the native but would conclude, as Speke does, that if the "best sort" of Europeans are sent out – ie. English gentlemen – then all will be well. But Brooke's thinking was more informed and complex. While he wanted to raise "these suffering people ... in the scale of civilization and happiness" (Keppel, *Expedition*, 1, p. 262), he understood – as would Stevenson and Haggard – that beliefs and customs, no matter how "barbaric," can not simply be removed without serious dislocation to the moral fabric of the people (Keppel, *Expedition*, 1, p. 274). In fact he warned himself against appearing the political or religious reformer, knowing the dangerous temptation for "people settled like myself" to "too often try to create a utopia." Rather, he interested himself in learning about the native peoples, even promising to "retrace the customs which once obtained ... long banished from this country ... the best of which I wish to restore."

Alfred Wallace, whose *The Malay Archipelago* (1869) was Conrad's "favorite bedside book," was another of Brooke's great champions. He defended the man, now dead, who was "sneered at by some who didn't know him" (p. 105). He felt that Brooke deserved the thanks of the whole archipelago for rescuing the inland Dyaks from the oppressive piratical Malays and for making trade possible. Like Brooke, Wallace advocated the development of colonies in Malaya, believing it advantageous to both colonizer and colonized. At the same time, his fears about the possible demoralization of the Dyaks – the "evil that too often arises in analogous cases" – were quieted only by the hopes of "education and a high-class European example" (p. 102). Quieted, not extinguished. Wallace goes beyond Cook's momentary envy of "the happy native" to wonder if in fact England could not benefit morally from the Malays, English society being plagued at the moment by crime and disease. In a moving conclusion to his book, he in fact questions the "progress" and moral development of "civilized" societies. Perhaps such societies as the Dyaks have something to teach us about respecting the rights of others and living together with few inequalities, Wallace writes. Livingstone too would note the attractions of a communal society where, as Wallace remarks, there "are none of those wide distinctions of education and ignorance, wealth and poverty, master and servant, which is the product of our civilization," where the cooperative, rather than the competitive, principle obviates the poverty and crime that "the dense population of civilized countries inevitably creates" (p. 597). Although these insights are confined to an afterthought, appended to the major study, they in fact confront the major tenets of that study. Hindsight permits us to see at work here the cognitive dissonance – to use Adrienne Rich's phrase – that allowed some of the more thoughtful of observers to advocate colonization and at the same time to be painfully aware of the concomitant destruction of apparently more successful economic and social structures.

## CAPTAIN JOHN HANNING SPEKE

Conrad announced himself a contemporary of the Great Lakes; the news of Burton and Speke's expeditions was "whispered to him in his cradle," and allowed him a few years later to enter "laboriously in pencil the outline of Tanganyika on [his] beloved old atlas" (*Last Essays*, p. 14). Did he read Burton's *The Lake Regions of Central Africa* (1860), or Speke's *What Led to the Discovery of the Source of the Nile* (1864), or someone else's account? In any case, the story told more than geographical truths. Along with all the other possible models for Kurtz – M. M. Mahood, for example, lists no fewer than nine –

certainly Burton's name must be added to the list, another multi-talented, polyglot European whose idealism had always harbored a brutal racism.

While earlier African explorers such as James Bruce or Mungo Park had been charged by the Royal Society with discovering new geographical knowledge which would contribute to the advancement of science – and of commerce – John Hanning Speke, as well as many other nineteenth-century explorers in Africa, saw himself as a seeker of geographical facts, but even more compellingly as an instrument of empire. Like Brooke, Speke had served his regiment in India. There he inherited the appropriate colonial views about the "problems of ruling blacks;" the step from imperial soldier in India to imperial explorer in Africa was a short one for him. In any case, as Said's analysis of the production of "the Orient" suggests, "Africa" also had been constructed, largely by nineteenth-century European writers, whose works Speke did not even have to read for himself, so pervasive was their influence:

By the 1850's the image [of Africa] had hardened. It was found in children's books, in Sunday school tracts, in the popular press. Its major affirmations were the "common knowledge" of the educated classes. (Curtin, *Work*, p. vi)

Speke brought with him to Africa, then, "the myth of the Dark Continent" – a myth whose genealogy Patrick Brantlinger carefully traces (see "Victorians and Africans") – and of course, his subsequent writings only contributed to its power.

The idea that Africa was a place of darkness, ignorance and savagery served, paradoxically, not only the movement for the abolition of slavery but also for the extension of empire, as Brantlinger shows. England's efforts to suppress the slave trade effectively committed its explorers, missionaries, traders, and finally colonial administrators to a more pervasive influence on the continent. And the attitude toward the Other accompanying this movement was that, somehow, slavery was in fact a manifestation of African savagery and inferiority itself. And thus the African needed the white man's help if he was to progress towards a more civilized and truly liberated state. Unlike Wallace who was writing several years earlier, Speke represented the prevailing Victorian attitude that doubted if "we" had anything to learn from "them." A cultural chauvinism, even arrogance, assured the English that their nation was superior not only technologically but also morally (Curtin, *Image*, p. 143). It was, after all, as a morally "advanced" people, that they opposed the slave trade. Out of necessity, Speke begrudgingly granted a respect to the peoples whose lands he needed to pass through to attain the Victoria Nyanza and thus the Nile, but he routinely describes their beliefs as "absurd," their religion as "obscure fetish," their language as "strange," and their incessant drumming as "ludicrous." Their "weak brains give way when questioned about geography" (*What Led to the Discovery*, p. 349), and even their family life is inferior to that of the English (p. 296). For the most part the natives annoy him; they present an obstacle to his desire, and he is impatient with their childish and "capricious barbarism" that prevents their direct answers to his question, "My mother, Queen Victoria, wishes to know if you want to open up trade with our country." Travelling as the prince, he was quite clear as to the benefits his mother, the Queen could confer upon these backward people.

Most Victorians agreed with him. The African, further down the evolutionary ladder, needed the more highly evolved European's help. As the writers of *The Africa That Never Was* make clear, racial differences had been noticed from as early as 1530. But it was not until the mid nineteenth century that race was used to explain the African's "savagery" (Hammond and Jablow, *Africa*, p. 61). That is, culture was racially transmitted; "race" became a trope that served the ideological function of signifying the inferiority of the conquered and the superiority of the conqueror (Gates "Writing"). Such an obviously inferior culture as the Europeans found in Africa must result from an inferior race, and such an innate inferiority justified imperial intrusion. Speke subscribed to the standard Biblical explanation of racial origins current at the time, made respectable by pseudo-scientific theories of monogenesis versus polygenesis. Thus, he felt moved to explain to Bombay – in Hindustani, the only language Speke took to Africa – why he had to serve, and "bow to the superior intellect of the European." Because Africans, and thus Bombay – the most "honest and conscientious black man" Speke had ever met, a regular "Friday" – had descended from Ham, "by the common order of nature, they, being the weakest, had to succumb to their superiors, the Japhetic and Semitic branches of [Noah's] family (*What Led to the Discovery*, p. 340). (It is hard to know what Bombay made of this explanation; his response, of course, is not included. In any case, the Bombays of this discourse are silenced by its very assumptions.) This explanation of racial origins allowed Speke and other believers in the "myth of the dark continent," to blame Africans for their own enslavement and find them morally culpable. While he duly calls for the suppression of the slave trade, he includes a matter-of-fact description of the slave market in Zanzibar, where he sees "unhappy-looking men and women, all hideously black and ugly" (*What Led to the Discovery*, p. 190). Somehow, the fault is theirs for being unhappy, black, and ugly. This convenient racial explanation permitted him to insert a criticism of the slave, while the occasion ostensibly called for a condemnation of the slave trade.

These observations, once again, are delivered as truth. In his introduction to *The Journal of Discovery of the Source of the Nile*, he professes "accurately to describe naked Africa – Africa in those places where it has not received the slightest impulse, whether for good or for evil, from European civilization." But looking at an "Africa" already produced for him, he sees only what confirms his unexamined ideas:

If the picture be a dark one, we should, when contemplating these sons of Noah, try and carry our mind back to that time when our poor elder brother Ham was cursed by his father, and condemned to be the slave of both Shem and Japheth; for as they were then, so they appear to be now – a strikingly existing proof of the Holy Scriptures. (*Journal of Discovery*, p. xvii)

Here again his racism is encoded as Scriptural Truth. Even the Nile is annexed to serve the Christian Bible and justify Speke's discovery of "that mighty stream that floated Father Moses on his first adventurous sail" (*What Led to the Discovery*, p. 259).

Such patriarchal engendering characterizes Speke's writing, as well as that of many other explorer/writers, and serves to justify the imperial intrusion. Again in his *Journal of Discovery*, he announces that "I saw that old Father Nile without any doubt rises in the Victoria N'yanza, and, as I had foretold, that lake is the great source of the holy river which cradled the first expounder of our religious belief" (p. 429). To the pantheon of Fathers – the Nile, Moses, God – Speke adds himself and other resourceful fathers, bearers of the sacred spark. Speke's advice to others is to understand that the African is a "grown child" whose sins are best cured with "great forbearance, occasionally tinctured with a little fatherly severity" (*Journal of Discovery*, p. xxx). It is difficult not to read "fatherly severity" euphemistically, knowing the Victorian "worship of force" generally (see Houghton, *Victorian Frame of Mind*, chapter 9), and the propensity of many Victorian travellers to encourage their native porters with regular floggings and pistol brandishings. (Livingstone's reluctance to use force is marked as exceptional; see Jeal, *Livingstone*, p. 303). Like Moses himself then, Speke led his "faithful children" – the eighteen native bearers who remained with him out of the original number, more than seventy-five, engaged in 1860 – down the Nile to Cairo. He then, at expedition's end in 1863, had them photographed at Shepherd's Hotel, and like a good Victorian paterfamilias, he "indulged them at public concerts, tableau vivants, etc." (*Journal of Discovery*, p. 551).

Before he had set out, he had justified the expedition to the readers of the conservative publication, *Blackwood's Magazine*. By expressing a confidence in progress, he paints a picture of the imperial endeavor as heroic and necessary: "if the N'yanza be really the Nile's fount, which I sincerely believe to be the case, what an advantage this will be to the English merchant on the Nile, and what a field is opened to the world, if, as I hope will be the case, England does not neglect this discovery!" (October–November 1859). The words here do not as finely disguise the project. Speke openly advertises his endeavors as advantageous to English merchants. But again, with "neglect," the moral note is sounded and transforms development and expansion from mere commercial advantages to moral duties. And if the European is morally upright in so persevering, then the native is not only backward but morally inferior for not having taken advantage himself of his own opportunities. This argument was already a familiar one to mid-Victorian audiences. Since at least the 1830s, missionaries justified their work by arguing that the land was Edenic and plentiful but that the people had failed to develop what God had given them. Thus the imperative to develop this moral wilderness through the conferring of the Christian light and Western culture, both made possible through trade (Curtin, *Image*, p. 327). Speke argues similarly:

To look upon its resources, one is struck with amazement at the waste of the world: if instead of this district being in the hands of its present owners, it were ruled by a few scores of Europeans, what an entire revolution a few years would bring forth! An extensive market would be opened to the world, the present nakedness of the land would have a covering, and industry and commerce would clear the way for civilization and enlightenment. At present the natural inert laziness and ignorance of the people is their own and their country's bane. They are all totally unaware of the treasures at their feet... they are, both morally and physically, little better than brutes... (*Blackwoods*, p. 65)

To oppose "resources" to "waste," "covering" to "nakedness," "industry and commerce" to "laziness and ignorance" is to privilege one of the terms over the other and thus make clear the superiority of the English claim. The discursive power here, as well as its proliferation, works to manufacture attitudes but also, as Said argues, to render the machinery itself invisible. Speke's imagery promotes his readers' acceptance, silently; as covering nakedness is a commendable action to this discourse's Victorian audience, so must be opening markets and clearing the way for those unquestionably privileged goals of civilization and enlightenment. Speke's use of contrast is continued in opposing the district's "present owners," later dismissed simply as "brutes," to "European rulers" and the contrast works to privilege the latter, only forty of whom could do the job at hand – civilizing – better than all the brutes put together.

The language of this discourse asserts a point of view; it is exclamatory, opinionated, argumentative and not particularly interested in limiting itself to factual "truths" although it makes its appeal, usually, as informational writing. Speke intends a particular message for a particular audience:

But I must not expatiate too much on the merits and capabilities of inner Africa, lest I mislead any commercial inquirers... That commerce does make wonderful improvements on the barbarous habits of the Africans can now be seen in the Masai country, and the countries extending north-westward from Mombas up through Kikuyu into the interior, where the process has been going on during the last few years. (*Blackwoods*, p. 102)

Speke uses "improvements" and "barbarous" as though they were objective terms, but of course they are highly contaminated. The Masai's "improvement," for example, evinces as much as anything the prevalent, almost obligatory English idealization of the aristocratic feudal warrior; thus the Masai was admired by "the best sort of white man" (Hammond and Jablow, *Africa*, p. 164). The image of the white man throughout Speke's discourse, then, is of a benign, even benevolent father figure and agent of improvement. The hypothetical "wrong sort" of Europeans lurk at the margins of Speke's writing, but the corruption they might be capable of will be offset by the labors of English gentlemen. The moral superiority he attributes to the imperial endeavor and its hero justifies, even necessitates, their incursion into Africa, for while being commercially advantageous to the British, it is morally beneficial to the African, an extremely convenient equation. And England evidently agreed with him, for at (con)quest's end, he was awarded the Royal Geographical Society's "Founder's Medal," for discovering the Victoria N'yanza, and was given a hero's welcome; as the crowds applauded him, church bells rang, and the band played "See the Conquering Hero Comes" (Maitland, *Speke*, pp. 180–181).

## DAVID LIVINGSTONE

The writings of David Livingstone also urged the twin projects of suppressing the slave trade and strengthening the Christian missions in Africa. Returning from his first exploration of the Zambesi, he published *Missionary Travels and Researches in South Africa* (1857). The remarkable success of that book and of his subsequent lectures, collected in *Dr. Livingstone's Cambridge Lectures* (1858) led to the establishment of the Universities' Mission to Central Africa in 1860. While Livingstone and Speke were poles apart, in many respects, both assumed that native Africans were doomed without English help. A devout Scotsman, Livingstone's initial response upon arriving in Africa was guilt that Christian Europe had not come sooner to deliver the heathen from darkness. He was appalled by the slow conversion rate, but by his next trip, his obsession had shifted from conversion to suppression of the slave trade. In 1858, he returned to Africa, this time as the British Consul to Quillimane for the Eastern Coast and independent districts of the interior, and as commander of an expedition for exploring eastern and central Africa, "proceeding to the West Coast, in order to find a path to the sea by which lawful commerce might be introduced to aid missionary operations," and thereby abolish the slave trade (*Narrative*, p. 6). Introducing his second work, *Narrative of an Expedition to the Zambesi and its Tributaries* (1865), Livingstone writes:

This account is written in the earnest hope that it may contribute to that information which will yet cause the great and fertile continent of Africa to be no longer kept wantonly sealed, but made available as the scene of European enterprise, and will enable its people to take a place among the nations of the earth, thus securing the happiness and prosperity of tribes now sunk in barbarism or debased by slavery; and, above all, I cherish the hope that it may lead to the introduction of the blessings of the Gospel. (p. 2)

"The blessings of civilization" and "the blessings of the Gospel" recur in this discourse, often synonymously. To help him "in opening up Africa," had been Burton's invitation to Speke, an image echoed by Livingstone. The great advantage to British trade of "opening up" that which had been "wantonly sealed" appeared to them a noble aim, and Christianity certainly served that aim well. Although apparently genuinely determined to eradicate slavery in Africa and concerned with the welfare of the natives, Livingstone does not question the compatibility of those goals with furthering British interests in Africa, establishing colonies and trade routes. Unfortunately, the paradox, analyzed by Brantlinger and referred to above, of the anti-slavery movement only deepening British influence in Africa, was not apparent to Livingstone. Quelling what Livingstone saw as "the open sore of the world" led inevitably to the expansion of empire, as Brantlinger demonstrates. But after thirty years in Africa and discovering the extent of European, especially Portuguese, influence, he resigned himself to English imperialism as the best solution to an already contaminated Africa.

In its matter-of-fact manner, one he apologizes for in the Preface in the conventional manner, this narrative urges the elimination of "that curse of Africa, and that shame... the slave trade" (*Narrative*, p. v), by means of colonization. The force of the writing, then, throughout is to argue for the richness of the land and the perniciousness of slavery, appealing to his readers' commercial and moral impulses simultaneously. He urges the development of the land, of missions, of settlements, and of legitimate trade as effective means of eliminating the slave trade and also as attractive alternatives to the underemployed in England's overcrowded cities and even to the large convict population in Britain. "Lawful commerce and Christian missions" would do the work of anti-slavery warships now cruising the coasts, and far more economically, he argued. In highlighting the land, Livingstone speaks of the abundance of game and the land's rich potential. He details the flourishing native production of indigo, cotton, sugar cane and the relatively untapped but proven mineral resources, especially of magnetic iron ore, of coal, and of gold. While echoing Speke's descriptions of the land's underdevelopment, he does not blame the native's laziness as much as his malaise due to the demoralizing influence of slavery and the ever-present danger of slave traders. But the effect of the writing is that the land will richly repay a settler's industry. At the same time Livingstone loses no opportunity to accuse the Portuguese and their continued, now illegal, conduct of the slave trade of multiple calamities, from the moral debasement and enervation of the native people, to the ruin of the Portuguese's own missions and settlements.

His attitude toward the natives shifted over time. Early on, in his *Private Journals* (1851), he reminded himself several times that he had come, like Jesus, "not to judge," but to teach peace and love. Yet, after living among native peoples for two years, he shuddered with disgust at their "heathenism." After thirty years in Africa, his views permitted gradations and some complexity. A constraint operating on all missionaries resulted from the current debate over the question "Is the African capable of receiving the light?" Obviously, as a missionary, Livingstone needed to image the African sympathetically enough, as educable and morally capable of receiving the blessings of civilization, to justify his own presence there (Curtin, *Image*, p. 268). At the same time, he never freed himself from Victorian racism and felt that natives were low down on the evolutionary scale. Yet he took issue with what he considered false reports made by and for the English about the native, and one feels that the impetus was not only rhetorical. A few years before his death, sick and dispirited, he read Speke's *Journal* and, not willing to let such a calumny remain undisputed, recorded in his own journal his disagreement with Speke's assertion that the native women willingly sold their own children to the slavers.

But he certainly shared many of his contemporary's belief in progress, that "the world is rolling on to the golden age" (*Private Journals*, p. 167). By 1872 he still believed that "progress would cure Africa's ills" (see *Last Journals*, II). It is the measure of the force of contemporary ideologies that Livingstone of all people could have suppressed the memory of the squalor and poverty of his early years in a Glasgow cotton mill to urge "progress" on the African. He justifies the rightness of the endeavor by writing that the "inmates of our workhouses have more comforts than rich African chieftains do" (*Private Journals*, p. 168). (Would his rescuer Stanley have agreed, who spent his formative years in a Welsh workhouse?) Soap, clean linen, glass windows, sugar, painless surgical operations, and advanced communications, are among "the fruits of God's love for us," Livingstone reasons, refusing to question the Victorian equation between free market economies and Christian morality. Somehow that the African peoples he has met lack these material "advancements" marks their moral debasement too. Consequently the imperial hero is depicted here as the bringer of light, who can and must illuminate the "dark minds" of these "depraved children of Ham."

Travel writing, then, was popular, officially sanctioned and high-minded. Among modern readers, Mary Louise Pratt has commented on this literature of exploration that "aspired to scientific status," intent as it was on producing "information" (Pratt, "Scratches," pp. 124–125). She observes that in "these information-producing travel accounts, the goal of expanding the capitalist world system is, as a rule, acknowledged in prefaces, but only there" (p. 125). She points out the near-obliteration of the explorer-traveller himself in the discourse, present only as "the deleted subjects of passive verbs," while the native is there "only in the abstract ('man')." As she points out, the anomalous situation in this travel writing is that place gets narrated and people get described; that is, natives are generalized in a universalizing ethnographic present tense and considered only as representative of various sub-groups, all belonging to the all-encompassing category, "African." The Bakâtla were "a cowardly people" (*Missionary Travels*, p. 11), Livingstone tells us. The Batlapi "were an insignificant and filthy people when first discovered" (p. 220). On the other hand, nowhere are the travellers' struggles, especially with native carriers, narrated. Livingstone, we know, had colossal problems managing his native crews, but such confrontations occupy the margins of his discourse, if at all. While it can be argued that Livingstone foregrounds the land, and effaces himself, as a strategy suitable to his avowed purpose, as discussed above, it is also true that such passive and abstract depictions can only help the project of justifying the European's presence in Africa, of minimizing his violent intrusion, of depersonalizing the native, thus glorifying the endeavor – ultimately commercial and political – while presenting it as objective, passively distanced information. That this highly descriptive writing is also meditative, as we saw in

Brooke's Sunday ruminations and Livingstone's moral reflections on the iniquities of the slave trade, increases its appeal and further shapes the imperial adventurer as a hero, a light-bearing emissary to the dark lands of the "other."

# CHAPTER 2

# Adventure fiction: a special case

> Once more the spirit of the age has found literary expression and
> the result is a whole revolving bookcase of literature charged
> with the spirit of imperialism.
>
> (*Blackwood's Edinburgh Magazine*, February, 1899)

Closely related to travel writing was the adventure fiction of the day.
In fact the line between the two discourses was often a thin one. Both
constructed the imperial subject similarly, applauding the same
heroic virtues of pluck and forthrightness in the conqueror, Othering
the native in familiar ways, and making use of similar expressions,
images, and plots. As Martin Green demonstrates, Victorian
adventure fiction chronicled, as did the travel writing we have just
looked at, "dreams of adventure and deeds of empire." Both genres
were tremendously popular, and both were well represented, side by
side, in the flourishing periodical literature of the day. The reviewer
quoted above, in *Blackwood's* celebratory millenial number, refers to
works by such popular writers as W. W. Jacobs and Rudyard
Kipling, and to Henry Newhall's *Drake's Drum* as examples of the
current interest in books "charged with the spirit of imperialism."
He also recommends a Mr. Vandervell's *Shuttle of an Empire's Loom* in
which the British tar is depicted as having "unfailing pluck" and
"indomitable good-humour" (p. 264), a familiar formula in travel
writing and adventure fiction alike. The enthusiasm of the reviewer's
contention that this "imperial" discourse was a literary expression of
the spirit of the age promoted the readers' desire for the literary
products while compelling their agreement with the beliefs that
inhered in the age's spirit. More dangerously, as we have come to see,
such authorizing of this discourse worked to silence any questions
that might have suggested themselves about the European intrusion
into non-European countries in the first place, for, in fact, both the
travel writing and the adventure fiction of the day served to

39

naturalize that intrusion and subsequent expansion "while inscribing
difference into the very body of discourse and social relations in far
from obvious ways" (Humphries, "Discourse," p. 114).

*Blackwood's* itself was a hearty participant in the imperial fervour,
and the accompanying pieces in this 1,000th number evince this
interest. For example, "From the New Gibbon" speaks triumphantly
of the British Empire now at "the highest pitch of its prosperity," "its
authority extended alike over the most dutiful of daughter peoples
and the wildest and most sequestered barbarians," and boasts that
even "two centuries of empire had seemed insufficient to oppress or
enervate the virile and adventurous spirit of the British race" (p.
241). A piece on Jamaica constructs the imperial subject in a manner
familiar to readers of travel writing in terms of the effaced European
author and the homogenized, dehistoricized Other; this writer calls
upon his readers to enjoy the sight of happy "negroes in their little
log-huts...all seemed to be busy with something or another. At the
doors women were sewing or men were cobbling" and "little
picaninies in a state of nature" could be seen chasing chickens and
pigs (p. 304). The facile and patronizing dismissal of "them," as
contented and busy children – the "dutiful daughter peoples"
presumably – in their "little" houses congratulates white writer and
reader alike as representatives of a truly benevolent, productive
empire. With "in a state of nature," we perceive the conspiratorial
wink of writer to reader, both of whom understand the euphemism;
not only are the children literally naked, and therefore uncivilized,
but all these people are in their natural state – i.e. under the gaze of
the European intruder and chronicler of imperial, civilized order.
Other articles here include several pieces – stories and travel articles
– on India, and on Malaysia, one by Hugh Clifford. All depict the
white man as "Sahib" or "Tuan" against a generalized native
population. Only the third item in *Blackwood's* 1,000th number failed
to sound imperialism's triumphant note, the first installment of
Joseph Conrad's "Heart of Darkness." Why its subversion was not
felt by most readers is central to this study and will be the direct
concern of later chapters.

In its construction of the imperial subject, then, adventure fiction
derived its authority not only from its popular appeal but also from
societal approval of its basic, and rather non-fictional, claims to be
educational and inspirational, for the extent to which this discourse
resembled the travel writing of the day, gave a special status to

adventure fiction. So closely allied with travel writing, a genre that aspired to fact, after all, adventure fiction came to be viewed as a special case, demanding more credibility than other fictions. That both appeared not only in such an important publication as *Blackwoods* – as we have seen – but also side by side in such popular periodicals as *The Graphic*, the *Illustrated London News*, *Cassel's*, *Cosmopolis*, *Cornhill*, *Fraser's*, *Longman's*, and *T.P.'s Weekly*, earned for both a special status, marking them as part of the factual, workaday world of newsprint, not fanciful but part of the informational machinery of the day. In fact, both adventure fiction and travel writing were considered far preferable to novels about which general suspicion traditionally hovered, and book reviewers in the various newspapers and journals recommended the fiction as educational. By mid-century, the abundance of "penny-dreadfuls," cheaply printed, sensational novels aimed at the working classes (Hogarth, *Artist*, p. 16), such as *Black Bess*, *Tyburn Dick*, and *Mysteries of London*, to which almost narcotic-like qualities were ascribed, made most works of imaginative fiction generally suspect.[1] Religious Evangelicals and Dissenters, whose influence grew throughout the nineteenth century, went so far as to condemn the novel as "the Devil's bible" (Cruse, *Victorians*, p. 67f). The utilitarian argument against fiction which prevailed was particularly strong in reference to the working classes. The 1878 issue of *Publishers' Circular* expressed this view:

Free libraries, which should only be provided for the poor and helpless, not for those who can help themselves, should be resorted to for education and inspiration, and should begin at elementary works, long antecedent to works of imaginative fiction. If the ratepayers are to provide imaginative fiction, or the luxuries of the mind, for slightly poorer classes, why should they not also provide free games, free plays, *panem et circenses*, free cakes and nuts for the boys? (Altick, *Common Reader*, p. 232)

"Luxuries of the mind," novels served no useful purpose. In his autobiography, *The Days of my Life*, H. Rider Haggard noted that in the year *King Solomon's Mines* appeared, 1886, the annual publication of novels was about 800. By 1894, Conrad could write his aunt in France that he had accepted his publisher's low terms for *Almayer's Folly* – £20 – because publication itself was becoming so difficult; "every week some dozens of novels appear" (Karl, *Letters*, I, p. 178). By 1912, the annual publication of novels was up to about 3,000, reflecting a significant change in attitudes towards fiction, or simply a growing disparity between professions of belief and actual behavior. But in 1884, career novelists such as Henry James still felt they had to argue for the respectability of the novel and commented that while "the old superstition about fiction being 'wicked' has doubtless died out in England...the spirit of it lingers" (James, *Future of the Novel*, pp. 4, 5).

To avoid the stigma of being "merely a story," then, adventure fiction purported to be informational and often came equipped with the same appurtenances of fact as travel writing – appended maps, scholarly footnotes and explanatory prefaces. While having an interpretive stance that espoused imperial views, adventure fiction, like travel writing, was perceived as primarily factual, reliable reporting within a narrative enacted by fictional or semi-historical characters. Indicative of this perception was its considered suitability for a newly enfranchised populace, and interestingly, travel narratives and adventure fiction were considered together in this respect also. One of the innovations resulting from the Reform Bill of 1867, empowering school inspectors to examine the students in the higher grades on works other than the Bible, was that works such as "*Robinson Crusoe*, Voyages and Travels, or Biographies of eminent men," were approved of because these texts were all read as fact (Altick, *Common Reader*, p. 7). Fiction, as we have seen, was a frowned-upon frivolity, "free cakes and nuts"; the literacy needs of the working classes in particular, it was argued, should be confined to practical information that would make them more devout in their religious duties and more productive, obedient, subjects. Like *Robinson Crusoe*, Charles Kingsley's *Westward Ho*! was also read as a healthy corrective to the moral blight caused by novel-reading, and in at least one case of a youth "seduced" by fiction, that novel was offered as a solution to his destructive addiction. Upon reading it, according to a contemporary report, he abandoned his former life, reformed, and soon was respectably employed, filling "an important post in a large City printing office" (Greenwood, *Sunday School*, p. 6) – a convincing utilitarian argument, indeed.

Again the moral and economic arguments get collapsed here, for the century's literacy battles – in a manner familiar to us today – equated the democratization of knowledge with national prosperity. Since the 1840s, reformers in the wake of the first reform bill advocated only educational material that praised contentment with one's appointed station as a patriotic duty; any call for education as a means of social mobility would have been a voice in the wilderness. Rather, teaching the working classes their role in the scheme of things, and giving them useful knowledge laced with warnings against dissatisfaction were the goals of educational reform. Arithmetic – particularly for boys – was stressed as was geography, in order to "stimulate enterprise at home and swell the stream of colonialization" (Kay-Shuttleworth, *Popular Education*, p. 101).

That particular stream had been swollen with the poor, the idle, the criminal and had served as a convenient solution to England's rising population problem; Peggoty and Little Emily emigrated to Australia as a kind of punishment, to escape her disgrace in a new life. But by the second half of the century, settling in the empire's outposts was being spoken of as a kind of duty for the best representatives of all classes, but increasingly for the upper-middle classes, so important had the project become. Professor of Modern History, Charles Kingsley, warned his Cambridge undergraduates against the corrupting effeteness and frivolousness of contemporary life in England, and advocated instead manly activities abroad. As we have seen, he wrote admiringly of Brooke of Sarawak and also of his own son who "is now working with his own hands at farming, previous to emigrating to South America, where he will do the drudgery of his own cattle-pens and sheepfolds; and if I were twenty-four and unmarried I would go out there too, and work like an Englishman, and live by the sweat of my brow" (Lang, *Essays*, p. 158. See also Green, *Dreams of Adventure*, p. 218). Thus, the belief that the stream of colonization should be swelled because it was morally improving was inscribed in the discourse, urged in such patriotic terms by such authorities as Professor (and later Canon) Kingsley, so as to effectively naturalize the colonist's presence and conceal the fact of his intrusiveness. In even loftier terms John Ruskin would appeal to the Oxford undergraduates as fellow members of a "race mingled of the best northern blood," who must, as "youths of England, make [their] country again a royal throne of kings; a sceptred isle, for all the world a source of light, a centre of peace; mistress of Learning and of the Arts..." If England was not to perish, he told them, "she must found colonies as fast and as far as she is able, formed of her most energetic and worthiest men; – seizing every piece of fruitful waste ground she can set her foot on, and there teaching these her colonists that their chief virtue is to be fidelity to their country, and that their first aim is to be to advance the power of England by land and sea"

(Ruskin, *Works*, p. 42). Consider the appeal: the moral obligation, the "destiny," of such a chosen people is to confer her light everywhere – and however – possible. This call to export British subjects, labor and ideas also repeated itself many times over in the magazine stories and adventure fiction of the day. Words are deeds and have consequences; whether Cecil Rhodes heard about Ruskin's lecture or read it – reportedly, Rhodes' library at Groot Schuur, Capetown included the works of Ruskin (Cloete, *African Portraits*, p. 151) – the discourse generally made a Rhodes inevitable, even though Ruskin later protested against the kind of empire-building he represented.[2] This appeal, then, was authorized in the educational discourse addressed to all classes, for a variety of reasons, under the guise of non-fictional Truth.

Travel narrative and adventure fiction, then, both enjoyed an elevated status and were read as similar discourses, subject to similar rules. Because of this association, the credibility and respectability of the one was also attributed to the other, thus gaining for adventure fiction an influential power that its predecessor, the Romance, lacked, one that shaped, with real consequences in attitude and policy, the outlook of generations of readers towards the imperial subject. Paradoxically though, adventure fiction and the travel writing that informed it were inscribed within the romance tradition. Both discourses were often framed as quest romance, thus necessitating the reader's view of the central protagonist as heroic and his endeavor as authorized, even divinely ordained. Interestingly, readers today respond with great strength to the travel adventure as romantic quest, particularly in regard to that paradigmatic saga of Livingstone and Stanley. Out of a possible multitude, a few examples: Marianna Torgovnick sees Livingstone as Stanley's "Grail" (*Gone Primitive*, p. 26), and similarly Jeal writes that Livingstone's search for the source of the Nile "had become a quest" and that it "would confirm the Sacred Oracles" (*Livingstone*, p. 329). Jacques Darras reads Stanley's quest for Livingstone as Marlow's for Kurtz, thus connecting the Belgian endeavor to the English one. Patrick Brantlinger locates common motives of quest romance in imperial adventure from *Treasure Island* to *Nostromo* (*Rule of Darkness*, p. 192f).

Victorian readers did not have to be familiar with medieval romance to understand the ideological appeal thus made, for Scott's historical romances had updated the genre for them, and by mid-century, the "Victorian mania for Scott had whetted the appetite for other adventure" (Cruse, *Victorians*, p. 296). Adventure was the essential plot element of romance; the successful quest included the perilous journey and the crucial struggle and exaltation of the hero (Frye, *Anatomy*, pp. 186–187), certainly a familiar feature to readers of both travel writing and adventure fiction as was the impetus of romance towards "grave idealizing of heroism and purity" (Frye, *Anatomy*, p. 306). And as Michael Nerlich shows, from its beginning as twelfth-century knightly romance, the discourse argued that adventure was the exclusive property of a special class (Nerlich, *Ideology*, p. 6). In fact, as he goes on to show, the discursive power of the genre developed over the next few centuries as a justification of the existence of an embattled upper class (which might otherwise have been considered unnecessary, even parasitic), and as a glorification of its deeds (which might otherwise have been viewed as disruptive). In Haggard, this appeal is overt, for his protagonists Quatermain and Curtis write as members of an embattled squire-archy. Thus to invoke the romance, was to divinely authorize the questor's mission and place it beyond interrogation. But the Gradgrindian emphasis on facts authorized works of adventure fiction as "realistic" and "true-to-life," even though the writers' traces marked their stories "the way the handprints of the potter cling to the clay vessel" (Benjamin, *Illuminations*, p. 92).

Furthermore, adventure fiction generally announced itself as fact. Part of the particular pleasure afforded by the genre was that it concerned real places with geographically verifiable names, not airy habitations without names. In the prefaces and throughout the discourse too, this fiction promoted itself as chronicles of actual experience. From *Robinson Crusoe* on, adventure fiction had purported to work directly from original sources, and thus made claims on its readers' belief, presenting itself as having the force of actual experience behind it. As a contemporary writer, Andrew Lang observed, these writers had been there; as the "new conquerors," they had gone out of "the streets of the over-populated lands into the open air" and had "seen new worlds for themselves." This claim to provide eye-witness, and therefore reliable, information can be seen in the writing of Captain Frederick Marryat, Robert Ballantine, G. A. Henty, and H. Rider Haggard in their major works of adventure fiction that span the second half of the nineteenth century. In each case, the claim for reliability also serves to re-inscribe the imperial subject already constructed by the travel writing.

After serving in the Royal Navy for twenty-four years, from the age of fourteen, Marryat retired in 1830 and started writing novels that came directly out of those years at sea. In the preface to his first children's book, *Masterman Ready* (1841–42), Marryat describes his work as written in the "style" of *Swiss Family Robinson*, but he quickly moves to distance himself from that work, explaining his chief objection, its improbability:

I pass over the seamanship, or rather the want of it, which occasions impossibilities to be performed on board of the wreck, as that is not a matter of any consequence: as in the comedy, where, when people did not understand Greek, Irish did just as well, so it is with a large portion of the seamanship displayed in naval writers. (p. v)

The preface makes further claims for the writer's authority. In it, Marryat goes on to object to the plants and animals inhabiting the supposed "temperate latitudes" of *Swiss Family Robinson*, plants and animals that he, from first-hand experience, knows are found only "in the interior of Africa or the torrid zone." These errors are inexcusable, he argues, for especially in works for children, "the author should be particular in what may appear to be trifles, but which really are not, when it is remembered how strong the impressions are upon the juvenile mind. Fiction, when written for young people, should, at all events, be based upon truth...." However, that "realism" is relative and not absolute is borne out by Robert Louis Stevenson's comment several years later that he aimed to avoid what he felt were the great improbabilities that marred Marryat's *The Phantom Ship* when he was at work on *Ebb Tide*, a novel he intended to be grimly realistic (Hillier, *South Seas Fiction*, p. 134).

Ballantyne's claims are similar. Most of his books celebrated a cause of some kind, either supporting missionary efforts in Canada (*Hudson Bay*, 1848), the South Seas (*The Coral Island*, 1857), and Africa (*Black Ivory*, 1873), or a testimonial to the good work of the Shipwrecked Mariners' Society (*Shifting Winds*, 1866), or the suppression of the slave trade in Africa (*Black Ivory*). But all of them, didactic and polemical as they are, claim to be fact rather than fiction. Another "new conqueror," Ballantyne went out of "the streets of the over-populated lands into the open air" of North America with the Hudson's Bay Company at the age of sixteen; his first book *Hudson Bay* was actually a travel diary kept during his years with the Company. He continued to travel the rest of his life, as clerk, trader, fireman, or miner, in search of authentic settings for his fiction. So chagrined was he after *The Coral Island*'s publication to learn of a factual error he had written into that book – that coconuts grew on trees in the same form as Englishmen at home saw them in the shops – an error caused by his never having been to the South Seas himself, that he determined never again to write of places about which he lacked first hand knowledge (Quayle, *Ballantyne*, pp. 142, 143). In his first three books, *Hudson Bay*, an autobiographical account of "everyday life in the wilds of North America," *The Young Fur-Traders* (1856) and *Ungava* (1857–58), Ballantyne assures his readers that his primary purpose is to inform, and he works to establish his credentials as an authority in prefaces, references to documented sources, footnotes, and purely informational asides. In his preface to *Ungava*, for example, he maintains that most of the major incidents are facts – "fiction being employed chiefly for the purpose of weaving these facts into a readable form," and that the intention of the story is "to illustrate one of the many phases of the fur-trader's life in those wild regions of North America which surround Hudson's Bay." He thanks the "Leader of the adventurous band" for his "kindness in placing at our disposal the ground work on which this story has been reared" (p. xi).

Interestingly, Ballantyne images books as factually informational within his fictions also. But he works to distance himself from those other, unreliable fictions; his heroes, he insists, are real, not heroes of "romance" (*Shifting Winds*, p. 17). Jack, the oldest of the trio of boys who shipwrecks on the Coral Island, frequently teases the youngest, Peterkin, that he would know more if he had read more. Because Jack has read a great deal, he has a store of handy information. "I have been a great reader of books of travel and adventure all my life, and that has put me up to a good many things that you are, perhaps, not acquainted with" (*CI*, p. 25). Thus he knows how coral is formed, he can identify the breadfruit tree and knows its many useful products, and he knows the coconut can contain a delicious liquid, to the awed delight of his two younger, thirsty friends. Like Marryat's Masterman Ready and Ned in Henty's *Under Drake's Flag*, Jack has that valued commodity in adventure fiction, practical lore. But he credits books with his knowledge, particular ones at that. Later when Ralph, the middle boy who tells the story, finds himself in sole charge of a schooner, he happens to find an old volume of Captain Cook's voyages from which he learns "much interesting knowledge about the sea in which I was sailing, but I had many of my own opinions, derived from experience, corroborated, and not a few of them corrected" (*CI*, pp. 268–269). Travel narratives, then, are represented in this fiction as so reliable that they are to be read as information manuals and trusted more than experience itself. Rhetorically, this internal self-endorsing works well; it privileges the genre from within while arguing convincingly for its reliability. And it certainly functions to silence any notions that might disturb a contemporary reader as to the presence of these British boys on an island in the middle of the Pacific Ocean. The only "unnatural" aspect of this encounter, it is made clear, are the "barbarisms" practiced by the inhabitants themselves.

In his preface to *Shifting Winds*, Ballantyne thanks "the Secretaries of the 'Shipwrecked Mariners' Society' and of the 'Sailors' Home,' Well Street, London, for their kindness in supplying me with reports, magazines, and other sources of information." And in introducing *Black Ivory*, he qualifies the "fictional" quality of the work by assuring his readers he has examined the "Parliamentary Blue-books which treat of this subject" as well as "various authoritative works to which reference is made in the foot-notes sprinkled throughout this book" (*BI*, p. 10). These texts and their accompanying apparatus of quoted sources, maps, prefaces and footnotes urge their readers' belief and demand their effectual complicity in validating the fiction and its imperial justifications. Ballantyne often used his fiction to argue against the deplorable lack of contemporary emphasis on geography. Interestingly, his boy-hero, Martin Rattler, who excels in school in only one subject, his favorite one – geography – anticipates Conrad's experience as a student.

G. A. Henty's titles themselves claim a direct relationship with actual experience: *The Young Franc-Tireurs and Their Adventures in the Franco-Prussian War* (1872), *Under Drake's Flag* (1882), *With Clive in India* (1884), *With Roberts to Pretoria* (1902), and *With Kitchener in the Soudan* (1903), to name a few. They represent historical or still living figures of national import in real places. His prefaces sustain the claim. Addressed to "My dear lads," they are manly chats in which the author establishes his credentials as a teller of important truths. But what else is to be expected from a discourse that set such store by truth-telling generally? Henty's lads, as we shall see, are above all, honest. In fact, such truth-telling is an essential ingredient in the adventure hero's depiction generally. The preface to *The Young Franc-*

*Tireurs* is typical in assuring the readers that in the following narrative, in the "guise of historical tales," he wants "to give...full and accurate accounts of all the leading events of great wars... While names, places and dates have been changed, circumstances and facts are true." Furthermore, he promises, he was there himself. He knew many of these irregulars or franc-tireurs personally, he promises his readers, and uses their own words often to tell his story, a story that would not otherwise have been recorded by main-stream historians. But we need to remember here, as Allen points out, that these were the days when the war correspondant was considered a gentleman adventurer, dependent usually on second hand information gleaned at day's end from the participants in cafés, beer gardens and barracks (Allen, "Henty," pp. 80–81). *By Sheer Pluck, A Tale of the Ashanti War* (1884) operates similarly, weaving together the fates of the fictional hero, Frank Hargate, with that of Sir Garnet Wolseley and his English troops. If Henty cannot give a first hand account himself, he cites eye-witnesses as sources, as in the preface to *On the Irrawaddy, A Story of the First Burmese War* (1897). Those witnesses include a Major Snodgrass, "the military secretary to the commander of the expedition." That such a source can only strengthen his claim for authenticity is Henty's conviction apparently; that it might indicate a severe bias is a question whose investigation the author-reader contract established in these prefaces does not permit. And his appeal was persuasive. As a biographer notes, as late as 1955 in Britain, Henty was being reproduced in the Collins Schoolboys' Library, and in American schools as well his works were read as history for many decades (Arnold, *Held Fast*, p. 19).

H. Rider Haggard makes another kind of claim on his readers' credibility, an almost conventional one by the time he wrote in 1885, the travel writer's apology. In his preface to *King Solomon's Mines*, Allan Quatermain, Haggard's narrator, apologizes for his "blunt" way of writing. More accustomed to a rifle than a pen, he is incapable of

the grand literary flights and flourishes which I see in novels – for I sometimes like to read a novel. I suppose they – the flights and flourishes – are desirable, and I regret not being able to supply them; but at the same time I cannot help thinking that simple things are always the most impressive, and books are easier to understand when they are written in plain language, though I have perhaps no right to set up an opinion on such a matter. 'A sharp spear,' runs the Kukuana saying, 'needs no polish'; and on the same principle I venture to hope that a true story, however, strange it may be, does not require to be decked out in fine words. (p. 20)

The disclaimer reminds us of Cook's who also felt that a plain style was appropriate for informational writing and hoped that "candour and fidelity [would] counterbalance the want of ornament" he was unable to provide. His authority, he maintains, derives from experience but also from factual travel accounts. If the travel writing of Cook and Livingstone informed Ballantyne, then Stanley was an important source for Haggard. *In Darkest Africa* certainly helped shape Haggard's belief in "the dark continent."

By thus disdaining any "literary" appeal, Haggard wisely broadens his audience and in fact disengages himself from the more literary *Treasure Island* on which he had originally modeled *King Solomon's Mines* (Cohen, *Rider Haggard*, p. 89). When Henry James referred to Haggard as Stevenson's "nascent rival" (Smith, *James and Stevenson*, p. 184), he acknowledged that those two writers were working in a similar vein, their chief difference being Haggard's lack of literary merit. While his remark intended to discredit Haggard for that failure, such was in fact Haggard's intention and one he often stated. The differences between those two works is revealing. Both were read as "adventure," but Haggard's followed the popular formula more closely and, consequently, enjoyed more success. In fact, Stevenson's quintessential adventure story, first published in *Young Folks* (October 1881), did not even sell well enough to boost the circulation of that periodical (Swearingen, *Stevenson*, p. 66). Certainly more literary than its companion pieces in *Young Folks* – "Sir Claude the Conqueror" or "Don Zalva the Brave" – it also refused to moralize, to include the "sayings of [Jim's] father or his mother" and passages of "a religious character" that Stevenson's father had advised him to add as a way "of harking back to something higher than mere incident" (Swearingen, *Stevenson*, p. 66). But it also refused to be "true-to-life" in certain ways. Its setting was distant but unnamed, and although inspired by Kingsley's *At Last* and well researched, it seemed improbable to many. Many readers found it too "fantastic" that a ten year old boy should be the hero of such bloody adventures and that the squire and doctor – English gentlemen, after all – should be so blind and gullible (Cohen, *Rider Haggard*, p. 89). Accused of not being factual, it was simply delivering the wrong fiction. That its sales were slow – a second edition was not required for two years – points up the essential ingredients of adventure fiction: at least a pretension to informational education and inspiration.

But eschewing the literary is also consistent with Quatermain's persona as a plainspoken, practical elephant hunter. In *Allan Quatermain* (1885), Haggard, in the guise of Editor, even corrects his narrator in a footnote, pointing out an instance of misquoted poetry (*AQ*, p. 90). To distance his telling from that of a novel – a work that needs added ornamentation to compensate for the barrenness of its content – also works to establish him as a reliable narrator of these events he took part in. Haggard acknowledges the tradition that holds that novels are frivolous fictions in order to characterize his narrator and the nature of his endeavor, but also to help counter objections to the believability of the events narrated. Such a disclaimer works for credibility, for it is an admission that the narrator has not the inventive powers necessary to bedeck and ornament, that his talents limit him to saying simply what happened. Like some simple primitive, his analogy suggests, all he can do is to trust that the unpolished spear he throws is so sharp and essentially sound that it will hit its target. He then goes on to construct his narration from his journal, from which he includes the occasional entry, to remind us of the journal's presence and therefore of the actuality of the events themselves.

In books Allan Quatermain does not narrate, Haggard avoids pretensions to the literary and sustains the fiction in other ways. In *She* (1886), for example, he establishes himself as "only the editor of this extraordinary history" (*She*, p. 17), working from papers left him by the original adventurer, including that writer's explanatory footnotes and only occasionally appending his own, citing learned Egyptologists and other scholars to corroborate otherwise amazing pieces of information. In some of those footnotes and throughout the discourse, careful and accurate descriptions of indigenous flora and fauna and explanations of various physical phenomena common to Africa but unknown to readers at home, inform and earn the readers' belief that these narratives are based on facts. Haggard's narrator frequently deplores his inability to describe the essentially indescribable; beyond "the wild invention of the romancer" (*She*, p. 306), these events, although stranger than fiction, did indeed occur.

This claim to realism, then, gave the genre great persuasive power.

Again, Lang speaks favorably of works such as Kipling's which "like all good work, is both real and romantic." While admitting of the possibility of adventure, it reveals "the seamy side of Anglo-Indian life" (Lang, *Essays*, p. 201). In fact the works themselves often addressed their readers' misinformation and sincerely tried to re-educate. Ballantyne, Henty, and Haggard all expressed concern that the English reading public knew so little about geographical matters. Isabella Bird, an intrepid late Victorian adventurer/writer, and Conrad also, complained that Europeans generally knew nothing about geography and were extremely short-sighted to place so little value on it. For Conrad it was not even a set subject but the only one he remembers being very interested in (*Last Essays*, p. 2). So concerned was Stevenson with the widespread lack of accurate information that he wrote a series of letters to the *London Times* over a period of several years to try to correct illusions about Samoa that readers at home labored under.

Although read as Truth, then, and resembling travel writing in certain particulars, adventure writing was certainly constructing fictions, ones that worked to justify the European, particularly the British, presence in other lands. Those writers who "had seen with their own eyes," as Lang had noted approvingly, had done so in such a way that their view was often predetermined. And perhaps as André Gide observed in his *Travels in the Congo* (1927), dedicated to "the Memory of Joseph Conrad,"

experience rarely teaches us anything. A man uses everything he comes across to strengthen him in his own opinion and sweeps everything into his net to prove his convictions.... No prejudice so absurd but finds its confirmation in experience. (p. 95)

These adventure writers, like other readers of travel narratives, were directly predisposed by those writers to view these other lands and the people who inhabited them in particular, predetermined ways. Like Kipling, Henty was a newspaper man, who, as a war correspondent for *The Standard* covered many colonial wars and on one such assignment joined up with H. M. Stanley, a fellow correspondent on the campaign and soon to become Commander of the Anglo-American Expedition for Exploration of Africa in charge of charting the Congo (Allen, "Henty," p. 90). Henty was covering the Ashanti campaign with Sir Garnet Wolseley (Gilbert's "model of a modern major general") – a campaign that left 4,000 Ashanti dead and 220

British and allied fatalities. "Covering" the war, as we have seen, is something of a euphemism, dependent as he was on second hand information. But even that term is too disinterested, for Henty certainly had attitudes already formed, and his accounts comprised less than objective reporting. Stanley returned to London and wrote *Through the Dark Continent* (1878), and whether Henty read Stanley's work or not is difficult to determine. The books Henty wrote out of the experience, *The March to Coomassie* (1874), *By Sheer Pluck* (1884) and much later *Through Three Campaigns* (1904) claimed to be factual accounts of historical, and fictional, characters in real places. But the attitudes towards the native and the Anglo-American presence in Africa were similar to those of Stanley and to many of the other writers of travel writing already discussed.

These writers, moreover, saw their fiction as continuations of real-life discussions in which they were personally participating. Kingsley, whose *Westward Ho!* celebrated Elizabethan England's imperialist ventures and successes, had read the journals of Rajah Brooke of Sarawak, as mentioned in the last chapter, and must have found himself in deep accord with that benevolent believer in progress, for he dedicated his work to Brooke, claiming he was "at once manful and godly, practical and enthusiastic, prudent and self-sacrificing..." (*WH*). As discussed earlier, Kingsley himself was a great promoter of colonization, issuing the call to England's youth in newspaper articles, fictions, and lectures. For Kingsley, Brooke was the colonizer *par excellence*, one Kingsley felt should be an inspiration to England's youth. Ballantyne also read much of the travel writing of his time; in *The Coral Island*, as we have seen, Jack extolls the virtues of Captain Cook's journals to Ralph, the central character, recommending it as containing much useful information. In Ballantyne's *Black Ivory*, the central characters frequently refer to Livingstone's work on the Zambesi, and editorial references are made in footnotes to other published works of "missionary enterprise." Haggard's first trips to Africa too were on official business; he accompanied Shepstone to South Africa to annex the Transvaal in 1877 and stayed on for a few years as a colonial officer (Cohen, *Rider Haggard*, p. 41). And since, as we have seen, the travel writers had their own reasons for defending the imperial project, from escaping the drabness of everyday life to establishing religious missions, their writing is other than objective. Whether these writers did "see new worlds for themselves," then, is doubtful. Even as they looked with their own eyes, they could not help, as we shall see, but view the landscape as beautiful and therefore worth annexing – or pestilential and thus in need of improving – the natives as inferior and therefore in need of enlightenment, and their own endeavors as benevolently heroic.

These writers were not spinning purely imaginary romances but were also informing the stay-at-homes in urban England of sunny foreign lands lately come into England's consciousness as acquisitions of empire. At the same time, however, adventure fiction argued powerfully for a particular interpretation of those realities, that the benefits of civilization merited British incursion into these lands. Influenced by the perspective from which travel narratives were often written, and by their own experiences in the outposts of empire, the writers of adventure fiction were intent both on revealing strange worlds to their readers, seen first-hand and additionally carefully researched, and also on shaping particular attitudes towards the imperial subject. That they did so with considerable effect derived in great part from the close association of adventure fiction with the highly esteemed and believed travel writing of the day. Indeed, this was "discourse" in Said's sense of writing that while manufacturing attitudes, rendered the machinery invisible.

But even though works such as *Masterman Ready*, *Westward Ho*, *The Coral Island*, *Under Drake's Flag*, and *King Solomon's Mines* worked in all these ways to be read not as novels, they were, in fact, clearly read as fictions, as exciting adventure stories about, in large part, fictionally constructed characters. Then why, in a culture that so distrusted novel-reading, did they become not only so popular and abundant but also officially validated? For they did indeed become recommended reading, especially for the young, and were, in fact, the prizes the culture conferred upon the young for good behavior. The answer must lie in their usefulness as inspirational literature, for they served the various utilitarian purposes of dispensing practical and historical information and of promoting an ideology of patriotic heroism and Christian dutifulness compatible with imperialistic aims.

The genre's ideology served imperial concerns so well, in fact, that it often became required reading. According to a biographer of Marryat, officers in H.M.S. Britannia were obliged to read and to memorize passages from *Peter Simple*, chapter 15 in particular, for in illustrating the value of a crew's unswerving obedience to a knowledgable, dutiful captain at sea, it both instructed and inspired

(Warner, *Marryat*, p. 157). In this chapter, the frigate Peter is serving on has just captured two or three French vessels when "we had an instance showing how very important it is that a captain of a man-of-war should be a good sailor, and have his ship in such discipline as to be strictly obeyed by his ship's company" (p. 99). The device of a fifteen year old midshipman who is too young to participate in some of the action but has the perfect vantage point for narrating is effective. A kind of Joseph Andrews ingénu, his youthful inexperience is a good part of his appeal, and he takes as his models, as the readers also should, the captain and the admirable Mr. Chucks, "the best boatswain in the navy," the first lieutenant tells the Captain (p. 129). During this particularly life-threatening maneuver, absolute obedience is demanded and received, even by the mate who had not agreed with the captain's orders but had obeyed, for

he was too good an officer, and knew that there was no time for discussion, to make any remark; and the event proved that the captain was right.

'My lads,' said the captain to the ship's company, 'you have behaved well, and I thank you; but I must tell you honestly that we have more difficulties to get through.'

'Mr. Falcon,' said he, at last, 'we must put the mainsail on her.'

'She never can bear it, sir.'

'She *must* bear it,' was the reply. (p. 103)

The mainsail is set and the ship careens so in the storm that the first lieutenant, still a "good officer" presumably, cannot restrain himself: "'If anything starts, we are lost, sir,' observed the first lieutenant." He is practically certain of death yet maintains his observance of the code, never forgetting his place in the hierarchy – "Sir" – and "observing" rather than "screaming," or "complaining." Calmly, the captain replied, "'I am perfectly aware of it...'" (p. 105). A reader would not have to memorize this passage in order to learn the lesson here; if anyone in this situation had neglected his duty, all would suffer, and it is the indomitable Mr. Chucks who concludes "'Private feelings must always be sacrificed for the public service'" (p. 108), the message officers and readers alike should heed.

Kingsley's *Westward Ho!* was also put to good use, as we have seen, to reform wayward youths. Its writing was inspired, he admitted, by the enthusiastic support he felt for England's participation in the Crimean War. He thought of *Westward Ho!* as "containing doctrine profitable for these times" (Kingsley, (ed.), *Letters*, p. 214), for it espoused the same anti-Catholicism that was an important force behind the war and, for Kingsley, helped to justify that war. A year later, in 1856, he wrote "Brave Words for British Soldiers and Sailors," a tract that was distributed among the troops in Crimea, the only one of many such inspirational tracts the men actually read, a correspondant assured him. As a result of its success, he was made one of the Queen's chaplains and was presented to Victoria and the Prince Consort.

In shaping attitudes essential to the imperial subject, then, adventure fiction was extremely useful. Increasingly abundant and popular, it came to be "the energyzing myth of English imperialism... the story England told itself as it went to sleep at night" (Green, *Dreams of Adventure*, p. 3). Even though much of this discourse was aimed at a general audience – only three of Marryat's twenty-seven books were specifically for "young people" – much of it was addressed particularly to future empire builders and often appeared in periodicals such as *Young Folks, Union Jack* and *Boy's Own Magazine*. And what Orwell was to note of the Boy's Weeklies in the early twentieth century pertains to their Victorian counterparts as well, that even more than the national dailies with large circulation, they "reflect[ed] the minds of their readers" (Orwell and Angus (eds.), *Collected Essays*, p. 461). Imperial literature, in fact, bore the same relationship to its readers as parents to children; it espoused a similar ideology of duty, discipline, honesty, obedience and responsibility. In fact we see the same relationship reflected in the language of the adventure fiction that starts to deal with the subject peoples, especially the exotic subjects of the empire's outposts, Mother/country and Daughter/colonies. If, as Brantlinger suggests, Africa let men act like boys ("Victorians and Africans," p/ 190), then similarly the fiction about Africa and other colonial outposts provided vicarious pleasures not only to young readers but also their fathers.[3]

G. A. Henty's more than eighty novels about the achievements of the British army in colonial settings were usually prefaced with "My dear lads." He actually aroused those dear lads to such a patriotic pitch that the generation reading him as Christmas gifts in 1900 were ready for the trenches fourteen years later (Allen, "Henty," p. 97). See also Fussell, *Great War*, p. 155f). In his preface, Ballantyne presents *The Coral Island* "specially to boys" and signs it "Ralph Rover," the involved narrator of the tale. Others of his novels are entitled after their young heroes such as *Martin Rattler*, or *The Young*

*Fur-Traders* (1856), making their intended audiences apparent. *Treasure Island* was addressed to "the wise youngsters of today" in the hope that youth had not become so studious as to forget its "ancient appetites" for Kingston or "Ballantyne the brave," and was signed "Captain George North." One of the great appeals of this fiction, then, was that it was delivered as truths passed on from one generation to the next. The persona of the speaker, a kindly and experienced older chap who appeared to know exactly what he was talking about and whose heart was obviously in the right place, did nothing to encourage disbelief or disobedience. The tone sustained in all of these works was of a manly chat or a kindly paternal lecture; as the dominant, officially approved discourse, it was appropriately men speaking to other men, or boys. Perhaps Benjamin's distinction between story and novel helps account for the nature of this fiction's appeal. Rather than the absent author of novels which described the modern world's perplexities, the story-teller – he who comes from afar – imparts practical counsel and the accumulated wisdom of the tribe (Benjamin, *Illuminations*, p. 84f).

Thus it came packaged as advice from a wise, good-natured father-figure. As espousing Truth and the requisite ideals, then, the culture used it as the prize for good behavior and in so doing conferred even more authority upon it. For taking academic firsts, for good conduct, for achievements in sports, this fiction was given as the prize. For example, a copy of Henty's *The Young Franc-Tireurs*, given as a Christmas present from "Momma and Papa" for "Xmas, 1901," must have been one of innumerable such parental gifts. A copy of Henty's *On the Irrawaddy* was also awarded as a prize on October of 1911 by the County Borough of Northampton's Education Committee to Arthur C. Tye, of the 2nd class "For excellent Work" and was signed by the Head Teacher. Pasted inside the cover of a copy of *Martin Rattler* is a bookplate from Glascow Academy, awarding this book as a Prize to H. M. Kay for "good work" in the First English Class and signed, E. Temple, Rector, 1916–17.[4]

These fictions arrived, then, with the blessings of the authorities; they and the ideals they espoused were not only endorsed by family, school and church, but were also promoted by the periodical publications that made this fiction so available. *The Illustrated London News* issue for November 30, 1901 in its article "Christmas Books for Boys," praised the "indefatigable Mr. Henty [who] has so skillfully blended fact with fiction in 'With Roberts to Pretoria'" and recommended it for being not only exciting but also educational. The other recommendations for Christmas fare for boys are other war books, *At the Point of the Bayonet*, about the Mahratta War and *To Herat and Cabul* about the first Afghan War, both by Henty. The genre arrived with great authority and all branches of the establishment endorsed it.

That it was a shaping fiction for several generations of Englishmen is easily attested to. Not only did the officers in H.M.S. Britannia read Marryat's *Peter Simple* and read it as a kind of rule book, but Conrad also admitted to an early admiration for that writer. In an early, laudatory article, "Tales of the Sea" (1898), he referred to Marryat as "the enslaver of youth" (*Notes*, p. 53). That frequent immersions in that writer, in abridged, translated versions, formed part of Conrad's obstinate resolve to go to sea, as suggested in *A Personal Record*, helps to support Martin Green's assertion that "Marryat was often said to be the best recruiting officer the British Navy had" (Green, *Dreams of Adventure*, p. 5). Marryat's influence on Conrad can also be measured in his writing itself. Conrad and Ford's collaborative effort, *Romance*, for example, contained obvious echoes of *Peter Simple*; a contemporary reader would certainly have remembered Seraphina and O'Brien from Marryat's novel. Kipling's allusions to Marryat, too, reveal that earlier writer's pervasive influence. In his story "At the End of the Passage" (1890), Kipling likens one of his characters, a civil servant in India, overburdened with the tasks of civilizing the natives, to "Chucks," recognizing in Marryat's common seaman – "the best boatswain in His Majesty's service" [*PS*, p. 129] – something akin to the figures he himself drew so well, the common soldier and the class-conscious civil servant, who, like Chucks, "had a great idea of bettering himself socially" (*Life's Handicap*, p. 161). Not only does Kipling assume his readers' ready understanding of "Chucks" and the world that comes with that allusion, but he also knows that the reference, made by one white man to three others within the fiction, is an illuminating one for them; these three Englishmen in India will hear the comparison and know exactly what the speaker means as will the readers of the fiction. Marryat was the common possession of a whole class of Englishmen involved in the Empire's business, and such invocations served indirectly to recall that "private feelings must always be sacrificed for the public service." Once that belief was in place, the idea of the White Man's burden as the selfless duty of responsible colonizers made perfect sense.

Writers and statesmen alike spoke as adults of the enormous influence these works exercised upon them throughout their lives. Speaking of his unhappiness at St. James School, Winston Churchill recalled many years later that reading provided him the greatest pleasure in his otherwise unhappy school days. When he was nine-and-a-half, his father gave him *Treasure Island* and that book particularly he remembered "devouring" "with delight" (Heath (ed.), *Churchill*, p. 22). So powerful were these books that they often preempted actual experience itself; not only were they shaping the metropolitan Englishman's ideas about these foreign places coming within England's sphere of influence, but they also predisposed the actual travellers themselves – as we have seen – to view these outposts in terms that derived more from travel writing, from the writers' own particular point of view as involved and therefore biased participants, and from adventure fiction, than from strictly factual information manuals. When Churchill, now a young British officer, first spotted Cuba from aboard ship, his vision of it was already colored:

When first in the dim light of early morning I saw the shores of Cuba rise and define themselves from dark-blue horizons, I felt as if I sailed with Captain Silver and first gazed on Treasure Island. Here was a place where real things were going on. Here was a scene of vital action. Here was a place where anything might happen. Here was a place where something would certainly happen. Here I might leave my bones. (*A Roving Commission*, p. 77)

Churchill also remembered reading *Kidnapped* while a prisoner of war of the Boers, and being so immersed in it that he felt David Balfour's adventures and mishaps as though they were his own (p. 290). So real was this fiction for many of its readers, that it exerted a kind of immediacy that life did not.

Even earlier Churchill had been reading Haggard, although he owns up to his reading of Stevenson more readily than to that of Haggard. But Haggard himself included a letter from the young Winston, aged fourteen, to the writer in his 1926 autobiography *The Days of My Life* (p. 8).

Thank you so much for sending me "Allan Quatermain," it was so good of you. I like AQ better than "King Solomon's Mines"; it is more amusing. I hope you will write a great many more books.
                    I remain,
                        Yours truly
                            Winston S. Churchill

Many attitudes held and espoused by the later Churchill can certainly be found in this fiction that promoted imperial prestige, expansion, and heroism. The same claims could be made about Harold Macmillan, who asserted in his *Winds of Change*, that "Henty was the prize," although he ranked Henty equally with Scott, Dickens, Conan Doyle and Haggard as the authors he most enjoyed (p. 176). In his critical biography of Haggard, Morton Cohen speaks of other prominent people who have acknowledged an admiration for Haggard in particular, among them, King Edward VII, who claimed to prefer Haggard to Hardy and Meredith. Cohen refers to the many writers who spoke of their debt to Haggard – D. H. Lawrence, C. S. Lewis, and Henry Miller (Cohen, *Rider Haggard*, p. 231). In his Introduction to a 1957 reprint of *She*, Stuart Cloete, a South African writer, maintains that he "was brought up on Rider Haggard and G. A. Henty," and that their books "were the literary milk of my boyhood from which I have never been weaned." But Haggard's influence was not purely literary. In remembering the impact on him of his early reading, Graham Greene recalls that the book "above all other books at that time of my life" was *King Solomon's Mines*.

This book did not perhaps provide the crisis, but it certainly influenced the future. If it had not been for that romantic tale of Allan Quatermain, Sir Henry Curtis, Captain Good, and above all, the ancient witch Gagool, would I at nineteen have studied the appointments list of the Colonial Office and very nearly picked on the Nigerian Navy for a career? (*The Lost Childhood*, p. 14)

But Greene was a reader, rather than a consumer, for whom, finally, the heroes seemed inordinately good.

They were men of such unyielding integrity (they would only admit to a fault in order to show how it might be overcome) that the wavering personality of a child could not rest for long against those monumental shoulders. These men were like Platonic ideas: they were not life as one had already begun to know it. (*The Lost Childhood*, p. 9)

But for many readers, as we have seen, the books were as palpable and convincingly real as actual experience itself, and in some cases, more so. Many of those who were persuaded to devour the fiction whole went into the military or government. Green was rather exceptional in doing neither; instead, he became a writer, a writer as it turned out, of a very different colonial fiction, one that challenged adventure fiction's construction of the imperial subject.[5] But at the moment, particularly the 1880s and 90s, the spirit of the age was expressing itself in a literature that applauded Britain's imperial ventures. How that discourse that made its appeal as inspirational and educational truth constructed the imperial subject, fictionally, will be our next concern.

CHAPTER 3

# Them and us: a useful and appealing fiction

While adventure fiction was officially validated, given as gifts, sanctioned, advertised, and recommended for its educational and inspiring attributes, and even assigned as required reading, its readership did not have to be sold, such were the immense attractions of this exotic fiction. The appeal it made was both to national, or racial, greatness and to personal fulfilment. Essentially nostalgic, adventure fiction yearned for an imagined golden moment in the nation's past, now endangered or lost completely, and at the same time argued for present outlooks and future courses of action that the fiction itself made especially attractive and justifiable. Thus, as we have seen, the fictions of the 1830s and 40s of Marryat reenacted the English successes against Napoleon's Mediterranean fleet, celebrating the English virtues of manly courage, duty, and continued conquest. In the early decades of the century, then, Marryat sounds the national note that links adventure with imperialism, a relationship that pertains throughout the century though one whose dark diminishment Conrad will record. Kingsley's *Westward Ho!* celebrated the triumph of Elizabethan England's naval forces over Spain's Armada and justified the parallel of Victorian England's anti-Catholic and expansionist venture in the Crimea. By referring back to the Elizabethan period, the great golden moment for England, he urged his readers to apply the glory of the one to the other. Most readers, apparently, found it agreeable to do so, since sales continued to mount throughout the century.

Adventure fiction celebrated, in its various "exotic" settings, a pre-industrial past, and particularly after mid-century, the nostalgia implicit in this fiction fulfilled the industrialized reader's desires for Edenic, unspoiled beauty – generally rendered in such explicitly male terms as "the virgin track," or "the unpenetrated forest" – and for an arena for manly, heroic action, uncomplicated by the complex

62

moralities of a modern, democratic world. Tennyson's Ulysses'
complaint about domestic life on Ithaca applied also to modern
England, for many people an increasingly "dull" place in which to
"pause." Industrial life was grey and dreary, and it was also
demanding and complex. The fictions of Scott and Cooper, the
names that hover at the back of this discourse and at the top of the
reading lists of most of these writers, created appetites for adventure
early in the century and took an admittedly anti-industrial stance.
Thus in contrast to the domestic and particularly urban fictions of
George Eliot, Dickens, Gaskell, Hardy, and Gissing that depicted the
deplorable Condition of England Question and the plight of the poor
against which their heroes were increasingly ineffectual, the arguments adventure fiction offered had great appeal. It offered a
pleasant change of scene from the fog-bound Victorian cities, from
the urban poverty of London's Tom-all-Alones and the dreary mills
of Manchester, and the picture of the Englishman, portrayed in the
adventure writing of the day, as morally admirable and physically
courageous, decisively exerting his superiority in sunny desert isles,
wide veldts, and tropical jungles was a welcome relief from the
agonized, self-defeating Jude Fawleys of the domestic fiction.[1] And in
reminding the English audience of its essentially upright moral
nature, adventure fiction helped assuage the guilt that the innumerable depressing Jo's of the domestic fiction aroused, mollify the
accompanying frustration at the apparent ineffectualness of reform,
eliminate the confusion of an increasingly complex world, and fulfil
the desires for forthright, heroic action.[2]

As we have seen, echoing other voices of authority announcing
imperialism as a patriotic duty, adventure fiction offered to – even
urged upon – its readers vicarious and real ways out of England's
dreary, overcrowded urban centers, and avenues of accomplishment
for upper class and upwardly mobile middle-class youth. While
Graham Greene resisted the temptation to sign up for colonial
service, posed by *King Solomon's Mines*, others did not. Many readers
could not help heed the call; if pluck was not lacking, possibilities
abounded in imperial outposts, for trade, for government positions,
for colonizing. The writers themselves were adventurers who had
enriched themselves considerably through their travels, and, of
course, through the writing that grew out of those travel experiences.
Similarly, the heroes of the fiction are depicted as enterprising men,
or boys, who advertise the advantages of their adventuring in various

ways. Such depictions appealed to one's national identity, and promised personal fulfilment, financial benefits, and status; if nothing else, there was always the racial advantage of being a white man in the tropics. Lingard, too, knows that such a life as he has chosen affords him a privilege unavailable to him at home: "I *am* an adventurer," he tells Travers in *The Rescue*, "and if I hadn't been an adventurer, I would have had to starve or work at home for such people as you" (134).

To a great extent, of course, England's imperial subject had already been shaped, and as we have seen the fiction writers themselves had already learned about the heroic Englishman and the "primitive" Other on various "dark" continents from journals of discovery such as Cook's, Livingstone's and Stanley's. By the close of the nineteenth century, Conrad was reading and writing out of a firmly established convention that went back at least to *Robinson Crusoe*, one that had been carrying on the cultural conversation about imperialism for over 150 years and one that addressed the questions confronting those who met the Other. The writing tried to answer those questions and usually did so by asserting the essential difference between "us" and "them," in order to promote, celebrate and justify the imperial project. The manichean nature of the colonialist literature that Abdul JanMohamed discusses – an elaboration of Frantz Fanon's argument in *The Wretched of the Earth* – pertains to Victorian adventure fiction as well. Both are rhetorics of difference that work through "the manichean allegory – a field of diverse yet interchangeable oppositions between white and black, good and evil, superiority and inferiority, civilization and savagery, intelligence and emotion, rationality and sensuality, self and Other, subject and object" ("Colonialist Literature," p. 63). The very form of the adventure novel, a story retold after the fact, usually by the adventurer himself who has successfully returned and can tell us of the wonders he has seen, the hardships endured, and of the moment at the heart of the Imperial subject – the encounter with the Other – is one that emphasizes these differences. As Andrew Lang had remarked about this literature, its subject was exotic, that is, strange, alien, foreign, outside, different, expressly not indigenous. Lang's formulation appears innocent, even appreciative. But, of course, in the fiction differentness was not neutral; rather it became a trope that worked against the possibility of reading "different" as "equal."

This fiction of difference, then, informed the Englishman at home about the Other in the outposts of empire through the conventions of the genre, chief among them the depiction of the white traveller-adventurer among those other people of different cultures, racial types and religions in exotic lands. The portrayals echoed those of the travel writing and appealed to the same feelings of national pride, moral obligation, and potentially, personal advantage. The depiction of the hero was fairly consistent and similar to those portrayals in the writings of Cook, McClintock, Brooke, Speke, and Livingstone. He was Christian, usually of a privileged, if not aristocratic, class and manly, that is, gentlemanly, brave, honest, decisive, hearty, and just. And this representation served to justify British incursion, for the Christian hero could only be viewed as benevolent and wise against native "savagery" and incompetence. Jeffrey Meyers points out that in these fictions there can be

no real involvement with the stereotyped native, who is important not as an individual but as an example of what the Englishman must overcome and suppress, nor with the traditional culture or the tropical setting, which merely serves as an exotic background. (*Fiction and the Colonial Experience*, p. vii)

These adventure heroes bring not only order and justice to the dark continent but also the light of Christian truth, and of course they have no compunction in doing so; no moral complexity confronts them, and the wilderness holds no temptation nor does it loosen any of their firmly held moral and religious convictions. They are always English gentlemen, i.e. Christian, and they always triumph. And from Jim Hawkins to Martin Rattler to Allen Quatermain, these heroes were precursors of that later idealist, Tuan Jim, a fictional victim of this fiction. For Conrad perceived a blur rather than a sharp distinction between them and us and thus distrusted these depictions and the rhetoric of heroism that devised them, a rhetoric which meant to inspire and stir Victorian readers.

More successfully than Jim, Conrad managed to escape – while greatly admiring – that "enslaver of youth," Captain Marryat, whose books were part of "the literary harvest" that followed Waterloo (Salman, *Literature of the Empire*, p. xi). The names of a few of Frederick Marryat's better known books – *Peter Simple* (1834), *Jacob Faithful* (1834), *Mr. Midshipman Easy* (1836), and *Masterman Ready or The Wreck of the "Pacific"* (1841) – emphasize these essential

qualities, and their heroes – Peter Simple, Jack Easy and Master
William Seagrave – display cheerful readiness and courage throughout their adventures. Martin Green argues that Captain Marryat's
heroes, rather than aristocratic as was characteristic of the heroes of
chivalric romance, derive for the most part from Robinson Crusoe
and Cooper's Natty Bumppo and are thus practical men of common
origin. This observation, while less true for Marryat's general fiction,
pertains particularly to the heroes of Marryat's juvenile fiction, such
as Masterman Ready who is a common sailor – son of a merchant
vessel captain – but whose practical knowledge saves the shipwrecked
Seagrave family from a fate their name had threatened. Perhaps it is
his very commonness, however, that finally makes him expendable,
for he alone dies saving the more genteel, better educated Seagraves.
It is the lore he practices in the wilderness and passes on to the
family's son, Master William – how to sink a well, how to turn
turtle, how to build a stockade and defend it against attack – that
enables them to survive their ordeal, and while delighting Captain
Marryat's readers, this practical knowledge of wilderness survival
also taught the values of readiness, manly self-defense, responsibility,
and discipline. In fact, Marryat's fiction written expressly for "young
people" engages in a great deal of moralizing and philosophizing
that is extraneous to the plot but that teaches values and attitudes
necessary to future empire builders. Although only a common sailor,
Ready is honest, avoids profanity and preaches his exemplary
morality to William. Mr. Seagrave also loses no opportunities to
moralize. In the following lecture he delivers to his son and heir, the
views on empire and on "us"/"them" relations are surprisingly
liberal. After explaining to his son that all empires come and go, he
argues the inevitability of colonies wresting independence from the
mother country by means of analogies to "a son, who has grown up
to manhood, leaves his father's house, and takes up a business to gain
his own livelihood," and to a "bird [who] as soon as it can fly will
leave its parents' nest" (p. 108). Disturbed by this prospect, William
expresses the hope that England's demise will not occur for a long
time. His father responds:

"And so does every Englishman who loves his country. Recollect that
when the Roman empire was in the height of its power, Great Britain was
peopled by mere barbarians and savages. Now Rome has disappeared, and
is only known in history, and by the relics of its former greatness, while
England ranks among the highest of nations. How is the major portion of the

continent of Africa peopled? by barbarians and savages; and who knows what they may become some future day?"

"What! the negroes become a great nation?"

"That is exactly what the Romans might have said in former days. What! the British barbarians become a great nation? and yet they have become so."

"But the negroes, father – they are blacks."

"Very true; but that is no reason to the contrary. As to darkness of the skin, the majority of the Moors are quite as black as the negroes; yet they were once a great nation, and, moreover, the most enlightened nation of their time, with a great many excellent qualities, full of honour, generosity, politeness, and chivalry. They conquered and held the major part of Spain for many hundred years; introduced arts and sciences then unknown, and were as brave and heroic as they were virtuous and honourable." (p. 109)

But Marryat takes away with one hand what he gives with the other, for the fiction has effectively discredited Mr. Seagrave throughout, depicting him as an ineffectual philosopher who, without Ready, would never have gotten his family safely onto the island or survived once there. He is often lost in thought, or prayer, while Ready is working. It is Ready's lore and first-hand knowledge of practical matters that convince here, not Mr. Seagrave's book-learning and enlightened musings. Described as "a well-informed, clever man," Mr. Seagrave, we are told, holds an office in Sydney in the colonial government and is very devout. But Ready is in charge, and we cannot attribute too much authorial weight to Mr. Seagrave's abstractions. In any case, as abstractions, their effect is to dehistoricize and normalize this rise and fall of empires. Since it is a natural process, we need not look too closely at the colonizing activities actually going on or at the means of conquest.

This idealism might either be the sort of qualified hopefulness we find at the end of Forster's *A Passage to India* – not here, not yet – or a kind of evasion. But in spite of these seemingly egalitarian future projections, for the time being, this fiction argues, "they" are "barbarians and savages" and pose a definite threat to "us." Under imminent native attack, William looks through his telescope over the top of the stockade to catch his first glimpse of the feared enemy. "The savages were all painted, with their war-cloaks and feathers on, and armed with spears and clubs, evidently having come with no peaceable intentions...." The understatement here reveals great stolidity in the face of a fearsome situation, somewhat belied by William's observation to Ready: "what a fierce, cruel set of wretches

they appear to be; if they overpower us they will certainly kill us."
"Of that there is no doubt, Master William; but we must fight hard,
and not let them overpower us. Kill us they certainly will, and I am
not sure that they may not eat us afterwards, but that is of little
consequence" (283). Their foreign appearance, their methods of
fighting, their utter faceless anonymity, the grammar of the language
itself with its frequent juxtaposition of "them" and "us," "our"
discipline, thoughtful preparedness and the courage of the individualized few against "their" uncivilized cruelty and large numbers –
all make those very distinctions that Mr. Seagrave's speech to
William purported to erase.

Even the natives Marryat does individualize are far from the noble
citizens of a great future nation that Mr. Seagrave envisions. Juno,
the Seagraves' faithful nanny, had been a slave. Her parents had
been owned by a "Dutch boor" [sic] – whether misprinted or
misspelled, the slip is a telling one, for it also reveals the otherness of
the boorish, non-English colonists – in the interior north of Cape
Town, and as *The Pacific* approaches the Cape of Good Hope, Mrs.
Seagrave assures Juno that she has nothing to fear. "'But you are free
now, Juno,' said Mrs. Seagrave; 'you have been to England, and
whoever puts his foot on shore in England, becomes from that
moment free'" (p. 7). This insistence upon England's aversion to the
practice of slavery echoes throughout the century's adventure fiction
but is made questionable not only by the economic dependence of
families such as Marryat's on the West Indian slave trade, but also by
the fictional depictions themselves.[3] Juno, if not a slave, is definitely
a dependent, a somewhat silly, childish, overly emotional one at that;
she is praiseworthy in so far as she is loyal and increasingly so as she
becomes more devout in her prayers and earnest in her attendance at
the family's Bible reading sessions. In spite of egalitarian musings,
then, the depiction of the native, in this fiction as in Defoe's, is either
that of an undifferentiated group of barbaric, threatening savages,
the faceless Other, or that of a faithful Friday, much improved
through domestication and Christian teaching.

In Marryat's adult fiction, such as *Peter Simple*, *Jacob Faithful*, and
*Mr. Midshipman Easy*, similar depictions are at work but without the
ambivalence of fathers whose moralizings are not questioned. In fact,
ideas of equality are ridiculed in *Mr. Midshipman Easy*. Jack Easy's
father, a kind of unrestrained, parodical Mr. Seagrave, presides over
a household as eccentric as Shandy Hall. The hobby he rides is the

equality of man, a doctrine that causes Jack a great deal of trouble and one that finally proves fatal to the father who goes mad, and dies a grotesque death. "They" are in evidence in this novel in the form of an Ashanti Jack befriends in his travels, an African made acceptable not only by his loyalty but also by his nobility, for he claims to be a prince in his native land, an aristocratic exotic. Prince or not, Mesty, like his ancestor Friday, never questions his subordinate position to Easy and is grateful to be his servant. As "a descendent of Ham," after all – a theory ascribed to by many writers in the nineteenth century other than Speke – Mesty and Juno are appropriately servants, in fact their "natural" role in much popular fiction of the day (Street, *Savage in Literature*, p. 59).[4] While the relationship between Mesty and Jack is mutually beneficial, it depends for its success on its inequality; "they" are still easy to distinguish from "us." To everyone's satisfaction, racial lines are maintained and class lines are restored. Not written expressly for young readers, as was *Masterman Ready*, *Mr. Midshipman Easy* and the other adult fictions make these distinctions without muting or disguising that message with didactic moralizings.

In the century's next generation of adventure fiction, the heroes of R. M. Ballantyne's fiction also are hearty, able adventurers who, although of rather common origin, enjoy the racial distinctions reserved for "one of us," and in any case, end up with a tidy income by the novel's conclusion. In fact, the hero of *Shifting Winds*, *A Story of the Sea* (1866), a typical Ballantyne book, eulogized early in the book as "not a hero of romance whose soul raised him above the fear of sudden death – no, he was only a true-hearted British tar, whose frame was very strong, whose nerves were tightly strung and used to danger…" (p. 17), is relieved when reminded by his daughter that the root of all evil is not money, but the love of it. Thus Stephen Gaff and his wife "did not find their fortune too much for them, being guided in the use thereof by the Bible." The didactic strain is blatant in Ballantyne, even though such adults as J. M. Barrie, recalling their actual reading experience of his most popular book, *The Coral Island*, remember only the boys' heroic exploits, not the heavy religious emphasis (*CI*, Preface).

Like other Ballantyne characters, the white fur-traders of *Ungava*, *Tale of Esquimaux-Land* (1857) must have appealed to middle-class readers as possible models. Not gentry, they nonetheless improve their fortunes through their adventures, and in doing so, command a respect from the native Eskimos who are described s "disconsolate" at the departure of the white fur-traders. Child-like, simple and loyal, they mourn the loss of their hunter-trapper friends. The fictional depiction here of native and white men in colonial outposts reminds us of the relationship portrayed in much of the travel writing. So too does the insistence upon cheerfulness and cooperation. Like McClintock, these fur-traders value above all things their compatibility and good spirits, a necessary condition of lonely outposts. This bond would later be questioned by Stevenson and Conrad – although it is a bond Conrad believed in – in works like *Ebb Tide* and "Outpost of Progress" particularly, in which the good feelings have somehow expended themselves and the white men do not stick together in a jolly, harmonious, unity that upholds their natural supremacy. Seemingly intent only on instructing his readers in native exotica, Ballantyne effectively emphasizes the differences between "them" and "us." Even though the white man and the native are on friendly terms, they live distinct existences. The Esquimos "dwell" in their igloo villages, apart, and eat their strange diet of blubber and fat, while the white men live in their wooden houses and supplement their diet with tinned goods from England. Unlike a later visitor, Gontran de Poncins who came to think of himself as the uncultured savage after his years among the Eskimo (*Kabloona*), Ballantyne – like Speke – never suffered that confusion. The traders themselves are a jolly, stout-hearted, uncomplaining lot, well supplied with backwoodsman lore and know-how. Cheerful and altruistic, that they are there for personal gain is not directly mentioned, but their motives are usually ascribed patriotically to the good of the company, i.e. The Hudson's Bay Co.

In his first book, *Hudson Bay or Everyday Life in the Wilds of North America* (1848), written directly from his journals, Ballantyne depicts the Indians as "the primitive children of the forest" (p. 70), who risk their lives for the white traders. Again, Victorian racist assumptions firmly underlie the portraits. That "they" should serve "us" and even sacrifice their lives in the line of what is made to seem their duty, is a depiction so common to this fiction that native inferiority gets inscribed here as natural. Exceptions to this rule are members of the wild Blackfoot tribe, much given to fighting and thieving (321) and others who have occasionally been guilty of such uncivilized excesses as cannibalism.[5] That they are, essentially, children, of course, requires that the more civilized colonizers use a firm hand in their management, for like children their savagery needs to be checked; even more important to the missionary argument Ballantyne is urging, like the essentially docile children they are, their savagery *can* be checked. While Ballantyne sees them all as "generally very lazy" (p. 78) and "morally degraded" (p. 80), and their religion as simply "unmeaning mummery of the medicine tent" (p. 355) – echoing the same superior religious stance of so much of the travel writing – he also makes it clear that civilized restraint and true religion can reform them. Although, as Street makes clear, the depiction in *The Coral Island* of the natives as "barbarians and blood-thirsty cannibals attempting, with uncontrolled frenzy, to tie every white man to the stake" actually constitutes an appeal to missionaries to come and help, the point is also to argue against detractors that such an effort could be successful (Street, *Savage in Literature*, p. 70f). Thus Ballantyne notes happily that the missionaries sent out so far – Christian Britain's duty, he insists (p. 355) – have effected some changes; "the light of the gospels is beginning to shine with beneficial influence" (p. 80). Against these inferior savages, the white trader takes on heroic dimensions, especially the Englishman whose ancestors were the frequently mentioned adventurer-explorers, Hudson, Frobisher, and Sir John Franklin. In *Shifting Winds*, also, Ballantyne interrupts the plot for a short lesson on geography and the history of exploration and the great advances "our current knowledge" allows. These Englishmen too, these references imply, serve in a proud tradition, one of "facilitating trade, saving time, and greatly improving the condition of mankind" (*Shifting Winds*, p. 240), all equally desirable and unquestioned benefits it is the Englishman's moral obligation to pursue.

Of course, "Darkest Africa" might well have originated out of geographical ignorance, but, as Curtin argues, "it was adhered to out of cultural arrogance." As we have seen, a great source of urgency and conviction in this imperial fiction came from the sense – especially strong by mid-century – of cultural confidence in Britain. Curtin points to the Great Exhibition of 1851 as marking "the pinnacle of pride" in Britain's achievements, from the defeat of Napoleon to material progress at home, and the accompanying sense of superiority in regard to British religion, race and culture (p. 293). *Pax Britannia*, then, was the moral duty of a nation so advanced in its religious beliefs and technological achievements; such a mission compelled "us" to "swell the stream" and illuminate the darkness of "their savagery" with "our civilization," the proponents of imperialism argued.

Even Ballantyne's *Black Ivory, A Tale of Adventure among the Slaves of East Africa* (1873), a work whose neutral-sounding title promising "slave adventures" somehow belies its professed dedication to the elimination of the African slave trade, devotes many of its pages to an examination of the differences between "civilized" and "savage" peoples and to stereotypical depictions of native Africans. But by 1873 with the abolition movement firmly under way and greatly influenced by Livingstone's writings, Ballantyne's depiction of the native shifts a bit. If his former purpose, to promote missionary work, necessitated its own rhetoric, then the goal now – to suppress the slave trade – called for some readjustment in the stereotype. "The nigger is naturally a jolly fellow," and "he's not that ugly really" (p. 166), Harold Seadrift, a young Englishman recently shipwrecked off Africa's east coast, informs the sailor Disco, his fellow traveller. Such magnanimity also seems to motivate Disco's observations of a young slave girl. He tells Harold he is surprised to find her pretty:

"Ay, but I mean *really* pretty, you know. I've always thought that all niggers had ugly flat noses an' thick blubber lips. But look at that one: her lips are scarce a bit thicker than those of many a good-looking lass in England, and they don't stick out at all, and her nose ain't flat a bit. It's quite as good as my Nancy's nose, an' that's sayin' a good deal, *I* tell 'ee. Moreover, she ain't black – she's brown." (p. 20)

Although Disco maintains a respectful distance from and respect for Harold, the shipowner's son, on this issue the faithful British tar expresses a working-class view very similar to that of his employer's son. Ballantyne's fiction, then, means to disabuse its readers of false notions abut the native's appearance; "they," surprisingly, are not ugly, but only to the extent that they resemble "us." In his attempt to characterize the native sympathetically, a view he sees necessary to his polemic against the slave trade, Ballantyne idealizes any differences that remain in spite of his efforts to represent the native as like "us." Thus he describes a selected representative:

If an enthusiastic member of the Royal Academy were in search of a model which should combine the strength of Hercules with the grace of Apollo, he could not find a better than the man before us, for, you will observe, the more objectionable points about *our* ideal of the negro are not very prominent in him. His lips are not thicker than the lips of many a roast-beef-loving John Bull. His nose is not flat, and his heels do not protrude unnecessarily. True, his hair is wooly, but that is scarcely a blemish. It might almost be regarded as the crisp and curly hair that surrounds a manly skull. His skin is black – no doubt about that, but then it is *intensely* black and glossy, suggestive of black satin, and having no savour of that dirtiness which is inseparably connected with whity-brown. (p. 166)

In order to dispose readers favourably toward the African, and thus towards the book's project of criticising the slave trade, "they" must seem less conspicuously other than "our" image has hitherto suggested, and the particular ways in which they fail to resemble John Bull – black skin and "wooly" hair, for example – are simply idealized. In this portrait, we recognize the phenomenon Pratt discusses (see chapter 1 above), the static ethnological Othering of the native, as though he were a kind of zoological specimen, one individual representing an entire group, frozen in time. This apparently benevolent view achieves two effects. In its attempt to enlist support for a strong anti-slavery argument, it depicts the native as safely, appealingly passive, an object to be gazed upon from a distance with condescension – after all, he cannot be absolutely like us – with curiosity and finally with pity when we learn of his treatment by sinister Portuguese slave traders. It enables a view of him as victim, childlike and innocent and in need of our protection, and the depiction safely neutralizes any possible assertiveness or independence on his part. At the same time, it enables a view of the Englishman as generous, well-intentioned, capable, and heroic as he calls for the suppression of the slave trade – referring to Livingstone's *Travels* here for support – and for more English colonists and missionaries to aid in the civilizing project.

As Brantlinger notes, the step from suppressing such savagery as the slave trade to suppressing all "savage" customs and bestowing the light of Christian civilization, was a short and seemingly natural one and involved Britain more deeply than ever in enforcing *Pax Britannia* ("Victorians and Africans," p. 175). These depictions, here, as elsewhere, attempt to justify England's imperial projects by arguing for the natural superiority and thus the moral obligation of the Englishman who can so ably benefit more "backward" nations. In this way also the fiction explains the understandable relief felt by such a representative of enlightenment upon seeing another of his kind. During a lengthy stint at an isolated Company outpost, Ballantyne writes that one day he saw a man trudging through the snow towards his lonely cabin. "This unusual sight created in me almost as strong, though not so unpleasant, a sensation as was awakened in the bosom of Robinson Crusoe when he discovered the footprint in the sand" (*Hudson Bay*, p. 358). But better than any Friday – he already has his "solitary man," a French Canadian guide – the newcomer turns out to be not only a "*white*" man, but a "gentleman," and a "fine good-natured" and "well educated" one at that. The marooned white man, cut off from his own kind in an uncivilized, exotic land, feels more of a kinship with a literary prototype than with those few Others around him.

In G. A. Henty's novels, the heroes are honest, gallant, cheerful, resourceful and full of pluck, all valued Victorian qualities. Pluckish, indeed, are the heroes of *By Sheer Pluck* (1874), traveller-naturalist Mr. Goodenough and his young assistant, Frank Hargate, who set off boldly for Africa's interior in search of specimens of natural history. Although Frank's mother and sister live on the meager pension left to an officer's widow, "a pittance that scarce sufficed" (p. 5), Frank ends up with a comfortable inheritance – from his mentor and friend Mr. Goodenough – and a snug West End medical practice, the fulfilment of a middle-class fantasy indeed. Henty's heroes are "gentlemen-adventurers," and even if their origins are not aristocratic, their social position is always mentioned and is always respectable. Ned's father of *Under Drake's Flag* (1883) is a schoolteacher, but Ned, along with all Henty heroes, retires on an ample income, and like many Henty heroes, to a secluded estate in Devon. Set against these sturdy English adventurers are the natives. Again difference is invoked in a series of manichean oppositions. Their religion Mr. Goodenough dismisses as "fetishes and negro trumpery," in a manner reminiscent of Ballantyne's "unmeaning mummery." Upon first arriving in Sierra Leone, Mr. Goodenough instructs Frank that the natives here are "the most indolent, the most worthless, the most insolent, in all of Africa" (p. 112). It is their disobedience, their insolence that seems to most displease Mr. Goodenough, for when he speaks well of natives – some others, he concedes, are "strong, willing and faithful" (p. 113) – it is in terms of their obedience and loyalty. A bit later, Mr. Goodenough more fully initiates his young assistant into these truths fundamental to every white man in the tropics:

"They are just like children," Mr. Goodenough said. "They are always either laughing or quarreling. They are good-natured and passionate, indolent, but will work hard for a time; clever up to a certain point, densely stupid beyond. The intelligence of an average negro is about equal to that of a European child of ten years old. A few, a very few, go beyond this, but these are exceptions.... They are fluent talkers, but their ideas are borrowed. They are absolutely without originality, absolutely without inventive power. Living among white men, their imitative faculties enable them to attain a considerable amount of civilization. Left alone to their own devices they retrograde into a state little above their native savagery." (pp. 117–118)

Recall that these were often school history texts – and prizes for good behavior – so factual and authoritative were Henty's works considered. But after all, this writing affirms current Victorian explanations of race, which by the 1870s and 80s, were being validated by science. Early anthropological thinking based on evolutionary theory served primarily to authorize the current racism by conferring upon it the status of scientific truth. That the "primitive" was connected to the "civilized" and that human thinking evolved through stages – from savage magic, through religion, to civilized science – was the prevailing ethnological thought of the day, propounded by Edward Tylor in *Primitive Culture* (1871) and ascribed to by many others. "Primitives," in other words, were earlier, simpler versions of more highly evolved "civilized" beings. In this way science confirmed the earlier depiction of natives as somehow stuck in time, a static, timeless view that privileged "progressive" societies. Early ethnographers such as Tylor worked out of the same basically racist notion as earlier discoverers had, that societies that lacked a written language were without a history, thus encouraging the view of the native as our original ancestor who had stood still, as it were, as Europeans evolved and progressed. Whether the language was in terms of lower/higher or simple/complex, the privileging was clear, as was the concomitant duty to civilize.[6]

In the passage quoted above, the European scrutinizes the native with an eye to his suitability as a servant, for once again, and in Henty particularly, the native is born to serve. The language here depicts the unchanging savage; punctuated by "always" and "absolutely," it declares, and these declarations delivered as incontestable statements of scientific fact by the unquestioned authority figure here to young Frank – and all of Henty's "dear lads" – are challenged by nothing in the fiction. The repetition of "they" and "them" relegates the native African to Otherness and effectively silences him. At a stroke, the repeated assertions depict "them" as helplessly childish and backward and "us" as decisive and enlightened. After all, "they" do not even have the intelligence and foresight to collect the important biological and geological specimens that exist right under their noses, so devoted are "they" to their quarrels and sloth. Written a year after Ballantyne's *Black Ivory*, *By Sheer Pluck* lacks the former's avowed purpose of criticizing the slave trade. But Henty proselytizes too, and even though the depictions differ, their effects are similar. Both are aware of speaking to an audience of home readers for whom "Africa" is gaining prominence in everyday reading and current thinking. Both views provide the British reader with a feeling of moral superiority and obligation, and both see the need to inform that reader on a subject that has heretofore been represented in the domestic fiction as improbably exotic or in caricature as the faraway and inconsequential peoples of Borrioboola Gha. It was this fictional African tribe that so absorbed *Bleak House*'s Mrs. Jellyby, to her family's despair and dissolution. But if Dickens spoke for Britain's uncertain commitment to empire at mid-century, the increasing popularity of this discourse spoke for a new appeal towards the end of the century as industrial grit intensified and the political and economic need for empire was being argued for.[7]

JanMohamed's remarks about such "racial romances" as Haggard's *She* and André Brink's *A Chain of Voices* pertain here, for Henty's fiction too depends on differences to naturalize British intrusion into Africa while justifying the "social function of the dominant class and ideal[izing] its acts of protection and responsibility" ("Colonialist Literature," p. 72). Thus Henty's fiction not only distinguishes between them and us, but it moves even further to distinguish some of us from the rest of us, and along national lines. The English are not to be confused with other, lesser white men whose imperial motives are not as pure. Thus Ned and Tom, the two boy heroes of *Under Drake's Flag*, succeed in organizing the hitherto ineffectual Indians of Puerto Rico and making a "stout resistance" against the Indians' cruel Spanish oppressors. Like Charles Kingsley's *Westward Ho!* (1855), *Under Drake's Flag* looks back to the Elizabethan days of greatness, and the depiction of the English is similarly solid, fair-minded, bold and sensibly Protestant. In the dedication of his book to the Rajah Sir James Brooke, K.C.B. – that same Rajah Brooke Conrad read and would write about as "one of my boyish admirations" (Watts, *Joseph Conrad*, p. 209) – and to George Augustus Selwyn, D.D., the Bishop of New Zealand, Kingsley expresses his "admiration and reverence for their characters," and thus sets forth the English ideal so at odds with these fictional depictions of natives and other Europeans: "That type of English virtue, at once manful and godly, practical and enthusiastic, prudent and self-sacrificing, which [Kingsley] has tried to depict in these pages, [Brooke and Selwyn] have exhibited in a form even purer and more heroic than that in which [Kingsley] has drest it, and than that in which it was exhibited by the worthies whom Elizabeth, without distinction of rank of age, gathered round her in the ever glorious war of her great reign" (p. xi). These are the traits that distinguish the Englishman in the tropics from all those Others, native or European, and privilege his imperial aspirations. An aspect of Conrad's subversion, then, can be anticipated here, for his admiration for Brooke provided more of a contrast than a comparison. Conrad's Europeans in Borneo, measured against Brooke, can only demonstrate diminishment not continuing glory. None of the "progress" Brooke called for, for example, came to pass with any permanence in either Lingard's Sambir or Jim's Patusan.

Like Lingard, Jim, Kurtz, and Marlow, Kingsley's and Henty's heroes are "educated" but not scholars. They are manly men, not "milksops," of whom Henty confessed a dread, those boys and men who were afraid of blood and would not fight for God and Country. Although Ned of *Under Drake's Flag* finds adventuring with Sir Francis Drake more compelling than his schoolbooks, he is knowledgable and full of useful lore. In fact he and Tom bring the secrets of fire-making and of cooking in calabashes over open fires to the unfortunate, backward natives of South America and are blessed for doing so, from Patagonia to Lima. Seen as gods by the natives, the fiction affirms, they would encounter no trouble at all if it were not for the diabolical Spanish, for whose heinous mistreatment of the Indians, all white men, even the English, must suffer. At point of death, our heroes' magnanimity allows them to sympathize with their Indian captors, knowing they are about to die for the sins of the Spanish and taking comfort in the knowledge that they have always avoided profanity and commonness and have done their duty and done it honestly. "Let us die as Englishmen and Christians," Ned tells Tom bravely (p. 197). Thus even though these heroes are engaged in adventure for booty and gain – as much is admitted at the beginning of the adventure – their self-sacrifice and good deeds dominate the narrative and set them apart from those Others. The benefits of empire to the governed under such men as Henty's heroes must surely outweigh any possible drawbacks, rarely even glimpsed, this fiction argues; the moral duty of the governers is clear.

The fiction of H. Rider Haggard, Henty's contemporary, also emphasizes the differences and insists that distinctions be made between "them" and "us." *King Solomon's Mines* (885), *Allan Quatermain* (1887) and *She* (1887) were all written out of his own African experiences and were all extremely popular. In the record-selling *Allan Quatermain*, Quatermain on his deathbed urges his second in command, Sir Henry Curtis, always to remember he is "first a Christian gentleman, and next a public servant, called by Providence to a great and almost unprecedented trust" (pp. 212–213) in his leadership of the Zu-Vendis people of Africa. After Quatermain's death, Curtis' eulogy to him repeats those ideals and reminds us of Kingsley's dedication to Rajah Brooke. Curtis mourns his friend as "the ablest man, the truest gentleman, the firmest friend, the finest sportsman, and, I believe, the best shot in Africa," high praise from Sir Henry in reiterating the by now familiar catalogue of desirable imperial traits. That they are distinctly English traits is insisted upon. Like Ballantyne's evocation of England's famous explorer-adventurers, a tradition the evocation places him firmly within, Haggard's Quatermain also reminds readers of this traditional, venerable connection: "that is what Englishmen are, adventurers to the backbone; and all our magnificent muster-roll of colonies, each of which will in time become a great nation, testify to the extraordinary value of the spirit of adventure..." (*AQ*, p. 80).[8]

As we have seen, the quest romance, in whose tradition these adventure fictions are inscribed, confers a powerful authority on them. Like the heroes of romance, Quatermain and his companions believe themselves to be divinely charged, "called by Providence to a great and almost unprecedented trust." Thus, they – like Henty's heroes too – are presented as extraordinary and, to the natives, even god-like. Consistently "our" superior knowledge is contrasted with "their" childish ignorance and awe of European technology – guns, spyglasses, and books. And when Captain Good, R.N., one of Quatermain's fellow adventurers in *King Solomon's Mines* predicts the sun's eclipse – with the help of his almanac – and the sky indeed darkens, the natives attribute to him superhuman powers (p. 126). Of course, that they do so only confirms the English reader's sense of superiority; "our" scientific explanation for such a phenomenon, according to contemporary thought, was clearly more advanced than "their" religious, superstitious one.

Throughout the fiction, then, Haggard's heroes, all English gentlemen, are described as being neither dishonest nor tempted by wealth, and as such different from most foreign adventurers or natives. Their integrity, as English gentlemen, sets them apart. When Holly, the leader of the expedition to the Amahaggar people of She-who-must-be-obeyed at Kor first enters the awful presence of She, or Ayesha, and is ordered to get down on hands and knees, he refuses. "I was an Englishman, and why, I asked myself, should I creep into the presence of some savage woman as though I were a monkey..." (*She*, p. 150).[9] Natives, on the other hand, are superstitious, quarrelsome, childish and generally untrustworthy. Echoing the racist beliefs and anthropological theories of the day, Holly opposes his "great respect for the infinite" whose truth was "always veiled from us" to "native superstition and foolishness" (*She*, p. 128). However, while Haggard does admit of an aristocracy even among native groups such as the Zulu and thus the possibility of concerted endeavors such as those undertaken by Allan Quatermain and Umslopogaas in *King Solomon's Mines*, his notions of equality are conditional. Here too, as in Marryat, the native is acceptable when he is loyal and obedient, and nobility always helps. The something different about the tall Zulu that Quatermain first detects is genuine, and in the course of the adventure the white men help restore to this Zulu chieftain his rightful crown. But Quatermain refuses Umslopogaas's offer to stay in his land and select wives from among his people, telling his Zulu companion that "we would seek our own place." The biblical language here helps to naturalize the observation. But Umslopogaas himself admits:

I do perceive that thy words are, now as ever, wise and full of reason, Macumazahn; that which flies in the air loves not to run along the ground; the white man loves not to live on the level of the black. (p. 207)

Without irony, Haggard's insistence here is on the natural differences, not any coincidental sameness that binds them in a common endeavor temporarily, a difference that also, comfortingly, asserts the white man's superiority.

In the same work, Quatermain records with undisguised relief the death of Foulata, a native woman who has marked for her own Captain Good, whose life Foulata has saved on more than one occasion. Her heroism finally costs her her life, and as she dies trying to save the adventurers from being locked into the diamond cave by a slowly descending door of solid rock, she instructs Quatermain:

Say to my lord, Bongwan, that I love him, and that I am glad to die because I know that he cannot cumber his life with such as me, for the sun cannot mate with the darkness, nor the white with the black. (p. 193)

As impenetrable as that rock door now sealing them in the cave, is the essential, natural difference that separates white from black, in this fiction, civilized from uncivilized, Englishman from native, "us" from "them." Significantly Haggard puts these observations in the mouths of the natives themselves whose natural analogies underscore the statements as essential truths.

As the adventure draws to its conclusion, Quatermain recalls Foulata's death:

I am bound to say that, looking at the thing from the point of view of an oldish man of the world, I consider her removal was a fortunate occurrence, since, otherwise, complications would have been sure to ensue. The poor creature was no ordinary native girl, but a person of great, I had almost said stately, beauty, and of considerable refinement of mind. But no amount of beauty or refinement could have made an entanglement between Good and herself a desirable occurrence; for, as she herself put it, "Can the sun mate with the darkness, or the white with the black?" (p. 204)

In spite of the "beauty" and "refinement" Quatermain grants her, his language reduces her to a thing whose "removal" was "fortunate." The "poor creature" was a burden that would "cumber" Good, an "entanglement" that would "complicate."[10] Finally, transforming Foulata's analogy into a rhetorical question closes it, and puts it beyond investigation. This insistence upon distinctions between them and us is at the heart of the imperial subject; it defends the enterprise and encourages its pursuit, and congratulates its participants both actual and vicarious.

In fact, the impetus toward democracy and reform of much of the domestic fiction was countered in this literature that decried such modern problems. Rather, it sang of England's past and present glories abroad and recognized natural hierarchies between peoples and among them as well, a simple order that made short shrift of the moral paralysis and complexities of the modern world. It questioned the values of the domestic world, seeing them as false and confining, and viewed the move towards democracy as dangerous and wrong-headed. Haggard's fiction, in fact, deplored the wane of Zulu aristocracy as well as that of the English gentry. Order, his fiction argued, is best maintained when those natural hierarchies are observed. In this fiction, metropolitan Englishmen could read of the adventures and endeavors of their countrymen in the outposts of empire, and congratulate themselves on their courage, good sense and benevolence. The white man in the tropics cut a strikingly impressive figure to his audience. Set against the dark native, routinely depicted as a childlike savage, he was masterful, knowledgeable, compassionate – in short, a Christian gentleman. He was "one of us." Thus adventure fiction served the various utilitarian purposes of dispensing practical and historical information and of promoting an officially endorsed ideology of patriotic heroism and Christian dutifulness compatible with imperialistic aims while framing and promoting the subject of empire; besides having great popular appeal, the works were also educational and inspirational, and thus escaped the stigma of being "merely stories."

# CHAPTER 4

# The shift toward subversion: the case of H. Rider Haggard

To better understand the shift adventure fiction underwent from a discourse that created and confirmed stereotypes supportive of British imperial ventures abroad, to one subversive of those endeavors, such as Conrad's was to become, we should look more closely at the literary context of the 1880s and 90s. As we have seen, adventure fiction had been officially approved and had admirably expressed a kind of *Zeitgeist* for many readers. Marryat's fiction of past and present national glories, Ballantyne's evangelical adventures, and Henty's tales of boyish pluck had occasioned only commendation, for the fiction informed, delighted, and inspired a home readership, and always sympathetically. Ballantyne gently chided his readers for not knowing their geography as they should, and Henty inserted a stern – but friendly – lecture now and again on the virtues of pluck and honesty, and thus applauded and reinforced home values. Just as the rightness of the adventurers' return to England was never questioned, so too were the readers' values never scrutinized. Adventure fiction had always supported the status quo; the arguments it advanced for continued and extended imperial activity were aimed at awakening desire, particularly in regards to Africa, rather than countering any real opposition. But Haggard's fiction, while celebrating the English adventure hero and applauding England's imperial endeavors abroad, also introduced an adversarial element, a contentious note, not present before.

While "realism" had validated adventure fiction and made it useful for promoting the imperial subject, Haggard's portrayal of savage realities was unnecessarily graphic, many readers felt. Even *Treasure Island* had met with some protests of "too bloody," but many reviewers found the "reek of blood" in almost everything Haggard wrote (Cohen, *Rider Haggard*, p. 226). Priding themselves, as we have seen, on bringing back true reports from imperial outposts, the writers of this fiction often had to defend themselves against accusations of being "decivilized," an attack Conrad also defended himself against in the Preface to his first novel, *Almayer's Folly*. But Haggard, "romance" writer that he was, was interested in assaulting his readership with "realities" he thought they ought to know about, rather than merely defending himself against their sensibilities. His writing evinced a growing distance between the adventurer/narrator and his readers, an antagonism rather than the former companionable informativeness. It was a distance that reflected his sense of the yawning chasm between the actual problems at imperial outposts, from the colonists' point of view, and the home readerships' conception of those problems. Specifically he was bitter about Gladstone's concessions to the Boers and Britain's subsequent loss of the Transvaal at Majuba Hill in 1881. The loss was England's, Haggard felt, and also his own, for he had gone out to Natal to serve under the Lieutenant-Governor, Sir Henry Bulwer, had helped Theophilus Shepstone, Secretary of Native Affairs, in Natal in his attempt to annex the Transvaal, and looked forward to a flourishing colonial career for himself there (Katz, *Fiction of Empire*, pp. 50–52). He wrote out of a sense, then, of urging the Home Government toward a more "enlightened" policy, and while he often felt frustrated in achieving that goal, he also despaired of effectively communicating to the rich and refined "idlers" of his day the actualities of colonial life in imperial outposts he knew so well, while growing more insistent upon doing so. But the reigning Victorian proprieties were not receptive to the kind of strident realism his fiction was dealing with increasingly.

However, the manly action that had characterized the appeal all along continued to do so for other readers who welcomed such fiction and championed it for its graphic forthrightness and saw it as a corrective to an effete decadence that bred unfitness in an age gone soft. *The (Scots) National Observer*, subtitled *The Imperial Review*, was an important Victorian literary weekly and represented the literary current of the time associated with Tory conservatism and imperialism. Its editor, William Ernest Henley, was drawn to this writing that was under attack, for political, literary, and temperamental reasons. With such influential champions, the fiction survived the criticism quite well. A militant Tory himself, Henley was as opposed politically to Gladstone's "Little Englanders" as he was literarily to the fact "that the theory and practice of British art [were] subject to the influence of the British schoolgirl... " (Buckley, *Henley*, p. 156). And the two issues were closely related for writers of empire like Henley. To deal only with domestic matters, as much contemporary fiction in fact did, was to turn the nation in on itself, a kind of insular suicide, they contended (Salmon, *Literature of the Empire*, p. 3). The writing that celebrated English achievements abroad appealed to the finest emotions, unified disparate interests, and infused new life into the nation, the argument continued. At the same time, such manly writing also usually served a "Unionism" that advocated expansion and union of colonial possessions. Never one to fear controversy in pursuit of his beliefs, Henley published many works considered too indelicate by many, such as Hardy's *Tess of the D'Urbervilles* when the *Graphic* refused to print the christening scene from that novel. And it was Henley's *National Observer* that published Stevenson's public correspondence concerning Father Damien and other items of "perdurable value" (Buckley, *Henley*, p. 154). It was he who first promoted Stevenson's *Treasure Island* and recommended *King Solomon's Mines* to Cassell's for publication. And he reacted strongly not only against the prudery that would silence this fiction, but also the bloodless aestheticism that he felt characterized *The Yellow Book*, his contemporary and rival, especially that of one of its contributors, "Henrietta James," whose pieces Henley himself grudgingly used when he felt his journal needed some respectability (Flora, *William Ernest Henley*, p. 78). The stances of the *National Observer* and *The Yellow Book* were similar; both seemed determined "épater les bourgeois." The anti-effeteness of the one and the aestheticism of the other were both responses to the grey utilitarianism of the day. Thus, Henley advocated a "robust" acceptance of reality and a reassertion of "the fundamental heroic human values," but his courage in doing so caused many readers to stop buying the *National Observer*.[1]

Even the less controversial material published in the *Observer* – essays by Andrew Lang, short stories by J. M. Barrie, Kipling's "Barrack Room Ballads," his own "London Voluntaries," the last verses of Robert Louis Stevenson, and the young Yeats' lyrics – failed to find a popular audience, and no single issue sold more than 1,000 copies (Buckley, *Henley*, p. 155). A certain truculence and willingness to offend popular taste caused the *National Observer* finally to fail. A similar fate awaited the *New Review* whose editorship Henley took over in 1895 and which folded shortly after *The Nigger of the "Narcissus"* completed its serial appearance there. A perceptive and courageous editor, if not a popular one, he commanded respect, admiration, and not a little fear; not only his one-leggedness served as Stevenson's inspiration for that fearsome pirate, Long John Silver. He had written Henley, May 1883, that it was "the sight of your maimed strength and masterfulness that begot John Silver in *Treasure Island*. Of course, he is not in any other quality or feature the least like you; but the idea of the maimed man, ruling and dreaded by the sound, was entirely taken from you" (Stevenson, *Letters*, 1, p. 242). Nor was Conrad spared a kind of awe of the man. When Henley first accepted *Nigger*, Conrad had written Garnett triumphantly: "Now I have conquered Henley, I aint fraid of the divvle himself" (Karl, *Letters*, 1, p. 323).[2] Ironically it was such forces for imperialism as Henley's, in large part, that first defended and published Conrad, whose writing in great part challenged the proponents of empire. But he viewed Conrad's work as he did that of Stevenson, Haggard, and Kipling, and while he, in fact, condemned Conrad's first two novels as inferior to the adventures of Kipling or Stevenson, he found in all of these works that which had usually promoted the imperial cause, the exotic subject manfully, not squeamishly, dealt with.

Appropriate to the "clubiness" of the writers who, after all, had traditionally helped to define "us" as opposed to "them," to identify those who were "one of us" and those who were not and who were aware of the discussion their fiction contributed to and carried on, and who were, in fact, each others' audiences and critics, most at one time or another found membership in the Savile Club. Teodor Josef Konrad Korzeniowski, an unknown Polish sailor, sailing under the Dutch flag in the Malay Archipelago, had undoubtedly not yet heard of the Savile Club when it elected Haggard into its membership in 1888 and would, a few years later upon Andrew Lang's recommendation, invite Rudyard Kipling, recently returned from India, to join. Sidney Colvin, another member, had proposed Stevenson's membership in 1874 and with Lang's support the proposal was approved. Henley was a member as were other writers, and representatives from most important literary reviews and journals. With characteristic picturesqueness, Stevenson had described its members as "swordsmen of the pen who are the pride and wonder of the world and the terror and envy of the effete pensionaires of the Athenaeum" (Cohen, *Rider Haggard*, p. 19). Actually, many years later, Conrad would join the Athenaeum – as did Haggard also in 1895 – but originally it was many Savile members who saw him as another forthright "swordsman of the pen," anything but "effete," and who claimed him as "one of us."

Stevenson's phrase implies the adversarial role this fiction was occupying, and the targets of these "swordsmen of the pen" were utilitarian effeteness and provincial narrowness, usually associated with a "Little Englander" attitude. From their association at the Savile, Haggard discovered Henley was not only interested in British achievements abroad but that he also generally "was extremely fond of war and fighting... [and] would insist upon my telling him stories by the yard about Zulus and their blood-thirsty battles and customs" (Haggard, *Days*, 1, p. 276). It was such scenes as the following, probably, from *King Solomon's Mines* that earned Henley's admiration for that book:

It was a splendid thing to see those brave battalions come on time after time over the barriers of their dead, sometimes holding corpses before them to receive our spear thrusts, only to leave their own corpses to swell the rising piles. It was a gallant sight to see that sturdy old warrior, Infadoos, as cool as though he were on parade, shouting out orders, taunts, and even jests, to keep up the spirit of his few remaining men, and then, as each charge rolled up, stepping forward to wherever the fighting was thickest, to bear his share in repelling it. (*KSM*, p. 159)

While the Mrs. Grundies of the day deplored such scenes for their bloodiness and savagery – referring to a swelling pile of corpses as "splendid" must have struck many readers as particularly offensive – Henley and others admired them for their fierce heroism. The "frail warrior," R.L.S. himself, was similarly fascinated. In his autobiography, Haggard includes a letter written to him by Stevenson from Bournemouth. Upon reading *King Solomon's Mines*, a work originally inspired by *Treasure Island*, Stevenson wrote to praise Haggard's book, especially the "reflections of your hero before the battle, the king's song of victory, the fine poetic use and command of the savage way of talking – all things that thrilled me" (Haggard, *Days*, 1, p. 235). Here Stevenson echoed Quatermain's own reflections upon hearing Ignosi's war chant, "uttered as it was in a language as beautiful and sonorous as the old Greek." And Ignosi's warriors' response, swelling with the self-importance of Biblical, as well as Greek, cadences and diction, must have thrilled these swordsmen of the pen as it did the gruff old elephant hunter, Allan Quatermain who witnessed it: "Their plumes covered the earth as the plumes of a bird cover her nest; they shook their spears and shouted, yea, they hurled their spears into the sunlight; they lusted for the battle and were glad." And as the enemy's head lay in the dust, Ignosi triumphantly chanted, with his foot upon the chest of his headless foe, "a paean of victory, so beautiful, and yet so utterly savage" (*KSM*, p. 166).

In neither Marryat's nor in Ballantyne's depictions of natives was there anything like this savage splendor. Rather than reaffirming the values of the dominant culture, as adventure fiction had done, this writing registers a discontent. For the subtext of these "thrilling" scenes of bloody violence and valor, one that Haggard actually makes overt in both his fiction and non-fiction, is not only a celebration of barbarism – a subject to which we will return – but also the belief in a militarism that condemns the effeteness of the times, a degeneration that leaves England militarily unprepared, a belief that, in fact, subverts the democratic values being promoted at home. While many argued that empire and democracy marched together compatibly (Salmon, *Literature of the Empire*, pp. 162–174), much of this writing indicates the opposite. As democracy grew and strengthened throughout the century, the writers engaged in carrying on the imperial conversation found themselves at odds in many respects with the basic tenets of democracy. For example, Haggard was convinced England's military forces were poorly manned and equipped and, for some time, had urged general conscription, a policy apparently at odds with the growing democratic temperament of the day. When war, in fact, did break out in 1914, he blamed "the madness of our nation which has steadily refused to bear the burden of any form of National Service" for England's unpreparedness (Haggard, *Private Diaries*, p. 3).[3]

That Haggard saw *King Solomon's Mines* as an opportunity to celebrate things military is clear from his introduction to that book. There he speaks of "the most interesting subject" that his book treats, as "the magnificent system of military organization in force in that country," and because "it permits of even more rapid mobilisation," it is even better than the system introduced by Chaka of Zululand, he contends (*KSM*, p. 19). While it can be argued that a strong military does not necessarily undermine democratic values, Haggard's enthusiasm for an immense number of easily mobilized fighting men probably struck many as excessive. He admired not only the military abilities of his fictional nation but also their militarism and the simple directness such an emphasis allowed, a system in which "the enemy" is easily identified and "is punished for his cruelty and misdeeds" (*KSM*, p. 162) without much thought to anything as cumbersome as "public opinion." To him, the simpler, more decisive, more hierarchical life of feudal savagery was far preferable to the liberal democratic values of the modern system. And for Haggard, this military organization accounted for military and economic security as well. At one point in *King Solomon's Mines*, as Quatermain, Curtis, and Good approach Kukuanaland along Solomon's Great Road, they notice the country becoming increasingly prosperous looking, the fields more cultivated, the kraals more numerous. This prosperity, we learn, can be attributed to an efficient military order in the land:

Each was guarded by ample garrisons of troops. Indeed, in Kukuanaland, as among the Germans, the Zulus, and the Masai, every able-bodied man is a soldier, so that the whole force of the nation is available for its wars, offensive or defensive. As we travelled along we were overtaken by thousands of warriors hurrying up to Loo to be present at the great annual review and festival, and a grander series of troops I never saw. (*KSM*, p. 100)

The comparison with Germany reflects both Haggard's admiration for the Kaiser's military force and his concern about England's complacency, especially about African affairs (Cohen, *RK to RH*, p. 40).[4] Once arrived at the King's encampment, the Englishmen saw these and more troops assembled:

All the rest was open ground; that is to say, it would have been open had it not been filled by company after company of warriors, who were mustered there to the number of seven or eight thousand. These men stood still as statues as we advanced through them, and it would be impossible to give an idea of the grandeur of the spectacle which they presented in their waving plumes, their glancing spears, and iron-backed ox-hide shields. (*KSM*, p. 105)

Haggard's militarism was prophetic; according to Paul Fussell, Henty and Haggard prepared a generation of young men for war in 1914 (Fussell, *Great War*, p. 155). But in the 1880s and 90s the militarism was excessive and even subversive. And the feudalism, with which that militarism was mixed, was nostalgic and out of step with the direction of modern democracies. Haggard was not the only Victorian who looked back on a pre-industrial age as attractively free of moral complexity in which the relationship between master and servant was a clearly defined bond between individuals based on rank, and characterized by service and responsibility, not the impersonal, vague associations and cash nexus of a mass culture; however, such a view opposed the impulse toward democracy current at the time and forced him into an embattled position.[5]

As an avowed imperialist, he served his country's concerns in various official capacities, travelling to various colonies for different Royal Commissions; he was even knighted in 1911 for his public services. It was as a servant of empire, then, who believed in the "divine right of a great civilizing people" (Cohen, *Rider Haggard*, p. 35), that he wrote and submitted his first published work, "A Zulu War-Dance," to *The Gentleman's Magazine* (1877). From his point of view as a nineteen-year-old on imperial business in South Africa under Bulwer and Shepstone, he speaks of the "spirit of justice" that always pertains when "the strong aggressive hand of England has grasped some fresh portion of the earth's surface," and that moves them to ask "how best and most fairly to deal by the natives of the newly-acquired land." What might strike us as paradoxical here – the "strong aggressive hand" that grasps, somehow validated by a "spirit of justice" that reflects – marks Haggard's particular vision of imperial authority and responsibility. Peculiar to that vision of fairness is a certain nostalgia for simpler times when "justice" was uncomplicated by such democratic innovations as public opinion:

In earlier times, when steam was not, and telegraphs and special correspondents were equally unknown agencies for getting at the truth of things, this question was more easily answered across a width of dividing ocean or continent. Then distant action might be prompt and sharp on emergency, and no one would be the wiser. But of late years, owing to these results of civilisation, harsh measures have, by the mere pressure of public opinion, and without consideration of their necessity in the eyes of the colonists, been set aside as impracticable and inhuman. ("A Zulu War-Dance," p. 94)

Did he consider Henty, who was covering colonial wars for *The Standard* from 1866 until 1876, one of those "special correspondents"? Such treatments, as we have seen, rarely challenged the official view. In any case, it is difficult to determine here whether Haggard puts more weight on "impracticable" or "inhuman," but the note of subversion is apparent. To celebrate the uncivilized subverted genre expectations most likely would have offended many, but to imply that the workings of democracies were unnecessarily cumbersome must have struck others as reactionary indeed. Hannah Arendt refers to this subversion as "the boomerang effect," whereby the conquerors' values in empire's outposts, of individual pluck, heroism, and self-resourcefulness facilitated by a hierarchical society in which "we" occupy a top rung, undermine the liberal values of a modern democracy and are smuggled home in the fiction. (Arendt, *Totalitarianism*, p. 223. See also Martin Green, *Dreams of Adventure*, p. 167 and n. 382). But the contraband virtues were cheered by some, as we have seen, as "manly forthrightness," much needed in an age gone soft and afflicted with effeteness.

In this early article, Haggard notes with apparent uneasiness the decline of the gulf, the distance reduced by telegraphs and other innovations of progress and civilization, for such a narrowing caused unsympathetic meddling rather than enlightened aid. From Shepstone to Jameson, colonial leaders in South Africa were increasingly countermanded by the Home Government, and in Haggard's view, announced in his fiction and non-fiction alike, such lack of support was short-sighted and irresponsible. Kingsley, too, we remember, carried on a similar argument with Rajah Brooke's parliamentary foes, who were uninformed and wrong-headed, in Kingsley's opinion. The awareness that modern democracies move in an undesirably complex, inefficient manner and that this new consideration of public opinion must now be listened to even when its demands are ill-advised is a note we hear frequently also in such stories by Kipling as "The Little Foxes." The democratic leaders at home – so this argument went – knew little about the actual situations in the empire's outposts and often enacted policies, influenced by their constituents' mostly uninformed opinions, detrimental to the concerns of empire and antagonistic to the more feudal view of noblesse oblige.

In "A Zulu War-Dance," Haggard applauds, as an on-the-spot imperialist, British attempts at colonization while working to remind his audience of the responsibility attending such an endeavor. Approaching the scene of the war dance, Haggard's party comes upon a scene of great natural beauty that he describes with care and understanding while acknowledging the depletion of its animal life:

But it was not always so lifeless and so still. Some few years ago many creatures roamed here...the traveller could have seen herds of elephants cooling themselves yonder after their day's travel, whilst the black-headed white-tusked sea-cow rose and plunged in the pool below. That bush-clad hill was the favourite haunt of droves of buffaloes and elands, and on that plain swarmed thousands upon thousands of springbok and of quagga, of hartebest and of oribi. All alien life must cease before the white man, and so these wild denizens of forest, stream, and plain have passed away never to return. ("A Zulu War-Dance," p. 99)

The admission is extraordinary, remarkable to us especially for its lack of criticism. He states the situation as a matter of fact, but through the language here that soars and swells with biblical import, we sense that along with a kind of perverse pride – such is the power of the white man – this cessation of life is to be regretted.

But his regret is more apparent and the subversion greater when he writes of the passing of another form of "alien life," the feudal system of allegiance that binds master to serf, chief to warrior. On the day of the war dance, the chief, Pagadi, has summoned his warriors, and they go, leaving their herds and fields untended. "Little reck they whether it be for festival or war; he needs them and has called them, and that is enough." Haggard's frank admiration for the old comitatus relationship of obedience to brave and responsible leaders is revealed by the archaic language here and again in his portrait of the Zulu warrior:

As he stood before us with lifted weapon and outstretched shield, his plume bending to the breeze, and his savage aspect made more savage still by the graceful, statuesque pose, the dilated eye and warlike mould of the set features, as he stood there, an emblem and a type of the times and the things which are passing away, his feet resting on ground which he held on sufferance, and his hands grasping weapons impotent as a child's toy against those of the white man, – he who was the rightful lord of all, – what reflections did he not induce, what a moral did he not teach! ("A Zulu War Dance," p. 102)

Here we get not only Ballantyne's romanticized, aesthetisized image of the Other, but also the sense that this portrait is not a static one but representative of an era already passing, that the characteristics described here will not, unfortunately, pertain for long. The strange inversions and negative constructions of Haggard's last phrases here work to mute his disapproval of what he reports. On the one hand, he regrets the passing of a way of life made admirable and attractive to him by its uncomplicated chieftain–warrior relationship – no complicated public-opinion problems here – while on the other he writes with a certain pride, mindful that he is among those stronger ones to whom the old order must give way, the "rightful" lords of all.

And perhaps with that feudal contract in mind, he calls on the readers of *The Gentleman's Magazine*, as the rightful lords, to be mindful of the responsibility of possession. The article's nostalgia only strengthens its call to conscience and action:

The various influences of the white man have eaten into the native system as rust into iron, and their action will never cease till all be destroyed. The bulwarks of barbarism, its minor customs and minor laws, are gone, or exist only in name; but its two great principles, polygamy and chieftainship, yet flourish and are strong... And it is the undoubted duty of us English, who absorb peoples and territories in the high name of civilization, to be true to our principles and our aim, and aid the great destroyer by any and every safe and justifiable means. But between the legitimate means and the rash, miscalculating uprootal of customs and principles, which are not the less venerable and good in their way because they do not accord with our own present ideas, there is a great gulf fixed. Such an uprootal might precipitate an outburst of the very evils it aims at destroying. ("A Zulu War-Dance," p. 107)

Any irony that might attend the phrase "high name of civilization" is, I believe, unconscious. On the basis of this passage, Haggard himself does not seem aware of the essential divisions in his own thinking. Within the next ten years, he will speak of the "blessings of barbarism" and the need to protect natives from civilization, but these after all are the first impressions of a nineteen-year-old on official business. In any case, a sense of regrettable inevitability marks the passage. In speaking of the English colony of Natal and of the social and political questions it raises, Haggard looks nostalgically at a vanishing way of life, but at the same time issues a kind of warning. While the savage ways will disappear – such is the nature of progress, whether we like it or not, he argues – how they do so is a matter of great importance. The war-dance, for example, is a keystone to the Zulu's moral and spiritual life. While colonizing and civilizing is our divine mission, he tells his readers, we must go about it carefully. It is interesting to note that his prophetic insights for Africa were Stevenson's for the South Seas. In "In The South Seas," Stevenson spoke of the white man's often fatal influence on those island people through disease and domination, and he noted that the groups among whom the fewest changes were imposed survived the most successfully. He went so far as to imply that when missionaries demanded the Marquesans to eradicate cannibalism as part of the progress conferred upon them, the way for general moral depravity in general was cleared. Upon that practice, "barbaric" or not, a whole morality depended; it had been a kind of moral keystone and when it was removed all rules for social order dissolved (*Works*, xviii, pp. 14, 40–43, 88f). In both, a significant shift in the racial stereotyping essential to this fiction has been made. No longer the fierce, threatening savage or doltish, backward sub-human, the native is seen for the first time in Haggard's fiction as a potential victim of colonial incursions, and in Stevenson's as a victim in fact.

Another way in which Haggard's fiction subverted genre expectations by questioning home values was in its criticism of commercialism. Haggard had least patience for that most democratic invention, the new commercial middle classes, the "money-grubbing reformers at home and the meddlers abroad," as he referred to them.[6] And of course, this complaint accompanied his admiration for the feudal relationship, for he saw that it was the more democratic, impersonal "cash nexus" that had come to supplant the traditional, hierarchical relationship of responsible chiefs/masters and loyal warriors/subjects. As Quatermain dies, he confides to his friends that he is glad to be out of a world in which "money is the moving power, and self-interest the guiding star" (*AQ*, p. 214). As we have seen, Haggard's fiction clearly demonstrates the superiority of the white man over the Other, but exceptions exist. Dining with their Majesties of Zu-Vendis, Quatermain notes that "the very highest in rank are always the most simple and kindly. It is from your half-and-half sort of people that you get pomposity and vulgarity, the difference between the two being very much what one sees every day in England between the old, out-at-elbows, broken-down county family, and the overbearing, purse-proud people who come and 'take the place'" (*AQ*, p. 141). Even though the Zu-Vendis are, conveniently, white, such sentiments certainly amount to subversion in a country whose passage of reform bills over the century continued to extend the suffrage to and aid in the creation of that very class of new rich, but were also probably welcomed by readers, embattled gentry like himself, who were disheartened with the increasingly commercial aspect of the growing middle classes newly enfranchised. For the first time, this fiction opposed itself to British values currently held, reflecting a basic rift in Victorian thinking as well. While Henty made potshots in passing at "milksops," and perhaps questioned the patriotism of a few, his fiction never opposed a central current in the culture as Haggard's was doing.

In spite of his imperialism and public service to his country, then, Haggard had misgivings about the modern "civilization" at home and that being exported to colonial outposts, and in doing so reversed genre expectations also. Quatermain is not content to remain in England after his first adventure in Africa, but in a most ungeneric fashion, must return. Constitutional restlessness propels him but also a discontent with conditions at home. He is "tired of playing the squire in a country that is sick of squires; he is tired of the tameness of things." Drawn back to the wilderness, and at odds with home values, he cannot stay in his Yorkshire estate, purchased with his share of the diamonds from King Solomon's Mines, and must return to Africa.

The thirst for the wilderness was on me; I could tolerate this place no more; I would go and die as I had lived, among the wild game and the savages...no man who has for forty years lived the life I have, can with impunity go coop himself in this prim English country, with its trim hedgerows and cultivated fields, its still formal manners, and its well-dressed crowds. He begins to long – ah, how he longs! – for the keen breath of the desert air; he dreams of the sight of Zulu impis breaking on their foes like surf upon the rocks, and his heart rises up in rebellion against the strict limits of the civilized life. (*AQ*, p. 11)

Even making allowances here for the Quatermain persona, we can detect an unconventional attitude. Henty's and Ballantyne's heroes long only for adventure, not to escape England, and always with the desire to return. But progress was indeed, to the Haggard/ Quatermain mind, a comfortable disease, one to escape and to protect native peoples from. After Quatermain's death, his companions Henry Curtis and Captain Good, stay on with the Zu-Vendi. They share their friend's attitudes towards the undesirability of civilized life, and as King-Consort, Curtis will devote himself to several projects – strengthening the central government and weakening the priesthood. Instead, he will "pave the road for the introduction of true religion in the place of this senseless Sun worship." The metaphor of road-paving is telling, for it be-speaks the very sort of "improvement" they proclaim to avoid, as they are dedicated to the "total exclusion of all foreigners from Zu-Vendis." Curtis writes his brother:

I am convinced of the sacred duty that rests upon me of preserving to this, on the whole, upright and generous-hearted people the blessings of comparative barbarism. Where would all my brave army be if some enterprising rascal were to attack us with field-guns and Martini-Henrys...I cannot see that gunpowder, telegraphs, steam, daily newspapers, universal suffrage, etc., etc., have made mankind one whit the happier than they used to be, and I am certain that they have brought many evils in their train. (*AQ*, pp. 218–219)

The feudal relationship once more asserts itself as proprietary and responsible. And it rests on the nostalgic, romantic view of the savage we have found celebrated throughout Haggard's work in a most unconventional manner. Barbarism is to be protected, this fiction argues, not maligned. While clearly Haggard's heroes distinguish themselves from those lesser beings who have let down the side by "going primitive," "going bush," "going fantee," "going native," the thin line is maintained by insisting on their obligations as superior beings. Readers are thus urged to understand their responsibility and, furthermore, to recognize their essential kinship with savagery, that the savage within us all is valuable and worth acknowledging. As we saw, his descriptions of the Zulus at war, although restrained by modern standards, did not attempt delicacy. In *Allan Quatermain*, in advancing the unconventional opinion at one point, that "in all essentials the savage and the child of civilization are identical," Quatermain immediately anticipates his readers' disapproval and speaks to them directly:

Ah! this civilization, what does it all come to? For forty years and more I lived among savages, and studied them and their ways; and now for several years I have lived here in England, and have in my own stupid manner done my best to learn the ways of the children of light; and what have I found? A great gulf fixed? No, only a very little one, that a plain man's thought may spring across. I say that as the savage is, so is the white man, only the latter is more inventive, and possesses the faculty of combination; save and except also that the savage, as I have known him, is to a large extent free from the greed of money, which eats like a cancer into the heart of the white man. It is a depressing conclusion, but in all essentials the savage and the child of civilization are identical. I dare say that the highly civilized lady reading this will smile at an old fool of a hunter's simplicity when she thinks of her black bead-bedecked sister; and so will the superfine cultured idler scientifically eating a dinner at his club, the cost of which would keep a starving family for a week. (*AQ*, pp. 11, 12)

Much here qualifies the original assertion, intended to be alarming, no doubt. It is hard to know exactly what he means by "the faculty of combination," but that the white man is more "inventive" seems to distinguish him negatively as much as positively, connected as it is with his "greed of money." If we would understand ourselves, he suggests to his audience of civilized ladies and cultured idlers, "we must look to the nineteen savage portions of our nature...not to the twentieth" civilized part. It is on those "nineteen rough serviceable savage portions that we fall back in emergencies, not on the polished but unsubstantial twentieth."

At another point in his narrative, Quatermain warns his readers that not only are they, in all essentials, very like the savages his fiction depicts, but that also their "civilization" they so pride themselves on provides only an illusory sort of protection against the vagaries of providence. Just because they are sitting "in a well-drained house with two policemen patrolling under the window" (*AQ*, p. 90), life is no more certain and controllable for them than if they were bead-bedecked African natives. Being "civilized" does not shield them from the darkness without. Nor, as another narrator will remind his listeners, does it provide any protection against the darkness within. Conrad's Marlow has trouble remaining "civil" in the face of what he too feels is an unbridgeable gap between him and his listeners, who, each being "moored with two good addresses, like a hulk with two anchors, a butcher round one corner, a policeman round another..." ("Heart of Darkness," p. 48), are thus incapable of understanding his tale about the heart of darkness.[7] And both Marlow and Quatermain confess a kind of bitter despair of connecting their listeners/readers with the savage experience. Inter- estingly, the policeman figures for both narrators as emblematic of a civilized society. Criticisms attend that depiction, especially in contrast with savage cultures that have no need for such forces of protection – from each other – and for artificially imposed restraint.

In an early address to his readers, Quatermain insists upon the similarity of civilization and savagery, that the one is simply the other "silver-gilt," and as subject to decay. But, he goes on:

Do not let me, however, be understood as decrying our modern institutions, representing as they do the gathered experience of humanity applied for the good of all. Of course they have great advantages – hospitals for instance; but then, remember, we breed the sickly people who fill them. In a savage land they do not exist... (*AQ*, pp. 11, 12)

Here he effectively takes away with the one hand what he grudgingly gives with the other, not a very enthusiastic hurrah for civilization and its modern institutions. In regard to modern education, he does not even make these small pretences of approval. He found that the young daughter of a missionary in Africa had more "courage, discretion, and power of mind than many a woman of mature age nurtured in idleness and luxury, with minds carefully drilled and educated out of any originality or self-resource that nature may have endowed them with" $(AQ,$ p. 76).[8]

Thus the celebration of the savage that lay at the heart of much of Haggard's writing worked against the traditional assumptions of the adventure genre. This admiration of native militarism and criticism of democratic values at home threatened the tenets of purported imperial rationale. The "blessings of barbarism" must have disturbed those who believed that the civilized life was Britain's gift to new imperial possessions. That white men had something of tremendous value to export was the assumption of imperial policy and of the travel writing and adventure fiction that discussed the subject. The aim of the voyage in both discourses had been to return to England having successfully exported the English way of life, returning intact to a better life than possible in the wilderness. The adventure story traditionally told of Englishmen leaving home to conquer, colonize and civilize, returning to be honored in various ways, but remaining essentially unaffected and certainly not questioning the superiority of the civilized life they returned to. Marryat's Peter Simple and Jacob Faithful, Ballantyne's Martin Rattler and Ralph Rover, Stevenson's Jim Hawkins and Henty's numberless stout lads all returned with their Englishness intact and their conviction untouched that their civilized lives were far superior to anything they had seen in various imperial outposts. They and the explorers before them in the travel literature were eager to lift "the veil of mystery," to discover virgin lands and follow untracked rivers for the glory and honor of the adventure and to bestow their civilization on native peoples, believing that in so doing they were conferring benefits on the land and its people, and always looking ahead to their return home to rewards of various sorts and to civilization. So the reluctance of Haggard's heroes to remain in England and their refusal to return sound a new note.

Either this subtext was successfully disguised, or many welcomed the subversion, for *Allan Quatermain* ran serially in *Longman's Magazine*, beginning in January of 1888 and set a record. "We have subscribed over 10,000 copies of *AQ* in London" (Cohen, *Rider Haggard*, p. 127). But the appeal of this thinking would fade by the early years of the twentieth century, when, disillusioned liberal England found the imperial idea a distasteful one. In his account of the shifts in political thinking going on at the time, historian George Dangerfield notes that the "Conservatives were drifting out of popularity like a swimmer caught in the undertow. Their prestige had suffered as the Boer War dragged on and England discovered how much blood it cost to run an Empire..." (*Strange Death*, p. 9). Conrad's thoughts on the matter in October of 1899 were prophetic. While no friend of the Dutch or the Germans, Conrad felt the war to be a mistake; as statecraft, it was ill-calculated for, he argued, it would "create a situation of which, unless I am much mistaken, the country will get weary. The victory, – unless it is to be thrown away, – shall have to be followed by ruthless repression. The situation will become repugnant to the nation" (Karl, *Letters*, II, pp. 210–211). In 1902, J. A. Hobson went so far as to argue that the imperialism being currently practised not only did not constitute progress, it was actually "a retrograde step fraught with grave perils to the cause of civilisation" (*Imperialism*, p. 13). At a time when the nations of the world were becoming increasingly interdependent, Hobson argued that imperialism worked against the general good and represented "a depraved choice of national life, imposed by self-seeking interests which appeal to the lusts of quantitative acquisitiveness and of forceful domination (p. 368). Although Hobson was not officially heeded at the time, his ideas did represent a growing dissatisfaction. The Liberal Party triumph in the general election of 1906 resulted, in large part, from the discontent occasioned by the Conservative imperial policies of Salisbury and Chamberlain in the South African war.

Thus, Haggard found himself in an increasingly antagonistic relationship to his audience. While he was certainly cheered by the support of writers and editors such as Henley and Stevenson, and by record sales in the 1880s and 90s, he was disturbed by the inhospitable reception his work found elsewhere but developed a defensive stance that gave more weight to certain arguments he was waging in his fiction. In a letter to Kipling, his friend, colleague, and neighbor, he said of his own novel, *Child of Storm* (1913): "You will see [it] described as a boys' story 'as usual too bloody for most tastes.' (Piff! What is blood in Zululand?) I believe there is a class of journalist who would have described the *Odyssey* as a boys' story – too bloody for most tastes!" (Cohen, *Rider Haggard*, p. 76). He insisted that he was merely delivering facts, facts "civilized" people did not want to admit to themselves, facts his "rose-water critics" had to face up to.

While we have heard previous writers from empire's outposts speak of the difficulty of adequately describing foreign scenes – Cook and McClintock both doubt they can ever convey to the home-audience the true aspect of the polar ice fields, for example – we have not heard this hostile tone before. Haggard's prose defended itself aggressively in assuming an embattled position and refused, as those before him had done in what had almost become a genre convention, to accept the failure as his alone.

Thus, Haggard initiated a certain shift in the genre of adventure fiction that subverted some of its most traditional claims concerning the imperial subject; his fiction helped to make the genre that had always defended the status quo capable of subverting it. The genre that had created and encouraged enthusiasm for imperialism found itself now defending itself against imperialism's angry opponents. Imperialist that he was, Haggard found himself advocating increasingly unpopular positions. His ideas on the primitive would be echoed by such anti-imperial modernists as Lawrence and Yeats, who also rejected the liberal idea of progress with its emphasis on commercialism and enlightened self interest and saw more to be hoped for from tapping back into our more intuitive, "primitive" natures than from modern civilization. Conrad, while not sharing Lawrence's "nostalgie de la boue," and while holding a very different attitude towards imperialism from Haggard's, also will record the loss that modern, civilized man has sustained.

# CHAPTER 5

# Travel writing and adventure fiction as shaping discourses for Conrad

The author who often spoke disparagingly of "boys' adventure tales" had probably consumed his share by the time he ran off to sea, as countless boys before him in the pages of adventure fiction had done.[1] From what he and others have written about his early reading, the sea stories of Hugo, of Marryat and of Cooper shaped many of his youthful imaginings, and Jacob Faithful, Masterman Ready, and Peter Simple must have been well known to Conrad from an early age as prototypes of heroic action. In "Tales of the Sea," a laudatory review of the works of Marryat and Cooper he wrote in 1898 for the *Outlook*, there was only the congratulatory in his description of Marryat's formula: "to his young heroes the beginning of life is a splendid and warlike lark, ending at last in inheritance and marriage." He admitted here to having been "enslaved," not only by the formulaic heroes, but also by the idealizing power of the work – both characteristics of adventure fiction – by Marryat's power to depict "the spirit animating the stirring time when the nineteenth century was young." To lose it, he claimed, would be "like the curtailment of national story or the loss of a historical document." He spoke of Marryat as a kind of irrational force, when he described that writer's "irresistible power to reach the adventurous side of the character" and of his power to "enslave," a power to which Conrad had to "surrender." And he defended that romantic conquest, claiming never to have regretted that surrender, for Marryat's stories "withstood the brutal shock of facts and the wear of laborious years" (Conrad, *Notes*, p. 53). Similarly, he never regretted the impulse that carried him from then land-locked, partitioned Poland to the sea, an impulse his family had so strongly and persistently counselled against as unwise and "Quixotic"; on the contrary, living out that fantasy, with its ideals of faithful duty and seamanship implicit in the dream, and working his way up to the rank of Master Mariner, remained his proudest achievement.

Not only the works of Cooper and Marryat but a variety of texts inspired those youthful dreams. In *A Personal Record*, published serially 1908–1909, after most of his major fiction had already been written, Conrad spoke of his early reading, in the chapter following his discussion of those "sea dreams" from which his family tried to dissuade him; it included much of Victor Hugo, in particular his father's translations of Hugo's *Toilers of the Sea*. He also admitted to the powerful influence of contemporary journals of discovery and to having read in "Polish and in French, history, voyages, novels" (*A Personal Record*, pp. 70, 71). At the end of his life, he looked back, in "Geography and Some Explorers," and recalled the particular effect those accounts of voyages had on him while still very young and what it meant to him to be contemporary with the explorations and discoveries of his time made by men to whom he ascribed the purest of motives. As we have seen in chapter 1, he admitted he could only have heard of the expedition of Burton and Speke and the news of the existence of Tanganyika and of Victoria Nyanza "whispered to [him] in [his] cradle," but to have been a contemporary of the discoveries of the Great Lakes and to have read those volumes of travel and exploration certainly colored his maturing imagination and forged for him certain ideals of character and conduct. In fact, in this same work, Conrad marked the diminishment from the heroic idealism of Cook, McClintock, Livingstone and others to the more recent, self-serving empire builders. He praised Captain James Cook as belonging to "the single-minded explorers of the nineteenth century, the late fathers of militant geography whose only object was the search for truth." To the polar explorers also he ascribed aims

as pure as the air of those high latitudes where not a few of them laid down their lives for the advancement of geography.... Seamen, men of science, it is difficult to speak of them without admirative emotion. (*Last Essays*, p. 10)

Among these polar explorers, as we saw, was Sir John Franklin, a name that recurs in Conrad's works as synonymous with a kind of pure heroism he contrasted with the opportunism of more contemporary adventurers, from the fictional members of The Eldorado Expedition to such "modern Conquistadores" as Belgium's King Leopold (Watts, *Letters*, p. 149). The effect on him, at ten years of age, of reading about Franklin in McClintock's *The Voyage of the Fox*, a book that let in "the breath of the stern romance of polar exploration," has already been discussed. And it was not only the polar regions that fascinated him but also the torrid zone. Such was the appeal of Africa, that his first friends in the "world of mentality and imagination," he claimed here, were the African explorers, Mungo Park, Bruce of Abyssinia, and David Livingstone.

And it was Africa, the continent out of which the Romans used to say some new thing was always coming, that got cleared of the dull imaginary wonders of the dark ages, which were replaced by exciting spaces of white paper. Regions unknown! My imagination could depict to itself these worthy, adventurous and devoted men, nibbling at the edges, attacking from north and south and east and west, conquering a bit of truth here and a bit of truth there, and sometimes swallowed up by the mystery their hearts were so persistently set on unveiling. (*Last Essays*, p. 13)

He saw them as worthy, adventurous and devoted, and did not question the "attacking" and "conquering"; instead he saw those actions motivated by the search for "truth, not for profit and gain."

Conrad appears determined in this essay to applaud the century's heroes. The work was originally titled "The Romance of Travel"; it was written as a preface to a volume called *Countries of the World* and only later collected in *Last Essays* which perhaps helps to explain Conrad's uncharacteristically uncritical stance. One might have thought that of all people, Conrad, whose scepticism usually controlled his idealism, would not have had this blind spot. For we have seen how even these men, admittedly shoulders above the later scramblers for empire in their search for geographical truth rather than personal gain, were not totally innocent in their intentions. But their prose was convincing, and the excitement generated by the publications of their narratives and journals of discovery was contagious at the time and reaffirmed the British reading public's sense of pride in empire. While he despised the engineers at Suez who, as we will see, "tore down the veil of the terrible beauty," and who destroyed the "mystery" (*An Outcast of the Islands*, p. 12), Conrad shared these explorers' excitement about "unveiling the mystery" of "unknown regions," and their ethnocentrism – these regions of course were quite well known to native peoples who had lived there for countless generations. While their interest usually came to be connected with concerns such as "trade," "commerce," "markets," and often proceeded at the expense of the Other, Conrad rightly

distinguished them from those less disinterested, more personally
motivated empire-builders – the "pilgrims" of "Heart of Darkness"
or the opportunistic members of that novel's Eldorado Expedition,
next to whom Kurtz was Marlow's "choice of nightmares." Even
Kurtz has something of "the sacred fire," and his idealism, as corrupt
as it becomes, serves to distinguish him from the rest. Kurtz
exemplifies idealism gone awry, but worse was to come, the presence
of the Eldorado Expedition appears to argue. Conrad thought of
himself as essentially an idealist; he admired idealism in others and
envied it in some, in Cunninghame Graham for example. but in the
same breath, he believed "every cause [to be] tainted" (Watts,
*Letters*, p. 68). No coherent philosopher, he was temperamentally
sceptical and profoundly idealistic; the one struggled with and
checked the other.

Other travel accounts that shaped his early thinking, as indicated
earlier, were the writings of James Brooke. Conrad admitted as much
in a letter to the Dowager Ranee of Sarawak (Lady Margaret
Brooke, the widow of Sir Charles Brooke, the second "White Rajah"
of Sarawak), who had written him an appreciation of *The Rescue*,
which he had finally completed in 1919. That book was the third,
preceded by *Almayer's Folly* and *An Outcast of the Islands*, in the trilogy
of the cycle of Lingard, the English sea captain whose prototype, the
actual Scots trader Tom Lingard, also inspired the character of Tuan
Jim. In that letter he told her that the

first Rajah Brooke has been one of my boyish admirations, a feeling I have
kept to this day strengthened by the better understanding of the greatness of
his character and the unstained rectitude of his purpose. The book which
has found favour in your eyes has been inspired in a great measure by the
history of the first Rajah's enterprise and even by the lecture of his journals
as partly reproduced by Captain Mundy and others. (Watts *Letters*, p. 210)

It was the Brookiana to a great extent that had inspired the early
Malay stories (see Gordan's "The Rajah Brooke and Joseph
Conrad"). Cunninghame Graham had given him a copy of *My Life
in Sarawak* in 1914, the Ranee's autobiography, and Conrad's reading
of it seems to have enabled him to return to the long abandoned
manuscript of *The Rescue*. The confrontation of "a proud and
cultivated young Englishwoman and the alien, exotic and primitive
world of the Malay Archipelago," the subject of the ranee's
autobiography, was also at the heart of Conrad's fictional depiction

of Mrs. Travers in *The Rescue*, and Brooke himself, referred to in Conrad's novel as "the disinterested adventurer," probably figured as a prototype of Lingard (Watts, *Letters*, p. 210).

Thus when Conrad came to Borneo, even his first glimpses of the actual half-caste Olmeijer, the model of his fictional Almayer, (Watt, *Conrad*, pp. 34–41) were already seen through a shaping lens. From the writings of Brooke and of others about Brooke, and from other accounts such as Alfred Wallace's *The Malay Archipelago* (1869) Conrad had already visited Borneo, had known of the local rivalries and struggles and the able colonial rule of the Englishman James Brooke, whose "greatness of... character" and "unstained rectitude of... purpose" so impressed him. But part of Conrad's greatness, and a large measure of his modernism, was the ability to hold in his mind simultaneously the ideal and the actual, and to admit the value and existence of both. Meeting Olmeijer and the other prototypes of his Malayan fictions did not erase his admiration for Brooke or his belief in the existence of such benevolence and heroism. In fact, in a contemporary review, he praises Hugh Clifford for being exactly the kind of colonial leader Brooke had been described as and congratulates him for being "to the Malays whom he governs, instructs, and guides... the embodiment of the intentions, of the conscience and might of his race" (Conrad, *Notes*, p. 58). Conrad did not let the one somehow negate the possibility of the other. He could see quite clearly that neither the prototypical – and thus the fictional – Almayers, Lingards and Jims came anywhere near the ideals of the actual Rajah Brooke, or for that matter, presumably, Hugh Clifford. In many ways he can be seen as using Brooke as a kind of reference point, against which to measure the distance Almayer, a disappointed, failed colonial, has plummeted. Even Lingard, or "Rajah Laut" as the natives refer to him, more closely inspired by Brooke, fails to attain the real heights of Rajah Brooke and marks a diminishment, a regrettable reduction.

As we have seen, adventure fiction was also a shaping discourse for Conrad. He was influenced by the genre, by its conventions and by its ideals, but he revealed his associations with much of it less directly than he did those with the even more reputable genre of travel writing. While he came to distance himself from "adventure yarns" and question some of the attitudes of the genre, as we shall see, he also accepted many of the conventions. In a letter to his first publisher, Fisher Unwin in 1896, he wrote about the book he was currently working on, *The Rescue*, and its central character, Tom Lingard, who had figured less prominently in the first two, *Almayer's Folly* and *The Outcast of the Islands*:

> If the virtues of Lingard please most of the critics, they shall have more of them. The theme of it shall be the rescue of a yacht from some Malay vagabonds and there will be a gentleman and a lady cut out according to the regulation pattern. (Quoted in Jean-Aubry, *Conrad*, 1, n.164).

Whether or not we understand what "regulation pattern" entailed exactly, it is clear that the phrase described a convention well known to Conrad and to his publisher. His familiarity with another conventional feature of the genre is the subject of another letter to Unwin, a few weeks later. Still working on *The Rescue* – he would struggle with it off and on for the next twenty-four years – he asked Unwin to send him a "Malay vocabulary," for he had forgotten many of the words and even though, he tells Unwin, he does not use much "language-colour," he wants to be correct (Karl, *Letters*, 1, pp. 276–277). Language-color, the exotic language that had become a familiar attraction of the genre, created pictures of faraway places with strange words and place names. As Marryat had named the nautical world, thus effectively creating it for readers who had never left inland towns and cities, and Ballantyne had brought into existence South Sea Islands through such exotica as taro-roots and coco-nuts, and Haggard had made his readers see an unknown world of veldts and kraals and scherms, so Conrad too used a new vocabulary to create a place in readers' imaginations of campongs, praus, and punkahs, sarangs, sarongs, and tindals, a place peopled by Others with such names as Babalatchi and Syed Abdulla bin Selim, a place where colonial traders dealt in guttah percha and rattans and met on the verandahs of colonial outposts to exchange reassuring fictions.

And he read and wrote of other writers of the genre. It is interesting to speculate on whether Conrad read Haggard or not. He claimed to despise that writer's work as "too horrible for words," yet an occasional echo of Haggard sounds in Conrad's fiction. The narrator of *She* – a best-seller and readily available since its initial publication in 1889–in one of the most compelling scenes in the novel, describes as "the heart of the darkness," a chasm they must cross on a narrow plank (p. 277). And could that novel's heroine, Ayesha, have suggested to Conrad "Aïssa," the native woman of his second novel?[2] But Conrad did confess, at least to his publisher Unwin, an admiration for the work of Louis Becke, a contemporary writer of exotic adventure in the South Seas, particularly his *Reef and Palm*. Both the matter and the manner of Becke's stories interested Conrad, and sufficiently so that he expressed disappointment (again to Unwin) when Becke failed to write up to his (Becke's) own high standards (Karl, *Letters*, I, pp. 298 and 302, 303).

A contemporary of Haggard and Conrad, Rudyard Kipling certainly brought new worlds into being for his readers and was as responsible as anyone for making "language-colour" a staple of adventure fiction. But in other ways also, Conrad's early fiction bore some resemblance to that of Kipling.[3] Unlike some of his literary associates, such as Edward Garnett, Conrad admired Kipling in certain respects, taking Kipling's works as inspiration for his own in some cases. Many have studied and written on Kipling's influence on Conrad; Watts' comments are representative:

*The Nigger of the " Narcissus, "* for example, was to resemble *Captains Courageous* not merely in the authority, sympathy and virtuosity with which the ship and her crew were presented, but also in the evident importance placed on the life of men at sea as an exemplar of initiation through trial-by-ordeal into a community whose moral sanctions arose chiefly from the discipline of cooperative labour in a challenging environment (Watts, *Letters*, p. 21).

A reader of both Kipling and John Buchan, Conrad wrote William Blackwood that he preferred the former. Upon being asked by Mr. Blackwood to review Buchan's "The Far Islands" which was serialized in *Blackwood's Magazine* in 1899, Conrad delivered his opinion of his fellow contributor and found him wanting, even dishonest; he accused him of stealing most of his ideas from Kipling's "The Finest Story in the World" (Karl, *Letters*, II, pp. 15, 16). Several years later, after reading *The Mirror of the Sea*, Kipling wrote Conrad an admiring letter also, about which Conrad commented in a letter to John Galsworthy, "The Age of Miracles is setting in!" (Karl, *Letters*, III, p. 366).

Thus, his experience with the form was not only through youthful reading, but also through the periodicals he was currently reading and appearing in, publications in which many fictions about colonial outposts were being serialized. He had been reading English newspapers at least since his Polish friend in Cardiff started sending him *The Standard*, the newspaper for which Henty was a correspondent, and we know he was reading others such as *Tit-Bits* to apprise himself of the current literary market in Britain. He was reading Stevenson's letters from Samoa to the *Times*, for he praised them highly to Colvin (Colvin, *Memories and Notes*, p. 149). Stevenson's South Sea fiction was also appearing in such important journals as *Scribner's Magazine* and *The Illustrated London News*, *The Wrecker* (1891–1892) and *The Beach of Falesa* (1893) respectively. Conrad's "Outpost of Progress" ran in the *Cornhill* in June and July of 1897, the issue following the one in which Kipling's "Slaves of the Lamp" appeared. In fact it was probably the contrast between these two somewhat similar fictions, both treating the imperial subject, that prompted Graham's letter of praise to Conrad that initiated their friendship.[4]

By the time he started writing he showed enough knowledge of the form to advise an aspiring writer, another sailor beginning to write fiction, a younger version of Conrad according to Karl (*Letters*, I, n.230), how to write "river stories," presumably having read many as well as having written one – *Almayer's Folly* – himself. He advised the young sailor, who had written Conrad an appreciative letter about his first novel and had inquired about his own chances for publication, to submit his manuscript to his own publisher, Fisher Unwin, for Unwin's Pseudonym Series. He himself had offered his first manuscript to Unwin on the basis of his familiarity with the Pseudonym Library, having read a few things in it, including *Mademoiselle Ixe* and *The Pope's Daughters* (Jean-Aubry, *Conrad*, I, p. 159 – in a 1918 letter to W. H. Chesson, one of Unwin's readers in 1895). He told the aspiring writer to make his work

purely river stories (about 30–40 thousand words). Only my dear Noble do not throw yourself away in fables. Talk about the river – the people – the events, as seen through your temperament … Death is not the most pathetic – the most poignant thing – and you must treat events only as illustrative of human sensation – as the outward sign of inward feelings, of live feelings – which alone are truly pathetic and interesting. (Karl, *Letters*, I, pp. 251, 252)

The advice is interesting; it reflects Conrad's general familiarity with the genre, but also his desire to avoid some of its pitfalls, to write a different kind of adventure fiction, one that insisted upon a greater complexity by resisting easy platitudes, refusing to moralize, and rendering rather than telling. While profoundly influenced by the travel writing and the adventure fiction of his time and by many of the ideals revealed and espoused in those works, he would challenge many of the convention's assumptions, affording and necessitating new ways of viewing the imperial subject.

Conrad's need to demythologize a genre that had so influenced him came from his public and personal awareness that the dream was over, that the possibilities for great aspirations and noble deeds were closing down; it was what Conrad made of, in Robert Frost's words, "a diminished thing." The nostalgia, the romantic yearning for a more heroic past, is mixed with the realistic appraisal of man's universal imperfection, an understanding that all men are base and that "into the noblest cause men manage to put something of their baseness" (Watts, *Letters*, p. 68). Recalling the time he was struggling to qualify as a first mate and master, Conrad wrote in a letter to R. B. Cunninghame Graham: "You are simply run down, and strong men feel it so much more than weaklings like me – who have felt over-tasked ever since the age of 28" (Watts, *Letters*, p. 82). Although Conrad was only twenty-eight, the struggle must have seemed especially difficult because of a certain futility and uncertainty that attended the endeavor. In 1886, a year later, Conrad became a British subject and did finally pass his British Master Mariner's exam, but while awarding him the long coveted Captain's Certificate, his examiner advised him to "go into steam." Since the opening of the Suez Canal in 1869, steam had become an important new technology, one that Conrad felt an aversion to and a reluctance to pursue (Jean-Aubry, *Conrad*, 1, p. 55). The canal "pierced" the Isthmus of Suez, as Conrad was fond of phrasing it – obviously he saw it as an inflicted violence – and connected the Mediterranean and the Red Seas, to facilitate the route to India and thus strengthen that imperial connection. But steam did not accord with Conrad's ideas of seamanship, forged as they had been by the fictions of Hugo, Marryat, and Cooper. And in the early pages of his second novel, *An Outcast of the Islands*, Conrad had eulogized the sea

before the time when the French mind set the Egyptian muscle in motion and produced a dismal but profitable ditch. Then a great pall of smoke sent out by countless steamboats was spread over the restless mirror of the Infinite. The hand of the engineer tore down the veil of the terrible beauty in order that greedy and faithless landlubbers might pocket dividends. The mystery was destroyed. (p. 12)

That he was reduced at one point to considering piloting at Suez marks his desperation, but at the moment of his triumph, the very sea-going tradition he had admired and had proudly earned his Captain's Certificate in was questioned and placed in jeopardy. Witnessing the dispersal of a romantic tradition, he felt that the Certificate, finally attained, was fast becoming a thing of the past.

Often finding it difficult to attain berths on sailing ships, not to mention commands, he was plagued for some years by the sense of his chosen career's uncertainty; his letters were filled with queries about alternate careers. In 1885, he wrote to his Polish friend in Cardiff, Spiridion Kliszczewski, of his desire to go into whaling in the polar seas. Anticipating success in his upcoming examination, he considered a way of making "a fresh start in the world" and decided:

> my soul is bent upon a whaling venture... I am brimfull [sic] with the most exhaustive information upon the subject. I have read, studied, pumped professional [sic] men and imbibed knowledge upon whale fishing and sealing for the last four years. I am acquainted with the practical part of the undertaking in a thorough manner... (Karl, *Letters*, 1, p. 14).

He considered, and then abandoned, the idea of gold mining and, at one point, in 1893 after leaving the "Torrens," he even wrote his aunt to ask her if she knew anyone "in the administration of the Suez Canal" who could help him obtain a post as a Canal pilot (Karl, *Letters*, 1, p. 135), and, a few days later, he wrote her again, telling her that he was "taking steps – or having them taken for me – to get a position in the pearl fisheries off the Australian coast. I rather fancy the idea..." (Karl, *Letters*, 1, p. 137). As we know, he also urged her to do what she could to procure for him the command of a steamer up the Congo in 1890, the year Henry Stanley was being enthusiastically received at Brussels and Antwerp by the King and Belgian people. As Jean-Aubry points out, Stanley's *Through the Dark Continent*, first published in 1878 in four volumes, was enjoying a revival, and as a result, the Congo was "the rage of Europe." Jean-Aubry reasons convincingly that "the atmosphere of adventure and discovery revived Conrad's childish enthusiasms and kindled the imagination of the young Pole, in whom the spirit of a novelist was just beginning to awake. He suddenly took it into his head that he must command a steamboat on the Congo" (Jean-Aubry, *Conrad*, 1, n. 121). As "Heart of Darkness" records, however, these awakened enthusiasms would be extinguished by his actual experiences in that imperial outpost.

But the same impulsive admiration for the heroic and adventurous could be found in his other schemes as well. According to Baines, his reading of Melville, whose influence in Conrad's work has been marked by many readers, probably had something to do with the whaling scheme, although Jean-Aubry credits it also with his meeting and discussing the work with the captain of the "Narcissus" (Jean-Aubry, *Conrad*, 1, p. 79), and as he himself admitted, he had been "imbibing knowledge upon whale fishing and sealing for four years." The other choices also seem the stuff of exploration and adventure inspired by a variety of texts, newspaper notices and advertisements, and talk with fellow sailor/wanderers. Although his qualms about his career were very real, his outlook was rather romantic, to the exasperation of his more practical uncle to whom he also confided some of these plans; his "soul" was "bent" on whaling, and he "fancies" the idea of pearl fishing in Australia. Of course no one in this young Pole's family, especially that uncle, approved his going off to sea in the first place, his original impulse for which had probably sprung – at least in great part – from a reading of Marryat. This was a youth for whom even arriving in London, at the age of nineteen, seemed an adventurous expedition into the land of the Other rendered in the manner of the travel writers he so admired:

Straight from the railway carriage I had walked into the great city with something of the feeling of a traveller penetrating into a vast and unexplored wilderness. No explorer could have been more lonely. I did not know a single soul of all these millions that all around me peopled the mysterious distances of the streets... All the help I had to get in touch with the world I was invading was a piece of paper, not much bigger than the palm of my hand – in which I held it – torn out of a larger plan of London.

As he took his "anxious bearings," he considered the consequence of a wrong turn: "I might have remained lost for days, for weeks, have left perhaps my bones to be discovered bleaching in some blind alley of the Whitechapel district, as it has happened to lonely travellers lost in the Bush..." (*Notes*, pp. 150, 152). When he did go ashore and become a writer, he referred to that new choice of profession as an "adventure" also. Later he was also to compare the enterprise of writing a novel to the "conquest of a colony" (*Last Essays*, p. 132).

Although accounts differ as to the exact date of Conrad's first story, "The Black Mate," according to Cunninghame Graham, in his preface to the 1925 collection *Tales of Hearsay*, in which "The Black Mate" was the last story, was written in 1884 and submitted to a *Tit-Bits* competition, unsuccessfully. Graham refers to the work only as Conrad's first work, "written about 1884, as a friend of Conrad's tells me" (Watts, *Letters*, p. ix). Jean-Aubry dates the story from 1885 (*Conrad*, 1, p. 89), and Baines and Graver conjecture 1886 for the story's appearance in its preliminary form and the present form – presumably the one in *Tales of Hearsay* – a revision for the *London Magazine* in 1908. Conrad's own memories of its publication are confused. Baines quotes him as saying in 1922, "the history of 'The Black Mate,' its origin etc., etc., need not be proclaimed on housetops, and *Almayer's Folly* may keep its place as my first serious work … I have a notion that it was first written some time in the late eighties and retouched later" (Baines, *Joseph Conrad*, pp. 84–86). Since Conrad's own memories of the story's origins are so confused and confusing, Baines examined *Tit-Bits* for the 1880s and found among its abundant and frequent competitions only one for which Conrad could appropriately have entered a version of "The Black Mate," in the May 1, 1886 issue, the "'Special Prize for Sailors'" … We will give the sum of Twenty guineas for the best article entitled "'My Experiences as a Sailor.'" In *A Personal Record*, Conrad states of *Almayer's Folly*, which he began to write in the fall of 1889 and worked on for five years: "Till I began to write that novel I had written nothing but letters, and not very many of these" (p. 68).

While this depiction increases the miraculous dimensions of Conrad's transformation from sailor to author and gives to his first writing endeavor a kind of disinterested air, it certainly obscures our precise dating of this story. But although here, as elsewhere, Conrad's dismissive remarks about his work must be taken with caution, since he deprecated some of his best writing, most readers, then and today also dismiss "The Black Mate" as derivative and lightweight. Jean-Aubry finds it "in the vein of W. W. Jacobs" (*Conrad*, 1, p. 89), and Graver calls it "a sport in the Conrad canon" (Graver, *Short Fiction*, p. 4) and faults it for a certain immorality: "Deceit in 'The Black Mate' is at bottom cheerful and Bunter is Conrad's only mischievous hero, a man whose well-being is momentarily menaced by nothing more terrible than broken bottles and the tedium of a captain's conversation" (4). Baines too dismisses it as "a trivial story, told in a breezily colloquial style" (Baines, *Joseph Conrad*, p. 85).

But, assuming that the 1908 story is just that, the original story merely "retouched," it is not without its significance to the student of Conrad. "The Black Mate" concerns a seaman no longer young, who in order to hold on to his job must continually dye his greying hair black. When, during a storm at sea, his bottles of black dye tumble out of their drawers and break, he plays upon the superstitious beliefs of his captain in order to prevent his ruse from being discovered. He concedes to his captain that a fall he has recently taken down the galley stairs was not really an accident, but that an unseen power had caused it as punishment for his disbelief. As though to verify the traumatic effects of the experience on him, his hair starts turning white, to the captain's great satisfaction, thus achieving the desired effect.

We can see in the unsympathetic depiction of Captain Johns, a familiar Conradian idea, the criticism of the foolishly gullible. But there is something of Conrad in Bunter also. He, like Bunter and other sailors no longer very young knew what it was to wear out "the soles of their last pair of boots on the pavements of the City in the heart-breaking search for a berth" (*Tales of Hearsay*, p. 88). Conrad, too, found refuge at the tobacconist's shop in Fenchurch Street where Bunter waited between berths for a new position, and in a passage characteristic of the whole in its nostalgic tone, Conrad measured the distance between then and now:

Willy, his shop, and the very house in Fenchurch Street, I believe, are gone now. In his time, wearing a careworn, absent-minded look on his pasty face, Willy served with tobacco many southern-going ships out of the Port of London. At certain times of the day the shop would be full of shipmasters. They sat on casks, they lounged against the counter. (p. 90)

The regretful, nostalgic note that characterized the contemporary adventure fiction also marked much of Conrad's writing, but that it appeared so early in his life and career is surprising. After all, whether he wrote it originally in 1884 or 1886, Conrad was only in his twenties, yet his glance was a backward one, towards a more glorious past when "London had plenty of fine ships in the docks, though not so many fine buildings in its streets" (*Tales of Hearsay*, p. 85). "The Black Mate" does reflect Conrad's plight at the time, and can be read as a first attempt by a sailor/author, no longer in his first flush of youth and already concerned about the future, investigating alternate careers, reading the periodicals in his newly adopted language, looking for various occupations, and entering story-writing contests – at least one that we know of – to test his skills and possible success in that area. His sense now of competing with time and his fear of being passed by in a world that was quickly changing was his perceived position, and even though, as Watt and others have noticed, the story derives a great deal from Daudet (Watt, *Conrad*, p. 48), the wistful nostalgia attributed to Daudet is also Conrad's.

The year after "The Black Mate" presumably was written, in the year of Victoria's Golden Jubilee, 1887, Conrad, then thirty years old, was hit by a falling spar on the sailing ship, the "Highland Forest," an accident he would consider of such significance that it would also incapacitate the hero of *Lord Jim*. A faintly ridiculous fate for an adventure-bound hero, it was certainly a come-down for Jim, and in treating the fictional accident ironically, Conrad perhaps revealed a similar attitude towards his own dreams of glory, for he, the Master Mariner, was immediately hospitalized for three months in Singapore and afterwards reduced to making routine passages on a Dutch coastal steamer, the "Vidar," from Singapore to Bulungan (his fictional Sambir) in Borneo, an easy berth after his accident. There he saw vagrant island traders and "wandering traders of good repute," Europeans of all descriptions, Arabs, Malays, and Chinese, all phenomena of an imperial island world that he had probably read about by now in Wallace, the various Brookiana, and current periodical accounts. It was during these trips that he first heard about and then saw the prototypes of Almayer, and of Babalatchi and Lakamba, two well-respected native merchants, of Willems, an alcoholic Dutch sailor who lived entirely "on Almayer's charity," and Tom Lingard and his nephew Jim, called by many Lord Jim for his swagger and physique. Conrad came to know also the hidden, twisted rivers and oppressive forests of that part of the Eastern Seas, from which he admitted to having "carried away into [his] writing life the greatest number of suggestions" (*The Shadow Line*, Author's Note, p. ix).

And it must have been at this point that Conrad vaguely projected the possibility of his also going nowhere fast, like Olmeijer/Almayer, a legendary failure, a victim of his own great expectations never realized, paralyzed by that despair and by vague, ridiculous hopes. In *A Personal Record*, Conrad remembered seeing him for the first time as the "Vidar" pulled closer to the river-side wharf at Bulungan one early, misty morning:

He was moving across a patch of burnt grass, a blurred, shadowy shape with the blurred bulk of a house behind him, a low house of mats, bamboos and palm-leaves with a high-pitched roof of grass. He stepped upon the jetty. He was clad simply in flapping pyjamas of cretonne pattern (enormous flowers with yellow petals on a disagreeable blue ground) and a thin cotton singlet with short sleeves... I had heard of him at Singapore, I had heard of him on board; I had heard of him early in the morning and late at night; I had heard of him at tiffin and at dinner.... (p. 74)

How Olmeijer must have engaged Conrad, interested as he was in multiple points of view! Already represented, Olmeijer's legend preceded him, and he came into existence through other people's stories about him. Meeting him, then, was like colliding with a legend and was a crucial experience for Conrad. According to his own account, he began work on *Almayer's Folly* in mid-1889 and, while working on it intermittently over the next five years, he never actually considered relinquishing his life at sea. But in *A Personal Record* again, written thirty years later, he equated the sun that sets in his novel's tenth chapter which he was writing while aboard the "Adowa," stalled in Rouen, with another kind of ending. "The sun of my sea-going was setting too, even as I wrote the words expressing the impatience of passionate youth bent on its desire" (p. 4). All he knew at the time, he wrote, was that the "necessity which impelled me [to write *Almayer's Folly*] was a hidden, obscure necessity, a completely masked and unaccountable phenomenon" (p. 68). His absorption with Almayer was not resolved with the writing of one novel either; something remained untreated that could only be purged by dealing with the subject yet again, and in his second novel, *An Outcast of the Islands*, he travelled backwards in time, delving into the sources of the legend, and dealt with a younger Almayer, getting at origins increasingly, and tracing possible explanations for such a phenomenon as Almayer and the sort of public loss and personal failure his story represented. In what he came to see as the cycle of Lingard, the third novel, *The Rescue*, was set even earlier in time and occupied Conrad on and off for the next twenty years. So, as he admitted, the man Olmeijer was to be credited with "some fourteen volumes so far" (*A Personal Record*, p. 87), and that was only in 1912.[5]

A vital connection existed for Conrad between getting this multi-volume story written and his sense of his own failing powers. As vague as his own dreams, the Eurasian Almayer must have been for Conrad a man who had been passed by, bitten and abandoned somehow on this remote twist of a hidden river, whose own ludicrous self-pity was a subject of fun for all who knew of him. Increasingly discontent with the disparity between his own dreams and the present reality he found himself in – a mate on a coastal steamer, bored with the monotonous passages and missing the promised excitement of the command of a sailing ship at sea – he resembled the captain in "The End of the Tether," worried about (possibly) failing eyesight, and the narrator of *The Shadow Line* who found himself in the grips of "the green sickness of late youth" when suddenly, "everything was gone – glamour, flavour, interest, contentment – everything" (p. 5). Thus Conrad must have been arrested by this figure of Almayer and have seen him as representative of the dream's demise, a rag-tag end in cretonne pyjamas, the public dream of pure, disinterested adventuring, and Conrad's own personal desire for heroic achievement shaped in large part by the imperial discourses of the day. While nostalgia often informs this early writing, reminding us of Conrad's own sense of loss, he nonetheless sees the absurdity of such a self-imposed paralysis as Almayer's. He must act; if not sail, then steam, if not the sea, then the writing desk.

# CHAPTER 6

# Almayer's Folly

> As a general rule, the British novel-reader likes the scenes of his
> story to be laid in British soil. He is insular in his tastes, not easily
> interested in places and people who are outside his experience.
> When a writer contrives to hold his attention with such topics it
> is proof that he has handled them exceptionally well. (Sherry
> (ed.), *Conrad*, p. 66)

Thus James Payn, a popular contemporary novelist, began his
review of *An Outcast of the Islands* for *The Illustrated London News* in
April 1896. Payn goes on to congratulate Conrad for his ability to
hold the reader's attention. But the observation that British novel-
readers are insular is puzzling when we remember Andrew Lang's
contention a few years earlier, borne out by sales figures, that exotic
literature enjoyed a great popularity (see chapter 1). Of course, as an
admirer of "Henley's Regatta," Lang opposed the Grundyism
abroad, a powerful faction that in the 1890s found the domestic
fiction to be more respectable and uplifting, dealing as it did with far
less objectionable matters than did the exotic fiction Lang championed. However, this reviewer must have noticed that the *News* itself
ran serially much of the adventure fiction and travel writing of the
day, contained numerous articles about colonial possessions, usually
elaborately illustrated, and reviewed and recommended books on
related subjects frequently. That he nonetheless found Conrad's work
"exceptional" suggests the contemporary resistance, already mentioned in chapter 4, to the popular adventure genre. Similarly
puzzling, juxtaposed with Lang's contention is Fisher Unwin's
response to Conrad's manuscript of *Almayer's Folly* and his reason for
paying the author so little for it, only £20. In a letter to his aunt,
Conrad quotes Unwin: "'We are paying you very little,' he told me,
'but, remember, dear Sir, that you are an unknown and your book
appeals to a very limited public. Then there is the question of taste.

Will the public like it?'" (Karl, *Letters*, I, p. 180). We hear in this protest the publisher's dodge, but also Unwin's sense, a reliable and well-developed one, we suspect, of the newness of Conrad's enterprise. But if the various discourses about the imperial subject were as popular as sales figures and contemporary contentions would lead us to believe, how could Unwin see *Almayer* as appealing to a small audience – unless, under the guise of adventure fiction, it was in fact doing something quite different?[1] Indeed, the apparent contradiction surrounding the reception of Conrad's early fiction provides a clue to the nature of its undertaking.

As Unwin feared, the novel did not sell well nor did its successor, *An Outcast of the Islands*, and he lost money on both of them. According to Edward Garnett, Unwin's manuscript reader, *Almayer* did not require a third impression for seven years, and "both *An Outcast of the Islands*, which received brilliant reviews, and *Tales of Unrest* took eleven years to reach a second impression" (Garnett, *Letters*, p. 16). Echoing the sentiments regarding British reading preferences recorded in Payn's review, Garnett admits that Conrad's early work, while it "appealed to the less insular 'honourable minority,'" was too exotic for most readers to whom the characters must have seemed "queer folk, outside the pale" (Conrad, *Prefaces*, p. 8). But what does this mean? How were Conrad's early novels so different from others written in the genre? While many readers expressed confusion over the early works and did not know how to place them, those novels were, in fact, referred to by most contemporary reviewers as exotic romances, and as adventure fiction, and frequently compared with works by such writers as Rider Haggard, Stevenson, and Kipling. Some readers found Conrad deficient next to these writers for offending such genre conventions as streamlined, swiftly moving plots, and accused him of slowing his narratives down with disordered chronologies, diffuse descriptions, and a psychological interest in interior monologues. As we have seen in chapter 4, such champions of the genre as W. E. Henley, for example, who read *Almayer's Folly* as adventure fiction, found it intolerably circuitous and long-winded; Henley told Unwin he could only get through sixty pages of it (Karl, *Letters*, I, p. 211). Several reviewers found that Conrad had surpassed other writers of the genre, that he was a masterful story teller who had "opened new worlds to the untravelled reader." One applauded his tales of strong men fighting the elements, of emotional crises, of settlers in foreign lands among alien people, [of] the conflict of the East and the West, of savagery and civilization ... It is Mr. Conrad's achievement to have brought the East to our very doors, not only its people – others have done that conspicuously well – but its feeling, its glamour, its beauty and wonder. He is one of the notable literary colonists. He has annexed the Malay Peninsula for us. (Sherry (ed.), *Conrad*, p. 110)

But whether his work was considered inferior or superior to others in the genre, the comparison implied the kinship of his work to contemporary adventure fiction and to travel writing. In his Preface to *Almayer's Folly*, Conrad himself defended his fiction as belonging to the genre some had accused of being "decivilized."

I am informed that in criticizing that literature which preys on strange people and prowls in far-off countries, under the shade of palms, in the unsheltered glare of sunbeaten beaches, amongst honest cannibals and the more sophisticated pioneers of our glorious virtues, a lady – distinguished in the world of letters – summed up her disapproval of it by saying that the tales it produced were 'decivilized.' And in that sentence not only the tales but, I apprehend, the strange people and the far-off countries also, are finally condemned in a verdict of contemptuous dislike. (*Almayer's Folly*, p. ix)

Perhaps the lady in question was part of that audience of detractors created particularly by Haggard's brand of offensively bloody militarism. To a certain extent, these otherwise puzzling pieces of evidence document the vortex of deepening and widening gaps occurring among diverse contemporary audiences,[2] a vortex in which Conrad became ensnared in spite of such disclaimers as this Preface to dissociate himself from the likes of Haggard. While he was quite alive to the market value of magazine fiction – particularly the exotic tales of imperial adventure – he was also aware of a certain antagonism toward the very discourse he knew his work would be read within. Interestingly, he made his disclaimer on grounds similar to Haggard's, the "bond between us and that humanity so far away."

I am content to sympathize with common mortals, no matter where they live; in houses or in tents, in the streets under a fog, or in the forests behind the dark line of dismal mangroves that fringe the vast solitude of the sea. For, their land – like ours – lies under the inscrutable eyes of the Most High. Their hearts – like ours – must endure the load of the gifts from Heaven: the curse of facts and blessing of illusions, the bitterness of our wisdom and the deceptive consolation of our folly. (*Almayer's Folly*, p. x)

From the beginning, then, Conrad felt moved to justify the writing of "far-off lands" against the attacks of "decivilized" often leveled at this literature, and he did so by unconventionally stressing the similarities between "us" and "them" rather than those differences that privilege "us". As it turned out, this Preface, or Author's Note, was not published when it was written in 1895 but in 1921 with the Collected Edition. Whether Unwin felt it inappropriate to the Six-Shilling Library *Almayer's Folly* was published in or Conrad withdrew it is not clear. Never a popular writer, he nonetheless was extremely aware of the market and tried to gauge that elusive entity, British taste. He had told Garnett, early on, that he "*won't* live in an attic!" (Garnett, *Letters*, p. 8) and at almost forty-years old, he undoubtedly meant it. He might simply have chosen to let his fiction work for him indirectly rather than to announce his subversion quite so overtly, for the Author's Note does strike several subversive notes. In a letter to one of his manuscript readers, W. H. Chesson, Conrad urged him to "say [in the advance publicity] something about being a 'civilized story in savage surroundings.' Something in that sense if not in those words" (Karl, *Letters*, 1, p. 199). In insisting on that point at least, he demonstrated his understanding of and interest in the current taste of British novel-readers.

The contradiction, then, is only apparent and not real if we read "insular" and "exotic" as possible synonyms, not antonyms. In fact, most works of popular travel writing and adventure fiction were essentially "insular," and certainly lay within the British reader's experience. No matter how far afield their travels took them, the vantage point of the adventure hero was consistently English, and the story of the Other was always told from the European point of view. Carrying English values and beliefs with him wherever he went, remaining stolidly untouched by his encounters with the Other in tropical outposts, the adventure hero essentially never left England behind. Thus any potential threat posed by the exotic was disarmed. Conrad's fiction was perceived as exotic, and disturbingly so, because its point of view was not purely insular. From the first, Conrad practised a certain amount of ventriloquism and never situated himself easily in one character. Perhaps it took a Polish sailor finally to tell the story of the white man in the tropics from alternative points of view, for through Conrad's multiple tellings, the story of the Other and the white man in the outposts of empire became theirs as well as ours. This was the final, to many the unforgivable, subversion. As

O. Mannoni has recently observed in his discussion of imperial Prosperos and native Calibans, "what the colonial in common with Prospero lacks is awareness of the world of Others, a world in which Others have to be respected" (p. 108); as Conrad showed, it was a world that at least needed to be represented.[3]

While it is probably true that Conrad's ventriloquism resulted more from his growing technical interest in writerly concerns than from any liberal consciousness, recording the dream's demise within the very genre that had so decisively shaped it was ironically appropriate. Working from within the genre that had constructed the imperial subject gave a particular poignancy to Conrad's attack on the tenets central to the discourse, for he was not a disinterested outsider. The dreams central to the subject had been his own, and he recorded their failure with reluctance but with candor. The first two novels, then, *Almayer's Folly* and *An Outcast of the Islands*, record the demise not only of the personal but also of the public dream. Although projected as "the cycle of Lingard," the third novel, *The Rescue*, was not completed until twenty years after the publication of *Outcast*. Sequels were not unusual in adventure fiction – Allan Quatermain saw action in several novels after *King Solomon's Mines* – but Conrad's "cycle" was unusual in that it ran backwards chronologically. The story of Almayer, suggested by the actual Eurasian inhabitant of Borneo, preoccupied him for six years, but after telling it, more remained. Coaxed into "writing another" by Garnett, he went over the same ground once again, as though compelled to seek explanations for such phenomena as he dealt with in *Almayer* in the origins of the characters involved. Sometime during the writing of *Outcast*, he projected the third.

In many ways, *Almayer's Folly* is a strange first novel, for it records an ending, not only of the cycle that had not yet been written, but of a dream shared by all writers of adventure and travel, and it effectively reverses the image of the white man in the tropics created by the travel writing and adventure fiction in periodicals and books. Conrad's novel employs many of the conventions of the discourse: an exotic setting, overheard plots and schemes – many concerning hidden rivers leading to hordes of gold – Taminah, the slave girl whose jealousy drives her to betray her beloved, and the crucial ring of identification, to name the most obvious. But, at the same time, the basic tenets of the genre are subverted. "We" are still defined in contrast to "them" and are still involved in colonial acquisition, but without any of the "fine words" that have accompanied such exploits in the past, a subversion of the genre that had always depicted the benevolent heroism and achievements of the white man in the outposts of empire. The European is represented by the most unheroic Almayer, the shadowy Lingard, the English gunrunner Captain Ford and the occasional naval officer. In terms of the novel, Dutch and English are fairly interchangeable since, whichever they are, they are outsiders here, meddlesome, potentially threatening and full of condescension for the natives, for the pitiable Almayer, and also for his half-caste daughter Nina.

The plot itself signals a major shift in genre convention. Adventure is only glimpsed, afar off, never in fact to be realized, at least not by Almayer. Instead of casting off with our hero from England for exotic lands, to seek glory and to light up the dark places of the world, and always to return to the hero's beloved native shores, we are confined to Borneo with Almayer throughout the fiction. Instead of journeying to open seas, wide veldts, or expanses of shimmering desert, we experience Almayer's claustrophobia in the forest-choked river village of Sambir. Instead of heroic deeds, Almayer accomplishes nothing; he starts a business that fails, and the grand house he has built in anticipation of his successes falls back into ruins; he raises a daughter who finally rejects him for the Malayan Dain Maroola and his more attractive native culture; Almayer alienates all potential allies through his own shortsightedness, lethargy, misplaced sense of racial superiority, and general blindness to things as they are, sinks into an opium coma, and dies, alone. Adventure has been severely reduced here to Lingard's promises of gold and diamonds that never materialize, to his vague allusions to hidden rivers, to intrigues among native Rajahs and rivalries with local Arab powers. For the most part, adventure takes place in the past, only faint echoes surviving in a few lingering legends and nostalgic reminiscences. As Lingard's exploits with the Sulu pirates are remembered, so Babalatchi, the resident native ruler's counsellor, looks back to a more heroic past. He tells the English Captain Ford, at the novel's end when the future should be illuminated with his news from Bali that Nina and Dain have had a son, the Rajah's grandson, that

the old times were best. Even I have sailed with Lanun men, and boarded in the night silent ships with white sails. That was before an English Rajah ruled in Kuching. Then we fought amongst ourselves and were happy. Now when we fight with you we can only die! (p. 206)

Although once Almayer might have looked the part of a white-clad hopeful, even the stuff of his dreams differed from his fictional and non-fictional predecessors. Standing amid the ruins of his hopes, early in the novel, he thinks back to twenty years before to

a young and slim Almayer, clad all in white and modest-looking, landing from the Dutch mail-boat on the dusty jetty of Macassar, coming to woo fortune in the godowns of old Hudig. It was an important epoch in his life, the beginning of a new existence for him...

Almayer had left his home with a light heart and a lighter pocket, speaking English well, and strong in arithmetic; ready to conquer the world, never doubting that he would. (p. 5)

We have come a great distance from the "merry chorus of the sailors" that attended the setting out of an adventure hero such as *The Coral Island*'s Ralph Rover, to the most musical sound Almayer hears in his newly chosen mercantile pursuit, "the musical chink of broad silver pieces streaming ceaselessly through the yellow fingers of the attentive Chinamen" (p. 6). And the difference is a telling one, for Almayer's dreams are the wrong ones. Domino-like, as Hudig's bank fails, so Lingard's chances fail, so Almayer's hopes fail. They were not only insubstantial, they were not the dreams of heroes. Others might have set out to "woo fortune" but not in trader's warehouses, but for glory and adventure – booty was also acceptable, but by the way. Being "screwed down to a desk" was the great fear of Martin Rattler, R. M. Ballantyne's boy hero (*MR*, p. 29). Stanley of G. A. Henty's *On the Irrawaddy* would prefer, at the age of fourteen, going off to India and conducting native barter up little-frequented rivers and occasionally beating off wild tribesmen to "having to go into some humdrum office," or "a dull counting-house" in England (p. 17). And in Henty's *By Right of Conquest*, Roger chose the dangers of life at sea fighting on the Spanish Main to the work that was offered to him in his cousin's prosperous counting house in Plymouth. The contrast illuminates the dream's diminishment; for Almayer, then, the heroic vision that informed the hopes and intentions of other adventurers has been reduced to a rather mean-spirited commercial endeavor.

Not only are his aspirations the unheroic ones of a gray, diminished commercial world, but the initially negative impulse that inspires Almayer's setting out further marks him as an uncharacteristic genre hero. Aside from the discontent with home values we have seen on the part of some of Haggard's heroes, from Marryat to Ballantyne to Henty, those same heroes intent on adventure in exotic lands mean to return to England. Martin Rattler is swept out to sea accidentally but makes the most of his new circumstances on a brig and conducts himself uncomplainingly, and adventures follow which provide ample opportunities for heroism and his triumphant return. But there is nothing accidental about Almayer's departure from his homeland. Almayer, we are told, is the son of Dutch colonials in Java:

> His father, a subordinate official employed in the Botanical Gardens of Buitenzorg, was no doubt delighted to place his son in [Hudig's] firm. The young man himself too was nothing loath to leave the poisonous shores of Java, and the meagre comforts of the parental bungalow, where the father grumbled all day at the stupidity of native gardeners, and the mother from the depths of her long easychair bewailed ·the lost glories of Amsterdam, where she had been brought up, and of her position as the daughter of a cigar dealer there. (p. 5)

Not even to disgruntled Allan Quatermain are England's shores "poisonous." Although Wiltshire, of Stevenson's *The Beach of Falesá* reluctantly admits by novel's end that a white man's country is no place for his half-caste daughters, his dream throughout has been to return to start up a public house in England. But nothing so altruistic powers Almayer's desires. The only tug toward homeland Almayer feels is for Amsterdam, the source of his mother's bitter nostalgia. His desires have been fueled by maternal discontent with anything less than the material and racial advantages of that European capital, so for Almayer too Amsterdam takes on an Edenic glow, but not out of any patriotic impulse. In fact, again contrasting greatly with Stevenson's character, Almayer accepts Lingard's proposal to marry Lingard's adopted native daughter for extremely unheroic reasons. He promises Almayer that nobody "will see the colour of your wife's skin. The dollars are too thick for that, I tell you! And mind you, they will be thicker yet before I die. There will be millions, Kaspar! Millions I say!" Almayer finds the offer a difficult one to refuse. He saw

> great piles of shining guilders, and realized all the possibilities of an opulent existence. The consideration, the indolent ease of life – for which he felt himself so well fitted – his ships, his warehouses, his merchandise (old Lingard would not live for ever), and crowning all, in the far future

gleamed like a fairy palace the big mansion in Amsterdam, that earthly paradise of his dreams, where, made king amongst men by old Lingard's money, he would pass the evening of his days in inexpressible splendour. (p. 10)

And like the King Midas of the fairy tale this passage hints at, who also dreamed the wrong dreams, everything Almayer touches withers and dies, particularly his daughter's love. The contrast with Stevenson's character is again telling, for Almayer's unheroic motives even surpass Wiltshire's initial reasons for "marrying" Uma. That South Sea trader at least redeems his unscrupulousness; he makes good on his pledge and grows to love his native wife, so much so that he will not jeopardise her well-being or that of their daughters in order to realize his own desire to return to England. Unlike Almayer, he finally refuses to see his marriage as simply another business transaction.

With this short sketch of the young Almayer, another truth promoted by adventure discourse is questioned, that of the glorious calling of the colonial life, for it was an able-bodied Englishman's duty, according to many of these writers, to carry on the good work in the far reaches of empire. Instead of being infused with any sense of patriotic pride – Mr. and Mrs. Almayer evidently had not read Kingsley or heard Ruskin's speeches and lectures on the subject – they only feel their material and social diminishment and general dissatisfaction. Almayer, understandably, wants to escape. A major effect of Almayer's transformation from a historical half-caste whom Conrad had actually seen, to the fictional Dutchman is that his past as a European colonial allows the narrative to suggest that this is the record not only of one white man's folly but of the misguidedness of the whole European venture in its imperial outposts.

Almayer's first desires to wander, then, are awakened by his great discontent at home and by the hope of becoming rich in a merchant's counting house, not the stuff that inspired adventure heroes. And consider the heroes of Almayer's hopes and dreams, those who shaped his desires. While Martin Rattler looked up to the likes of Vasco da Gama and Columbus, and Harold Seadrift of Ballantyne's *Black Ivory* revered Mungo Park and David Livingstone, Almayer, initially at least, admires Lingard for the "enormous profits of his ventures" (p. 8). He has heard the stories "of his smart business transactions," and to Almayer the noisy business dealings of Lingard and Hudig carried on in Hudig's back room, sound like the talk of

"Titans – a battle of the gods" (p. 8). Lingard is as close to a hero as we get here. Indeed, he is something of a legend:

At that time, Macassar was teeming with life and commerce. It was the point in the island where tended all those bold spirits who, fitting out schooners on the Australian coast, invaded the Malay Archipelago in search of money and adventure. Bold, reckless, keen in business, not disinclined for a brush with the pirates that were to be found on many a coast as yet, making money fast, they used to have a general 'rendezvous' in the bay for purposes of trade and dissipation. The Dutch merchants called those men English pedlars; some of them were undoubtedly gentlemen for whom that kind of life had a charm; most were seamen; the acknowledged king of them all was Tom Lingard, he whom the Malays, honest or dishonest, quiet fishermen or desperate cutthroats, recognized as "the Rajah-Laut" – the King of the Sea. (pp. 6–7)

While the description contains familiar echoes of legendary daring-do, it introduces a complexity; no singleness of vision is permitted here, but an awareness that point of view has everything to do with depictions. "Merchant" or "pedlar" depends on who is doing the naming. And while Henty's heroes were bold, and even reckless on occasion and certainly ready for a "brush with the pirates," it would not be said of them that they gathered for "purposes of dissipation," or if so, those who did were relegated to an inferior status, not truly "one of us." And "dissipation" would not be so quietly coupled with the "trade" which many of our heroes engaged in. But Lingard is clearly one of these "English pedlars," in the eyes of the Dutch merchants in the area and "Rajah-Laut" to the Malays. And while he is a titan to Almayer, to us his heroism is suspect. Almayer has heard the stories of Lingard's

desperate fights with the Sulu pirates, together with the romantic tale of some child – a girl – found in a piratical prau by the victorious Lingard, when, after a long contest, he boarded the craft, driving the crew overboard. This girl, it was generally known, Lingard had adopted, was having her educated in some convent in Java, and spoke of her as "my daughter". (p. 7)

But this heroism of the great Rajah Laut, and Almayer's admiration of it, is immediately undercut. The fiction subverts genre expectations by giving a voice to the formerly voiceless, for the point of view shifts here from the white version of the story as "rescue" to the native view as "capture." And the shift is something of a jolt, for the discourse so far has prepared us only for her gratitude; that this undeserving pirate's daughter is fortunate to be given the advantages of the white man's civilization has been the conventional construction of the situation. But now we are given a glimpse of the world through that native woman's eyes, and a different world it is:

> no one knew that on the day when the interesting young convert had lost all her natural relations and found a white father, she had been fighting desperately like the rest of them on board the prau, and was only prevented from leaping overboard, like the few other survivors, by a severe wound in the leg. There, on the fore-deck of the prau, old Lingard found her under a heap of dead and dying pirates, and had her carried on the poop of the *Flash* before the Malay craft was set on fire and sent adrift. She was conscious, and in the great peace and stillness of the tropical evening succeeding the turmoil of the battle, she watched all she held dear on earth after her own savage manner drift away into the gloom in a great roar of flame and smoke. She lay there unheeding the careful hands attending to her wound, silent and absorbed in gazing at the funeral pile of those brave men she had so much admired and so well helped in their contest with the redoubtable "Rajah-Laut." (p. 21)

The parallel structure of the first phrase here, of lost and found, readies us to easily accept the possibility of such a facile replacement. And to the European mind, for and by whom this story is framed, replacing piratical relations with a white father such as Rajah-Laut could only be advantageous. This is the stuff of legend, of white men's stories told to one another in various colonial stations and ports and on tropical verandahs – the "broad verandah of the Sunda Hotel" in Macassar, for example, where Lingard often held forth, Marlow-like, to "a scratch audience of shore loafers" (p. 23) – wherever Europeans met and exchanged the tales and anecdotes that shaped imperial consciousnesses and reinforced the conventional roles. But this easy acquiescence with the traditional formula is immediately questioned. Although we suppose that it is the European participants in this story who see the Malay girl as "the interesting young convert," by the end of the passage, the point of view has shifted, and the irony made apparent that the subject of this passage is actually the limited knowledge of those very European minds that are shaping the story. It is all about what they do not know. The narration distances us from those figures a traditional adventure tale would render clearly as the heroes; "old Lingard," "the redoubtable 'Rajah-Laut'," is opposed to "those brave men she had so much admired." Although we are also somewhat distanced from the Malay girl whose loss here is qualified by "after her own savage manner," that she is afforded a point of view at all sets up a tension not present in this discourse heretofore. Even in the rare instances "they" are given a voice, as is Juno, the family's black servant in Marryat's *Masterman Ready*, the point of view is obedient and predictable and, in all essentials, indistinguishable from "ours."

And in giving the formerly voiceless a voice, the monolithic nature of the white man's account of these events is again questioned. His telling becomes simply one version among others, and this subversion is central to the novel. After the wedding, when the *Flash*, Lingard's ship,

freighted with materials for building a new house left the harbour of Batavia, taking away the young couple into the unknown Borneo, she did not carry on her deck so much love and happiness as old Lingard was wont to boast of before his casual friends in the verandahs of various hotels. (p. 23)

Instead of seeing it as the crowning achievement of her life, this native woman views her marriage to Almayer with submissive contempt. The idea Forster was to parody in *A Passage to India*, that "the darker races are physically attracted by the fairer, but not vice versa" (pp. 218–219), is first questioned here. Whenever this discourse has even hinted at the delicate subject of miscegenation, it has imaged the white man as an object of desire for the native woman. Although we are never given the native "wife" Uma's point of view in Stevenson's *The Beach of Falesa*, her words and actions reveal only a trusting affection for the white trader Wiltshire. And consider Foulata's suicidal adoration of Captain Good in Haggard's *King Solomon's Mines*. But such is not the case here. Not only is Almayer not the object of this native woman's desire, he disrupts her dreams of the future. They

were dispelled by the Rajah-Laut's "fiat", which made Almayer's fortune, as that young man fondly hoped. And dressed in the hateful finery of Europe, the centre of an interested circle of Batavian society, the young convert stood before the altar with an unknown and sulky-looking white man. (p. 23)

The native of this fiction, then, is no longer voiceless and part of an undifferentiated, faceless group of Others, and the dialogic possibilities permitted by the discrepancies of multiple viewpoints begin to dislodge the authority of the white man's telling, the only version heretofore available through this discourse. Can we imagine the essential authority of Quatermain's telling undermined in such a way? of Amyas Leigh's of Kingsley's *Westward Ho!*, of Ralph Rover's or Jim Hawkins's? The stories of white adventurers, fictionalized or not, were treated as believable fact. The texts never asked us to doubt the narratives of Henty or Ballantyne; they did not allow us to question Quatermain's judgment or Martin Rattler's insights, as Conrad tells us we must do in the case of Lingard and Almayer. When Jim Hawkins picks up his pen, "to write the whole particulars about Treasure Island," we know what he will write will not allow of another point of view. Certainly nothing in the narrative itself asks us to doubt that truthfulness. But with Conrad's first novel, the adventure of the white man in the tropics is no longer solely "our" story. New voices, new points of view – the "techniques of evasion" Albert Guerard sees Conrad moving toward even in this early fiction (Guerard, *Conrad the Novelist*, p. 62) – intrude upon and question the monologic telling, shaped by the popular travel writing and adventure fiction of the day and by such influential periodicals as *The Illustrated London News*, *The Graphic* and *Blackwood's Magazine*. Such narrative distancing as he achieves here and his insistence upon multiple story-tellers disrupt the authorial center and interrupt the monologic repetitions of the white man's story, marking the demise of the dream those tellings shaped.

Conrad accomplishes his subversion not only through narrative technique but also through characterization. In large part, it had been the hero's reliability and decisiveness that asked for belief in adventure fiction. Lingard grows increasingly shadowy in this fiction and finally disappears, his promises having also evaporated. Almayer himself is the essence of indecisiveness. Convinced by Lingard that Nina must be educated in Singapore and brought up in a European culture, he sends his daughter off but misses her sorely:

He longed to see her, and planned a voyage to Singapore, but put off his departure from year to year, always expecting some favourable turn of fortune. He did not want to meet her with empty hands and with no words of hope on his lips. He could not take her back into that savage life to which he was condemned himself...He asked himself what was going to be her future. He could not answer that question yet, and he dared not face her. And yet he longed after her. He hesitated for years. (p. 29)

Indecisive, impotent, he is a person to whom things happen or not. He effects little. He certainly becomes that disoriented figure in cretonne pajamas Conrad first saw from on board the "Vidar," but imagining his beginnings as a white-clad, hopeful young colonial come to seek his fortune in a distant outpost asks us to view him in the light of other young hopefuls dealt with in this discourse, and in so doing asks us to measure the distance of his diminishment. Partially prepared for by the reprobates of Stevenson's later fictions – Case and Randall of *The Beach of Falesá* or the trio of dissolute outcasts in *The Ebb Tide* – he comes to bear less and less resemblance to those other fictional heroes.

The words quoted above are not those of a Masterman Ready or of a Sir Henry Curtis. This indecisiveness and dependence on vague expectations is not the stuff of imperial greatness. Again, in the case of Almayer as with Lingard, Conrad's narrative focuses on what the white man does not know. Practically everything that happens to Almayer does so without his prior knowledge; his desires are so uninformed by the actual maneuverings taking place around him, that events befall him. For example, we learn before he does – he is indeed the last to know – of the love between Dain and Nina. If it is the wise parent that knows his own child, he is as blind as Lear. He does not even suspect that his wife has already promised Nina to Dain and has been accepting Dain's silver as dowry. As Almayer lies in his hammock one evening dreaming of the expedition Dain has promised to help him with, at last, to claim the gold Lingard has always spoken of, his wife, in the adjoining room, leans over her large wooden chest, rummaging "in the interior, where a soft clink as of silver money could be heard." Audible to us, or presumably to anyone nearby, the actual presence of silver is unnoticed by the oblivious Almayer wrapped up in his much less substantial dreams of gold. The juxtaposition is cruelly ironic here and elsewhere when his ignorance of native plots and intrigues renders him impotent and essentially outside the action. Unlike other heroes of this discourse, Almayer does not possess the knowledge, and lacks even the requisite information, to make effective decisions.

As the white man is unreliable, impotent, and indecisive, so European civilization is scrutinized unsympathetically; as to its benefits, there is not a glimmer. While Hugh Clifford objected to the "unreality" of Nina's going back to her mother's people's savage ways (Karl, *Letters*, II, n. 130), such a move suited Conrad's intention, for it demonstrated that the white man's civilization had nothing to offer her. In fact, her silent presence after her sudden return from

Singapore serves as a constant reproach to the spurious advantages of the white man's education. She appears, after ten years, to have carried none with her, only scars of the white man's prejudice and his culture's inadequacies. Rather than the reputed moral degradation of the native, much discussed in the travel writing and adventure fiction, it is the European civilization that Nina condemns for its narrowness, its moral emptiness, racial exclusiveness, and lack of vigour. Represented by the high convent walls that confined Mrs. Almayer in her girlhood, or by Mrs. Vinck's house in Singapore where Nina lived and suffered the slights and prejudices of colonial society while attending a Protestant school, that European culture has less vitality for Nina than the memory of her mother's, and Dain's, Malay culture so threatened by the white man:

And listening to the recital of those savage glories, those barbarous fights and savage feasting, to the story of deeds valorous, albeit somewhat bloodthirsty, where men of her mother's race shone far above the Orang Blanda, she felt herself irresistibly fascinated... (p. 42)

Her mother's stories of "the departed glories of the Rajahs," her mother's and her own ancestors after all, were far more attractive than "the white side of her descent represented by a feeble and traditionless father" (p. 43). Almayer has nothing to pass on to his daughter, neither dowry nor stories of a heroic past, and Nina is another of Conrad's "victims" of fictions that both seduce and illuminate. But it is also the actuality of "the savage and uncompromising sincerity of purpose shown by her Malay kinsmen" that she found preferable to "the sleek hypocrisy, to the polite disguises, to the virtuous pretences of such white people as she had had the misfortune to come in contact with" (p. 43). Babalatchi, as we have seen, also deplored the coming of the white man, and he and Mrs. Almayer repeatedly share their enmity hunched over the kitchen fire in the Almayer campong. They both had experienced a more glorious youth, in their view, before the coming of the hated Orang Blanda, the white man, who now to their disgust, they see everywhere, on every sea. Part of Mrs. Almayer's hope for Nina's union with Dain is that her son-in-law will drive the white man away. She has never forgotten her bitterness that all the brave men of her youth have been killed by the Dutch. She confides these hopes to Nina as she urges her daughter's escape with Dain away from her father's house forever, in the dark of night:

Let him slay the white men that come to us to trade, with prayers on their lips and loaded guns in their hands. Ah... they are on every sea, and on every shore; and they are very many! (p. 153)

This is not the accustomed message. The white man, as depicted here, is no bringer of light, but a duplicitous, destructive opportunist.

Nor is the native idealized. While Babalatchi, in particular, emerges as a credible force, individualized and interesting, neither he nor Mrs. Almayer is particularly sympathetic, and the unsavouriness of their ways is made more explicit in *Outcast*. In many respects, Mrs. Almayer is treated as the stereotypical Other. Existing as a kind of antagonism to Almayer – her only name is his – she is the conventional "primitive," superstitious and impulsive. But her words break the former silence, for they record – albeit in the stiff, archaic "native" language of this discourse – a counter version of the familiar story.[4] Nina, herself a kind of half-caste compromise, is more individualized and has a less absolute insight, one that echoes Conrad's pronouncements in his preface. Even though she casts her lot with her mother's people, she sees that nefarious plots for gain were common to both cultures. Upon her return to Sambir, she is afflicted with double vision:

Her young mind having been unskilfully permitted to glance at better things, and then thrown back again into the hopeless quagmire of barbarism, full of strong and uncontrolled passions, had lost the power to discriminate. It seemed to Nina that there was no change and no difference. Whether they traded in brick godowns or on the muddy river bank; whether they reached after much or little; whether they made love under the shadows of the great trees or in the shadow of the cathedral on the Singapore promenade; whether they plotted for their own ends under the protection of laws and according to the rules of Christian conduct, or whether they sought the gratification of their desires with the savage cunning and the unrestrained fierceness of natures as innocent of culture as their own immense and gloomy forests, Nina saw only the same manifestations of love and hate and of sordid greed chasing the uncertain dollar in all its multifarious and vanishing shapes. (pp. 42–3)

How are we to read this? Are we to believe that this vision of sameness results from a failure to discriminate, induced by the blinding and "hopeless quagmire of barbarism"? Since the text frequently challenges the superiority of "civilized" cultures, without necessarily romanticising the native, we must assume that the narrator's voice here, presumably telling the white man's story of them and us, is ironic – that she was exposed to "better things" in Singapore has already been disputed. Nina's insight does not demonstrate an inability to discriminate but rather a willingness to look through the mythology of difference that surrounds her and see, in fact, similarities. Like the author, she is something of a privileged observer; one of many, her view here disturbs the conventional solitary telling.

In fact, the fiction reveals a willingness to see "us" as outsiders, as transitory interlopers, thus rejecting the simplistic view that anyone can be actually native. As the Europeans invaded the Arab held coastal trading centers, so the Arabs had driven the Dyaks further upriver, so the Dyaks had also usurped the land from former residents. The fiction is not surprised at this turn of events nor does it award prices. One conquering people is very much like another with the same inglorious motives in mind. The novel, then, refuses to glamorize the most recent invasions of Dutch and English. The white man is the intruder, not the heroic, benevolent bringer of light. He brings gunpowder and opium, not religion. In fact his religion is practically non-existent, rarely referred to and certainly not relied on, while the religions of the others are always present. Whether the gods are Dyak spirits or Allah, they are alive, respected and prayed to. Nor is there any thought here of improving the natives through the Christian message. As we have seen, the impact of the white man's intrusion has been anything but beneficial.

In certain respects, *Almayer's Folly* might strike us as another version of "The Black Mate," but without the facile conclusion. Both fictions look nostalgically to a past not to be recovered, *Almayer* with even more finality. Conrad had described his last chapter as moving from a "trio" of Almayer, Dain and Nina to a long "solo" (Karl, *Letters*, I, p. 156). After watching Dain lead Nina down to the canoe and paddle away until the prau's sail was merely a glint of reflected sunlight on the horizon, Almayer stood alone:

Now she was gone his business was to forget, and he had a strange notion that it should be done systematically and in order. To Ali's great dismay he fell on his hands and knees, and, creeping along the sand, erased carefully with his hand all traces of Nina's footsteps. He piled up small heaps of sand, leaving behind him a line of miniature graves right down to the water. (p. 195)

A few months after completing *Almayer*, in a letter to his aunt, Marguerite Poradowska, he replied: "I well understand this yearning for the past which vanishes little by little, marking its route in tombs and regrets. Only that goes on forever" (Karl, *Letters*, 1, p. 162). To forget seemed to Almayer the only defense against the collapse of his dreams, and although that solitude and sense of isolation in one's own life and time was Conrad's too, the novelist records as a defensive tactic against extinction. Knowing that, in effect, life dies in one's wake unceasingly, Conrad began writing, a way of remembering, out of a need to mourn and record that ever-vanishing past. And if those first two fictions concerned men who saw the world as rushing forward without them, that sense is even stronger in *An Outcast of the Islands*. In this novel, Conrad returned to the time he passed over in silence in *Almayer*, when Nina was a small child and had not yet been sent off to school in Singapore, when Almayer was closer to that first figure of a white-clad hopeful, farther from the disabused opium victim we last saw, and Lingard is younger and more in evidence. But Almayer is already desperately out of touch with that greater world he hopes to return to loaded down with the spoils of conquest. One of the only two white men on the East coast now, his watch has run down, and since he depends on the odd back copy of *The North China Herald* that Lingard might bring, his newspapers are like his dreams, already outdated and irrelevant. This second novel can be read as an attempt to explain what has gone wrong, and the nostalgic note sounded immediately announces a deep regret that things have gone as awry as they have.

# CHAPTER 7

# An Outcast of the Islands

While the political accusations will intensify with the African stories, still to be written at this point, they are already present in these early Malay fictions also. But what occasioned the shift in Conrad from a believer in the dream of disinterested adventure to a denouncer of its consequences in "Heart of Darkness?" To a great extent, his changing relationship to the endeavor itself, giving up the sea and the particular role that career required him to play, freed him effectively, if not entirely consciously, to subvert the usual celebration of the white man in the tropics.

In agreement with Jean-Aubry, Garnett contended that Conrad's Congo experiences were "the turning-point in his mental life and that their effects on him determined his transformation from a sailor to a writer" (Garnett, Letters, p. 8). Not only the African books but also the first Malayan ones were the fruits of his trip up the Congo. He later stated that in his early years at sea he had "not a thought in his head...I was a perfect animal." His Congo journey had forced a more reflective point of view. Garnett had seen that the "sinister voice of the Congo with its murmuring undertone of human fatuity, baseness and greed had swept away the generous illusions of his youth, and had left him gazing into the heart of an immense darkness" (Garnett, Letters, p. 8). But his objectivity concerning the imperial ventures he was engaged in was also enabled by his actual distance – ever increasing – from a maritime career. The disaffection with the imperial enterprise he had arrived at by "Heart of Darkness" was permitted in part by the fact that that novel's subject was at least ostensibly Belgian treachery rather than British, and his particular position as a self-imposed exile in England made his attitudes toward that host country extremely complex. But it was also enabled by his increasing separation from a career at sea. The process of transformation he underwent in these years was a gradual one, but with the changing self-image from seaman to writer, came a broader vision of European imperial undertakings and a willingness to depict the unwarranted consequences of their lofty professions and aspirations.

On July 4, 1894, Conrad had submitted the manuscript of *Almayer's Folly* to Fisher Unwin for inclusion in that publisher's Pseudonym Series. In August he still had not heard when he wrote his aunt from Champel, France where he had gone for hydrotherapy treatments. He had requested the return of the manuscript, he told her, from Unwin, and would pass it on to her. She was already a successfully published novelist in France, and he hoped that it would be published in France under her name; his would be represented only by the pseudonym "Kamudi" – Malay for "rudder" – printed in small type. So before he even knew the fate of that first novel, he wrote to tell her that he was still looking for a command, and that if she should find him something he would be willing to take an examination in Belgium. In the same letter he told her he had begun writing:

I want to make this thing very short – let us say twenty to twenty-five pages, like those in the Revue. I am calling it "Two Vagabonds", and I want to describe in broad strokes, without shading or details, two human outcasts such as one finds in the lost corners of the world. A white man and a Malay. You see how Malays cling to me! I am devoted to Borneo. What bothers me most is that my characters are so true. I know them so well that they shackle the imagination. The white is a friend of Almayer – the Malay is our old friend Babalatchi before he arrived at the dignity of prime minister and confidential adviser to the Rajah. There they are. But I can't find a dramatic climax. My head is empty, and even the beginning is heavy going. I won't inflict more on you. I already feel like letting everything drop. Do you think one can make something interesting without any women?! (Karl, *Letters*, I, p. 171)

That which begins as an investigation of "a friend of Almayer" – Willems – and a backward glance at a character already encountered – Babalatchi – a white man and a Malay, an almost neutral sounding, ethnographic look at "them and us," turns out to be an indictment of Lingard's benevolent paternalism and that of the white man's endeavor generally. Even after October, when Unwin accepted *Almayer* for publication, Conrad was still so busy "chasing ships" that "The Two Vagabonds" are idle," he wrote his aunt (Karl, *Letters*, I, p. 178). But Unwin had indicated that anything else he wrote, especially something shorter for the Pseudonym Library, would be seriously considered. Garnett had encouraged Conrad to "write another." So between revisions of *Almayer*, he pursued his "maritime affairs" with less persistence, but was still negotiating with some Liverpool people about a "pretty little ship" named *Primera*, and kept at "Vagabonds" (Karl, *Letters*, 1, n.185).

Thus at first he saw his second novel as magazine fiction, something short for a journal like the *Revue de deux mondes*, and influenced by the constraints of that genre. Then, he confided to his aunt, his title was stolen and his concept of the novel changed accordingly:

As for the idea of this work, so far untitled...First, the theme is the unrestrained, fierce vanity of an ignorant man who has had some success but neither principles nor any other line of conduct than the satisfaction of his vanity. In addition, he is not even faithful to himself. Whence a fall, a sudden descent to physical enslavement by an absolutely untamed woman. I have seen that! The catastrophe will be brought about by the intrigues of a little Malay state where poisoning has the last word. The denouement is: suicide, again because of vanity. All this will only be sketched, because, as I am writing for the Pseudonym Library, I am restricted to 36,000 words per volume. (Karl, *Letters*, 1, p. 185)

Having to relinquish the title allowed him to rethink the work, and in doing so concentrate on one figure. This description now sounds closer to one of Stevenson's South Seas letters or fictions that depicted dissipated and demoralized white men attracted through a kind of innate hollowness to the fringes of empire, and these were being serialized and published in the early 1890s; the final installment of *The Ebb Tide*, for example, had just been published in *To-Day* in February of 1894, eight months before this letter to his cousin, and we know he had read Stevenson's *In the South Seas*, for he spoke of it approvingly to Sidney Colvin (Colvin, *Memories*, p. 149). But his willingness to see the writing still as a short piece of adventure fiction with all the trappings – native intrigues, poisoning, and the "savage" native woman – results perhaps from his abiding self-image as a sailor. As long as he saw himself as a master mariner, he seemed less willing to distance himself in certain externals from the conventions and constraints of the discourse his writing belonged to. He was both testing the literary market and engaged, quite actively still, in finding a ship. We can also mark a certain psychological disjunction here as elsewhere between his artistic psyche whose intentions to prepare subversive novels apparently remained concealed from him and his more conscious intentions to write generic short stories characterized by the melodramatic devices of intrigues, poisonings, and suicide.

Reviewed as a romance in contemporary notices, Conrad's second novel, *An Outcast of the Islands* (1896), was likened favorably to works by Melville, Stevenson, and Kipling, although Henley's *National Observer* found it lacked Kipling's "rapid delineation of character," and his "vivid directness of style" (Sherry (ed.), *Conrad*, p. 69). Again, by genre standards, it was too diffuse. But generally it looked like an imperial fiction whose accustomed task it was to applaud the white man's endeavors in the outposts of empire. It certainly was filled with the requisite intrigue and lush vegetation, and the "absolutely untamed" native woman, Aïssa. Aïssa's adoration for Willems, the white man, is genre material; it was a devotion that caused her also, Foulata-like, to save his life. But finally she is no Foulata, and, more to the point, Willems is certainly no Captain Good, R.N.

"When he stepped off the straight and narrow path of his peculiar honesty, it was with an inward assertion of unflinching resolve to fall back again into the monotonous but safe stride of virtue..." (*Outcast*, p. 3). In this opening sentence of the novel, we know the "he" can refer to no conventional hero. Heroes, in this discourse, do not step off the path of honesty. Nor do they fool themselves into believing that moral consequences do not inevitably follow any action. We have read enough to know otherwise. Never even a white-clad hopeful like Almayer who was, after all, a privileged son of colonials of definite standing in the official hierarchy, Willems, son of a hard-working but unforgivably poor father, is a barefoot waif, a runaway from Rotterdam, in need of the paternal help he asks for, and receives, from Lingard. While Almayer was unheroic in a pathetic sort of way, Willems is corrupt. He is not just a symptom of the disease imperialism proliferates, he is a contributing cause. No adventure hero, he may be adored by Aïssa, but of course he is as passionately ensnared himself and finally becomes the fatal victim not only of her desire but also of his own corruption, not a victorious hero. He is eminently corruptible, as we learn in the first sentence, and Willems' fall is due to his own intrinsic hollowness, a hollowness the discourse has only begun to intimate, in Stevenson's late fiction, for example, but which Conrad depicts along with all its unsavoury consequences in Almayer, and Willems, and again in Carlier, Kayerts, and Kurtz in the African stories.

Lingard replicates, or anticipates, his first mistake with Almayer, setting up Willems as Hudig's confidential clerk, just as he formerly had done for Almayer. And if the distance between Almayer and the young hopefuls of adventure fiction was great, the gap has widened considerably with Willems. He feels he has secured his reputation in town with his prowess at mixing cocktails and playing billiards, not exactly the contributions to civilization envisioned by McClintock, Rajah Brooke, or David Livingstone. And the kind of work he does as Hudig's confidential clerk contrasts greatly with the ennobling work of empire the fiction has always proudly proclaimed. Indeed, Willems congratulates himself as he reviews the tasks he has already accomplished for Hudig:

the quiet deal in opium; the illegal traffic in gunpowder, the great affair of smuggled firearms, the difficult business of the Rajah of Goak. He carried that last through by sheer pluck; he had bearded the savage old ruler in his council room; he had bribed him with a gilt glass coach, which, rumour said, was used as a hen-coop now; he had overpersuaded him; he had bested him in every way. That was the way to get on... the wise, the strong, the respected, have no scruples. Where there are scruples there can be no power. On that text he preached often to the young men. It was his doctrine, and he, himself, was a shining example of its truth. (p. 8)

Here Willems impugns the heroic code and uses the language of that discourse to do so. But his "sheer pluck" serves only inglorious ends, and he sets a "shining example" for all the wrong reasons. To describe Willems, the first in a long line of dissolutes and betrayers, in the language of adventure fiction is to mark the heroic assumptions of the discourse as now mere empty pretensions, as only "fine words."

Of course, Willems becomes instead a rather tarnished example of the stupidity of being unscrupulous with those who are equally bereft of scruples but who are more powerful and able. When Hudig detects Willem's thefts and turns him out, Lingard once again rescues the worthless young man and deposits him in Sambir, for want of a better course of action, where that former protégé – now his partner, Almayer – is operating their trading station. There, in the hiatus created by his own moral vacuousness, Willems confronts the wilderness, within and without. An idea Conrad will deal with further in the African stories, that the white adventurer is indeed susceptible to the wilderness, is at work here.[1] Contrary to the representations in the discourse so far, the white adventurer does not remain unaffected and return home unscathed, particularly not if he leaves the ship, or the camp, or the path, all of which Willems does. Better men than Willems, Martin Decoud for example, that other study in solitude, will completely unravel from the intolerable strain of aloneness. Disturbed by the lack of familiar, sustaining activity and society, Willems curses his own uselessness and resents the "neat fences" of Almayer's courtyard. He takes to wandering around the settlement, then up the various branches of the river in Almayer's canoe, and roaming farther and farther afield, he follows unfamiliar, faint paths into the tangled forests.

Thus he meets Aïssa, daughter of the blind old Omar whom Babalatchi, Omar's fellow pirate from more heroic days, serves and protects. Even Willems' initial resistance to his attraction to her is in terms of loss, of "the flight of one's old self." His essential hollowness affords no resistance to such an unknown force, so strong it fragments him and sets his disparate selves at dangerous variance. "He had a vivid illusion – as vivid as reality almost – of being in charge of a slippery prisoner" (p. 78). He is reluctant to submit to the attractions of a woman, an unfamiliar kind of weakness to him, but he especially resists yielding to a savage woman, the final ignominy felt by his civilized self" (p. 78). "He, a white man..."

whose worst fault till then had been a little want of judgment and too much confidence on the rectitude of his kind. That woman was a complete savage, and ... He tried to tell himself that the thing was of no consequence. It was a vain effort. The novelty of the sensations he had never experienced before in the slightest degree, yet had despised on hearsay from his safe position of a civilized man, destroyed his courage. He was disappointed with himself. He seemed to be surrendering to a wild creature the unstained purity of his life, of his race, of his civilization. He had a notion of being lost amongst shapeless things that were dangerous and ghastly. He struggled with the sense of certain defeat – lost his footing – fell back into the darkness. (pp. 80–81)

And his final capitulation, following his betrayal of Lingard and Almayer, is marked by him in terms of the fatal conclusion of this image which has continued to haunt him: he had an "indistinct vision of a man going away from him... like a prisoner breaking his parole – that thing slinking off stealthily while he slept" (p. 145).

No single-minded, determined hero, Willems is confronted with several, antithetical selves, and to his chagrin, the more civilized self, the one he comes to bemoan the loss of, escapes from him. The image is a striking one, and no doubt it serves as a convenient psychological evasion, for Willems need not take the responsibility for actually relinquishing it. But without that self, essentially alone, he expresses disgust with the remaining, more primitive self and admits, "I am a lost man." The idea of civilized and savage selves has already been suggested by Haggard's narrator Allan Quatermain, but we have not actually seen that idea realized in the fiction; after all, such dividedness has not characterized "one of us." The discourse has not before revealed the representatives of European empires as having such easily corrupted and divided natures, and the enlightened single-mindedness of the imperial endeavor itself is thus effectively called into question. In any case, an interesting reversal occurs here. While according to Haggard's paradigm, it is the "savage" self that presumably would escape the constraints of the "civilized one," the self assigned to civilized society and responsibilities is shown here effectively escaping the fetters of the law. Such is the force of Aïssa's powers to enslave and overpower. Like "the great revolution at Sambir" which Almayer reports to Lingard and will later narrate to any chance visitor, with no government in Sambir, there was "nothing to restrain those fellows," the natives (p. 171). Willems' "governor" has slinked off like "a prisoner breaking his parole." How ineffectual, then, is this "civilization," that precious possession that had protected and distinguished the white adventurer as "one of us"?

While this "enslavement" by a native woman is melodramatic and engenders some of Conrad's worst writing – "the fragments of her supplicating sentences were as if tossed on the crest of her sobs" (p. 253), for example – it is the betrayal of self and of community that lets loose anarchy and that marks the depths of Willems' fall. For he has promised Babalatchi to reveal the whereabouts of Captain Lingard's secret river to Abdullah, the rival Arab trader, in order to regain Aïssa whom Babalatchi has temporarily withheld from him. Thus Willems betrays Lingard and Almayer and also himself. Five weeks after he first left Almayer's campong to be with Aïssa, he reappears, a changed man, raving abut Aïssa's disappearance. In fact, Almayer thinks he is seeing a ghost:

a masquerading spectre of the once so very confidential clerk of the richest merchant in the islands. His jacket was soiled and torn; below the waist he was clothed in a worn-out and faded sarong. He flung off his hat, uncovering his long, tangled hair that stuck in wisps on his perspiring forehead and straggled over his eyes, which glittered deep down in the sockets like the last sparks amongst the black embers of a burntout fire. An unclean beard grew out of the caverns of his sunburnt cheeks...he was barefoot. (pp. 87–88)

This condition is beginning to represent Willems' natural state, or at least the state to which he naturally, inevitably returns. But this time Lingard is not at hand to rescue him. As it turns out, he is beyond rescue already, and rejects even Almayer's perfunctory offer of hospitality. Untrue even to himself, this apparition is some remnant of Willems, all that is left. Reduced almost beyond recognition, he does not resemble anyone who ever had Pluck. Finally Almayer drives the specter away, threatening it with death should it return to his house, "a civilized man's house. A white man's" (p. 88).

Juxtaposed with Willems, Tom Lingard, the English sea captain, seems more the stuff of adventure fiction. In great contrast to Willems, Lingard, like so many adventure heroes before him, is admired for his unswerving honesty. But even though a more heroic past is evoked with Lingard, particularly when viewed next to Willems' unheroic present that binds him to his unexpected but inevitable future, the heroism is seriously qualified.

Tom Lingard was a master, a lover, a servant of the sea. The sea took him young, fashioned him body and soul; gave him his fierce aspect, his loud voice, his fearless eyes, his stupidly guileless heart. Generously it gave him his absurd faith in himself, his universal love of creation, his wide indulgence, his contemptuous severity, his straight forward simplicity of motive and honesty of aim...He loved [the sea]...he was grateful to it, with the gratitude of an honest heart. His greatest pride lay in his profound conviction of its faithfulness – in the deep sense of his unerring knowledge of its treachery. (p. 13)

It is only in great contrast to the outcast Dutch vagabond, Willems, the subject of chapter 1 that the English sea captain, Lingard, the subject of chapter 2 seems the genuine adventure hero. Although his honesty, capability, and courage place him in a familiar tradition, the abrupt shift in tone from the opening elegiac sentiments to "stupidly guileless heart" and "absurd faith in himself" indicates an unfamiliar authorial attitude and a more qualified hero. Lingard certainly anticipates Marlow in his misplaced faith in "one of us." While Marlow rescues Jim because he seemed to be "one of us" – the Conway graduate clothed all in white – so Lingard, even less discriminating, sees a young white man in trouble, and acts out of his "stupidly guileless heart" and the conventional wisdom of a racial cohesiveness that defines itself through the distinction between Them and Us, as constructed by the discourse of the day. If we had not already known, from *Almayer's Folly*, that the Rajah Laut's judgment was fallible, we come to realize that shortcoming here quite soon. Again, this fiction concerns the white man's ignorance and the unrest and tumult that follow in the wake of Lingard's misplaced benevolence. And he is not only wrong about Willems, twice, but he is also mistaken about the sea which, at the opening of chapter 2 has been compared to an unscrupulous woman, illogical, capricious, irresponsible, so we suspect already that his "profound conviction of its faithfulness," although tempered by his "knowledge of its treachery," is misplaced. Our suspicions are confirmed when we learn soon after that he has lost his brig, the "Flash" at sea, his great pride and the main source of his advantage over the Arab traders of the area.

But while Marlow comes to admit that he "would have been wrong" to have left the decks to Jim, Lingard is not as shrewd, and his good intentions bring only destruction to Sambir. The misguidedness of Lingard's idealism prefigures not only Marlow's but also Jim's and that of the British imperial enterprise. His good intentions amount to "meddling" and ultimately bring disaster down on the heads of the very people he seeks to protect, contributing to the chaos of the local rivalries and intrigues that plague Sambir and the eventual revolution there. The fictions he lives by were shaped not by books, as Jim's will be, but by the Sunday School teachings, equally misleading it would seem,

of his native village and the discourses of the black-coated gentleman connected with the Mission to Fishermen and Seamen, whose yawl-rigged boat darting through rain squalls amongst the coasters wind-bound in Falmouth Bay, was part of those precious pictures of his youthful days that lingered in his memory...Such were the agencies that had roughly shaped his young soul before he went away to see the world in a southern-going ship – before he went, ignorant and happy, heavy of hand, pure in heart, profane in speech, to give himself up to the great sea that took his life and gave him his fortune. (p. 198)

Much of this makes Captain Tom, then, seem the white man adventure fiction had always celebrated. His idealism, not unlike the idealism of Livingstone's writings that had shaped the desires of Ballantyne's heroes and served Ralph Rover and others well, led to his own conviction that he was indeed the bringer of enlightenment. Lingard dreamed of Arcadian happiness for that little corner of the world which he loved to think all his own. His deep-seated and immovable conviction that only he – he, Lingard – knew what was good for them was characteristic of him, and, after all, not so very far wrong. He would make them happy whether or no, he said, and he meant it. His trade brought prosperity to the young state, and the fear of his heavy hand secured its internal peace for many years. He looked proudly upon his work. With every passing year he loved more the land, the people, the muddy river that, it he could help it, would carry no other craft but the "Flash" on its unclean and friendly surface... he knew every settler on the banks between the sea and Sambir; he knew their wives, their children; he knew every individual of the multi-coloured groups that, standing on the flimsy platforms of tiny reed dwellings built over the water, waved their hands and shouted shrilly: 'O! Kapal layer! Haï!' while the "Flash" swept slowly through the populated reach... (p. 200)

The Rajah Laut's proud ruminations here certainly embody the white man's dream of magnanimously conferring prosperity on and reaping gratitude from the "multi-coloured" Other, jealously guarding his exclusive rights, as parent/lover/conqueror, to the "young state." But the condescension and self-congratulation in the view – "the flimsy platform," the "tiny dwellings," the undifferentiated Other seen as a mass of friendly, grateful greeters – become more apparent as the paternalistic musings turn into loud boasts on various colonial verandahs, that "paralyze" and "startle" the native population:

His thunderous laughter filled the verandah, rolled over the hotel garden, overflowed into the street, paralyzing for a short moment the noiseless traffic of bare brown feet; and its loud reverberations would even startle the landlord's tame bird – a shameless mynah – into a momentary propriety of behavior under the nearest chair. In the big billiard-room perspiring men in thin cotton singlets would stop the game, listen, cue in hand, for a while through the open windows, then nod their moist faces at each other sagaciously and whisper: "The old fellow is talking abut his river." (pp. 201–202)

The Rajah Laut is revealed here as a braggart, and the perspiring billiard players' somewhat patronizing comment further reduces him to "the old fellow." This is no Arcadia, nor is he the generic hero who would bring the light or restore the order.

In certain respects, Lingard's ruminations remind us of that actual ancestor of his, James Brooke, the first White Rajah of Sarawak. As we saw in chapter 5, Brooke had been one of Conrad's "boyish" admirations. In his journal, Brooke spoke as though the native were a kind of blank slate to write upon. How glad he was that the Dyaks did not have "an established religion of their own." How much "easier is it to dispel darkness with light, than to overcome the false blaze with the rays of truth!" (Keppel, *Expedition*, I, p. 57). And even though Lingard does not concern himself with impressing religion on the natives, he takes a similar pleasure in shaping their lives otherwise. Like Lingard, Brooke also was struck by the beauty of the place, made infinitely more attractive by his sense of ownership. He too found it "admirably suited for purposes of navigation and trade" (Keppel, *Expedition*, I, p. 48). But Lingard, whose short-sightedness and ethnocentricity contribute to his ineffectiveness, marks a diminishment from Brooke. Like Brooke, Lingard fought and vanquished the local pirates, but Brooke at least entertained such questions as what constitutes piracy, and was willing to view British action as possibly "interference with the right of native states to war one upon another." While Brooke hoped that the suppression of piracy in Borneo would result in opening that country "to commerce and civilization," he also saw that it "[might] bestow happiness on its inhabitants" (Keppel, *Expedition*, I, p. 164). That it might not was also a possibility that occurred to the more subtle Brooke. While Conrad wrote nothing but praise for James Brooke, and for his own contemporary, Hugh Clifford, he found it easier to fictionalize his reservations about the imperial endeavor. Unlike his more public pronouncements about Brooke and Clifford, Conrad depicted the fictional Lingard's actions as a kind of meddling that brought only enmity, intrigue, and death, and his own loss of power. Like Conrad's other idealists, Lingard is not spared the consequences of actual experience. While illusions are blessings, as Conrad wrote in the preface to *Almayer*, that redeem and illuminate, the facts are the curse we must live with. Romantic dreaming in the real world is not free, and although its expense was never measured by the adventure fiction, it is calculated here. Lingard's dreams of good deeds are as commendable as those of Rajah Brooke, Captain Cook or David Livingstone. But the actual consequences of those dreams, once put in effect, are disastrous. A failed Brooke, Lingard's dreams of benevolent despotism are only momentarily realized.

And again, here as in *Almayer's Folly*, it is the voices of the Other that tell a different story and make us view Lingard's heroism in a harsher light. When Lingard first tells Willems that he will take him to Sambir, he explains that it was he who brought prosperity there, settled the people's quarrels, and watched them grow. "There's peace and happiness there. I am more master there than his Dutch Excellency down in Batavia ever will be when some day a lazy man-of-war blunders at last against the river" (p. 45), he boasts to Willems. But the next voice we hear is Babalatchi's, and a very different voice it is, telling a different story. While Lingard thinks himself master of Sambir and is given his due as "Rajah Laut" when he makes his occasional visits, the master schemer in residence is in actual control. He is about to put into action plans that will reverse Lingard's own projections for Sambir. The proverbial white man's dream of his own island and his own grateful and subservient native population – colonial children to his imperial parent – is challenged by this new telling. The juxtaposition of viewpoints here confirms our sense that Lingard's paternalistic control is only imagined. It is through Babalatchi's eyes that we first see Willems in Sambir and learn of the alliance struck up between him and Aïssa. While brief native insights were afforded us in *Almayer's Folly*, the voices of the Other are telling significant portions of the story now, affording new, sub-versions.

Emblematic of Lingard's failing powers is the already mentioned loss of his brig. And when he returns to Sambir, at one point, midway through the novel, to hear from Almayer the extent of Willems' fall and of his treachery, Lingard admits to feeling "jammed on a lee shore this time, if ever I was" (p. 190). Betrayed by Willems, by the sea, and by his own conception of how "one of us" can be expected to act, the failure of the enterprise is anticipated in the collapsing house of cards he builds for Almayer's little daughter, Nina. Remembering the wonderful structure of playing cards the Rajah Laut had built for her on his last visit, she pleads that he once again build her a house, "and another house on the roof, and another on the roof – high. High! Like the places where they dwell – my brothers – in the land where the sun sleeps'" (p. 194). As we can see, Almayer has already visited his own longings for Europe and white society upon his daughter. As Lingard complies with her request, he speaks encouragingly to Almayer who is exceedingly disgruntled with Willems' ruinous betrayal. Lingard holds out the same promises he always has – wealth, a return to Europe for all of them, a "civilized" education for Nina – trying to reassure Almayer that their dreams will still be realized.

"I know what I am talking about...Been in California in forty-nine...Not that I made much...then in Victoria in the early days...I know all about it. Trust me. Moreover a blind man could...Be quiet, little sister, or you will knock this affair down...My hand pretty steady yet! Hey, Kaspar?...Now, delight of my heart, we shall put a third house on the top of these two...keep very quiet...As I was saying, you got only to stoop and gather handfuls of gold...dust...there. Now here we are. Three houses on top on one another. Grand!" (p. 195)

But the doom of the plans he projects here seems implicit in the fall of Lingard's house, a few moments later; as insubstantial and ill-conceived as those future projections, the house of cards "collapsed suddenly before the child's light breath. Lingard looked discomposed for a moment. Almayer laughed, but the little girl began to cry." And the crash echoes, reminding us of Willems' own fall, the one that indeed precipitated this collapse of Lingard's plans and that, earlier on in the novel, was described similarly: "When the longed-for day came at last, when she sank on the grass by his side and with a quick gesture took his hand in hers, he sat up suddenly with the movement and look of a man awakened by the crash of his own falling house" (p. 77).

Lingard and Willems are thus connected, most unheroically. And what brothers in adventure fiction – both Almayer and Willems refer to Lingard as "Father" – could serve as precedents for these two? Not only are the rancor and bitter enmity between these two "sons" subversive of genre expectations, but that they are exacerbated to the point of fratricide by native manipulation, further distances these imperial representatives from any others we have known in the fiction or travel writing. Like *Almayer's Folly*, *An Outcast of the Islands* tells more than the white man's story; in fact, here the native telling takes over. Like the players of chess in Babalatchi's campong, huddled about the chessboard drawn on a mat with red clay, Babalatchi manipulates the white men. Neither solitary tellers of the tales nor central players of the game, they have become simply pawns. Having just engineered and witnessed Willems' first conversation with Abdullah, the one in which Willems reveals the location of Lingard's river in order to regain Aïssa, left alone after its successful conclusion. Babalatchi is inspired to sing:

[The song] had all the imperfections of unskillful improvisation and its subject was gruesome. It told a tale of shipwreck and of thirst, and of one brother killing another for the sake of a gourd of water. A repulsive story which might have had a purpose but possessed no moral whatever. Yet it must have pleased Babalatchi for he repeated it twice, the second time even in louder tones than at first, causing a disturbance amongst the white rice-birds and the wild fruit-pigeons which roosted on the boughs of the big tree growing in Omar's compound. (p. 138)

In Conrad's original conception of the tale, Babalatchi was to be the other "vagabond." Although the altered title indicates a more solitary focus, Conrad's "ghosts" ran away from him again, as he would explain to his aunt, for Babalatchi is still a strong force in the novel, and the shadow he casts is a long one. In contrast to Willems', the story of his arrival in Sambir is more truly the stuff of adventure, albeit a different, anti-imperial version. "he was a vagabond of the seas, a true Orang-Laut," we are told:

He was brave and bloodthirsty without any affection, and he hated the white men who interfered with the manly pursuits of throat-cutting, kidnapping, slave-dealing, and fire-raising, that were the only possible occupation for a true man of the sea. He found favour in the eyes of his chief, the fearless Omar el Badavi, the leader of Brunei rovers, whom he followed with unquestioning loyalty through the long years of successful depredation. (p. 52)

While the irony of Babalatchi's "manly" deeds qualifies his heroism, his courage and fierce loyalty in the face of an oppressive enemy bespeak at least an idealism unknown to Willems and make them a fit subject for many tellings. And Babalatchi's rescue of Omar, blinded in battle with the white men in which all his other companions were killed, and of Omar's daughter, Aïssa has become the stuff of legend:

The story of that escape lives in the hearts of brave men even to this day. They talk of Babalatchi and of the strong woman who carried her blind father through the surf under the fire of the warship from the north. The companions of that piratical and son-less Aeneas are dead now, but their ghosts wander over the waters and the islands at night – after the manner of ghosts – and haunt the fires by which sit armed men, as is meet for the spirits of fearless warriors who died in battle. There they may hear the story of their own deeds, of their own courage, suffering and death, on the lips of living men. That story is told in many places. On the cool mats in breezy verandahs of Rajah's houses it is alluded to disdainfully by impassive statesmen, but amongst armed men that throng the courtyards it is a tale which stills the murmur of voices and the tinkle of anklets; arrests the passage of the siri-vessel, and fixes the eyes in absorbed gaze. They talk of the fight, of the fearless woman, of the wise man; of long suffering on the thirsty sea in leaky canoes; of those who died...Many died. A few survived. The chief, the woman, and another one who became great. (pp. 54–55)

The passage is interesting for it shifts the telling and forces a new viewpoint. Now we must view "our" warship from the view of native survivors, wading through surf trying to evade "our" fire, and we take a sympathetic view of their heroism in doing so. The shifting vantage point asks us to see the imperial intruders as dangerous and life-threatening. And the language itself is appropriate to a legend recalled repeatedly, for it makes large, over-generalized claims. The story "lives in the hearts of brave men," and concerns "another who became great," its allusion makes an Aeneas of Omar, and it affects a formal, even archaic diction that distances and enlarges; "after the manner of" and "as is meet" is the language of other heroic tellings and help to remind us of another blind man whose tales of greatness and heroism contributed to legends as inspiriting as this one. Thus stories other than the white man's inform this multi-voiced narrative. And the story of Willems' treachery, Lingard's loss of power, and Willems' murder at the hands of that woman who had once saved his life, becomes, by novel's end, another story among many told in the tropics, but a mean and sordid one next to Babalatchi's. There is nothing heroic in the tale or in the telling. As the narration of Willems' death ends, told from without and from within in a mixture of direct observation and stream of consciousness, the narrator abruptly removes his story in time and makes it Almayer's. "Many years afterward Almayer was telling the story of the great revolution in Sambir to a chance visitor from Europe" (p. 360). And it is along with this listener, a drunken Romanian, ostensibly a naturalist, but actually a commercial orchid-hunter, that we learn the grimy particulars that led to Willems' death, narrated flatly by the embittered, cynical Almayer. But even this telling becomes a re-telling, for Almayer must rely on Mahmat – the first-hand witness here as he also was in *Almayer's Folly* – to supply much of the information. "That's what Mahmat said. Never varied. You ask him yourself," Almayer assures the visitor. The monologic telling is even more effectively disturbed, for the stories have proliferated, necessitating multiple narrators, and the voices of the different tellings can be clearly distinguished. The heroic discourse of the white man in the tropics is absent.

This technique of creating multiple story tellers who recall events, effectively distances Conrad's work from the genre so many read him in. Henley was not alone in finding the novel diffuse, thickened as it was with disparate tellings. More recently, such readers as Guerard find these various retrospective reportings "evasive," and consider Conrad's inability to describe action directly in the present, a shortcoming (Guerard, *Conrad*, p. 84). This apparent weakness, however, certainly served Conrad's purpose. Refusing to narrate the scenes in the dramatic present is very much to the point here and serves Conrad's subversion well. He could have done it otherwise and did so, most impressively in *Typhoon*, for example, but in the face of dissolute imperial endeavor, such adventure is no longer possible. It is something remembered, recalled, sometimes nostalgically and heroically and sometimes bitterly, as Almayer's carping and disgruntled telling becomes.

It was probably Lingard, and Conrad's ambivalence toward this figure originally inspired by Rajah Brooke, that held him up and made work on *An Outcast of the Islands* initially difficult and progress on the third novel in "the cycle of Lingard," *The Rescue*, impossible for many years. But as he separated from the sea and came to see himself increasingly as a writer, he became more able, perhaps, to distance himself from traditional points of view and genre concerns. In spite of his efforts to remain a seaman, the links were loosening. He complained in the letters written during the period he was first tackling *Outpost* of his general despair caused both by being bogged down in his writing and by the absence of available ships. Finally in December he wrote his aunt that

The thing is done. I have changed my title. It will be: *An Outcast of the Islands*. And the thing itself has been changed. Everything has been changed except doubt. Everything, except the fear of the ghosts which one evokes oneself and which often refuse to obey the brain that has created them. Here is Chapter VIII finished at last. Four to go! (Karl, *Letters*, I, p. 193)

His awareness of a certain psychological disjunction here is revealing. As it turned out, the final version actually came to 26 chapters, divided into 5 parts of 4–6 chapters each, but as he approached the final conception, one that denounced the European endeavor in tropical outposts, the sea as a lifetime career for him was receding. Also, during the final months he was working on *An Outcast of the Islands* he was reading the reviews of *Almayer's Folly*; many of them were highly congratulatory and could only have encouraged him to take himself more seriously as a writer. Shortly after the writing of *Outcast*, the transformation from sailor to writer would be complete. Although in March of 1896 when he announced to a Polish friend that he was getting married and had given up the sea and meant to make his living at writing, a few months later, still on his honeymoon and working on *The Rescuer*, he wrote to the manager of the Sailors' Home that he had not given up his seafaring days. "I do hanker after the sea – it's only the want of opportunity that keeps me on shore. I am now writing my third novel" (Karl, *Letters*, 1, p. 283).

And opportunities apparently failed to offer themselves, for he remained on shore, and worked increasingly as a self-conscious writer. He abandoned *The Rescue* and in a subsequent work, a story that remained a story, "An Outpost of Progress" (1897), he admitted to working on such writerly aspects as control and concision. In fact he was to refer to this work as his "best story," because he had succeeded, at last, in his resolve "not to be led astray by my subject" (Conrad, *Congo Diary*, p. 82). In this work and in "Heart of Darkness" (1899), the condemnation of the genre's essential approval of the imperial subject would become overt. Conrad's early fiction ensured the shift toward a different kind of colonial fiction, a discourse that challenged adventure fiction's construction of the imperial subject.

# CHAPTER 8

# The African fictions (I): "An Outpost of Progress"

On the eve of his first command, the first-person narrator of "The Secret Sharer" wondered how far he "should turn out faithful to that ideal conception of one's own personality every man sets up for himself secretly" (Conrad, 'Twixt Land and Sea, p. 94). Although he almost fails to realize that ideal, he does finally achieve what he sees as "the perfect communion of a seaman with his first command" (p. 143). But, pursuing that ideal more often has fatal consequences for Conrad's characters who dream the wrong dreams. More significantly, they remain innocent of the understanding, revealed through the fiction, that the dream, the ideal, has been shaped. A man might believe he is setting up that ideal "for himself," or that the ideal simply exists as a monolithic absolute, an unquestioned truth, but in fact, the provenance is more complex. What creates the desire? In Conrad's fiction, in large part, it is constructed and carried on by the dreams and narratives of others, oral texts and written ones, especially by the adventure fiction and travel writing of the day. On the margins of Almayer's story but crucial to it is the shaping of Nina's desires by her mother's stories of a heroic past. Similarly, Lingard's ideals of heroic conduct are shaped by the narratives of sea-going missionaries. So too are constructed the ideal self-conceptions of Kayerts and Carlier, the central figures of Conrad's "An Outpost of Progress" (1897), thus presenting a powerful revision, one that counters the conventional heroism of the white man in the tropics.

The Graphic, an illustrated weekly newspaper that had written about the meeting in Africa of Henry Stanley, correspondent for the New York Herald, with explorer-missionary David Livingstone in November of 1871, and had been covering their travels together since then, featured prominently in its November 26, 1872 edition, a large illustration of Stanley and Livingstone sitting in their hut reading copies of The Graphic and The Times amid tall stacks of other back issues. Four natives are depicted here, standing aside and looking on amazed, as rapt in their observation of the two white men engaged in this strange activity as the white men are in their reading. One native, a child, holds a copy of *Punch* upside down in uncomprehending imitation. The drawing's apparently neutral caption – "Dr. Livingstone and Mr. Stanley – Receiving Newspapers in Central Africa" (*The Graphic*, 6, no. 155 [Nov. 1872], p. 460) – belies the fact that this text, like others, "is part of a network of power" (Said, "Textuality," p. 675). Simply the receiving of newspapers is seen as newsworthy and becomes an endeavor hallowed by the imposing engraving, a self-serving icon of the imperial enterprise. Although purporting to inform, the picture misrepresents the fact that Stanley had left the ailing Livingstone behind in March of 1872, and interests itself instead in arguing for the appropriateness of the Anglo-American presence in Central Africa.[1]

Itself a crucial vehicle of the imperial dream's construction, European literacy and particularly the periodical press here image the imperial endeavor in a manner that provides the exclusionary definition of Them and Us, that permits and even validates the project. The conversation carried on in the pages of these periodicals, suggested by the valorizing treatment of newspaper articles as factual information, a kind of God's Truth, to which They have no access – or so the illustration here suggests – necessarily excludes Them and thus creates a vacuum that justifies and even requires the white man's presence. The conversation, of necessity, is being carried on without Them. A badge of the conquerors' superiority, this show of literacy also demonstrates to *The Graphic*'s readers (circulation *c.* 200,000 in 1872, according to Altick, *Common Reader*, p. 395), the enlightenment they are duty-bound to share. The drawing depicts the imperial endeavor and its representatives as literate, in possession of Truth and Power, and thus designates the native Other as illiterate and thus dispossessed. Literacy itself privileges. It distinguishes Them from Us, confers power, and shapes our ideal conception of ourselves.

It is such newspapers, or perhaps their Belgian counterparts, that have been left behind at the river station in the Congo that Kayerts and Carlier are sent out to manage. "Our Colonial Expansion," one such article they come upon, spoke of

the rights and duties of civilization, of the sacredness of the civilizing work, and extolled the merits of those who went about bringing light, and faith and commerce to the dark places of the earth. Carlier and Kayerts read, wondered, and began to think better of themselves. (Conrad, *Tales of Unrest*, pp. 94–95)

The article has a self-aggrandizing reality that the lived existence of these two characters at this imperial outpost lacks; it tells a different, more heroic story, and they accept that version of reality with smug contentment. It offers them more palatable self-images, ones that illuminate their otherwise dismal existence. That the absurdly glaring contrast between those written-about ideals, part of a perhaps outdated construction available only in old, back-issues of newspapers, and their own selfish motives and unheroic inactivity is lost on them, sustains the ironic note that informs this story throughout. Under attack is Kayerts' and Carlier's readiness to accept slogans as truths, which contributes to the general criticism here of all the "fine words" the rhetoric of idealism has spawned, the "masquerade" Conrad is trying to unmask (Karl, *Letters*, I, p. 294).

Although still read as adventure fiction, or measured against it and found wanting in comparison to Stevenson and Haggard and Kipling, "Outpost" presents deliberate subversions of the generic hero in the figures of Kayerts and Carlier. Everything in the story conspires to represent them as inept, and the post itself, "a lonely station of the Kassai," as Conrad wrote his publisher, Fisher Unwin (Karl, *Letters*, I, p. 294), as insignificant, dwarfed by the surrounding forests and river that suggest a dense life beyond, one that Kayerts and Carlier find forbiddingly hostile and inaccessible. The director who drops them off at the station observes as he pulls away from the shore,

"Look at those two imbeciles. They must be mad at home to send me such specimens. I told those fellows to plant a vegetable garden, build new storehouses and construct a landing-stage. I bet nothing will be done! They won't know how to begin. I always thought the station on this river useless, and they just fit the station!" (p. 88)

These men inspire confidence in no one, not even the managing director. In his opinion, neither they nor their particular endeavor is at all noteworthy. We must conclude, then, that Kayerts and Carlier do not rank among "those who went about bringing light, and faith and commerce to the dark places of the earth," for they evidently have no merits to extol. Bringing neither light nor faith to this dark place, these two come only for personal gain. And they are equally ineffectual at bringing commerce, for although the first sentence of the story introduces them as the "managers," we learn quickly that the real manager, the "third man on the staff," is the native storeroom keeper who calls himself Henry Price but who is referred to by the other natives and the white company members as Makola. It is he, along with his wife, who effect the few trades with native tribes described here. And it is only through the good-will of the neighboring chieftain Gobila whose village women bear food and palm wine to the station daily, that they survive as long as they do, for the company does not provide these necessary stores, and they appear incapable of procuring food for themselves. Regarded as "imbeciles" by the director, a mystery that needs to be pacified by Gobila, despised by Price/Makola, considered "perfectly insignificant and incapable" by the narrator, and utterly disregarded by the native station men supposedly under their direction, Kayerts and Carlier can only be read as subversions of the hegemonic discourse's hero. Neither their motives, their actions, nor their abilities remind us of Henty's heroes or those of Ballantyne or Haggard. And they certainly belie any such publicly admired notions of heroism as celebrated in such African explorers as Mungo Park, David Livingstone, or John Hanning Speke. The rhetoric that had always accompanied the European Imperial endeavor in Africa is present here only in the old newspapers, and those fine words mask the men's actual reasons for being there and feed their self importance. But while the words serve to form their ideal conception of themselves, they mark the distance between that constructed ideal and these actual "pioneers of trade and progress."

In physical stature alone, these two are unprepossessing. Kayerts, a minor official in the Administration of the Telegraphs, is short and fat. Although Carlier was "a military man," that heroic calling is immediately undercut; he was actually "an ex-non-commissioned officer of cavalry in an army guaranteed from harm by several European Powers" (p. 88). And they both degenerate in a decidedly unheroic fashion, Kayert's legs finally so swollen he can hardly walk, and Carlier so "undermined by fever, [he] could not swagger any more," and is reduced to "tottering" about uncertainly (p. 108).

But even more marked is their moral decline; a Conradian deterioration in the wilderness that is even more commented on and explained than that of Willems, is that of Kayerts and Carlier. Unlike any of the heroes of the adventure/travel discourse, they do not carry with them an impregnable, sustaining sense of self and purpose that allows them to accomplish the assigned tasks and return home intact. The wilderness will act upon them in a most unheroic fashion, but their intrinsic vacuousness renders them especially susceptible. As failed civilian and soldier, they represent both the civil and the military branches of the imperial endeavor. It was their ineffectualness at home, not any patriotic zeal, that caused them to come out to this desolate station, and like the destructive discord between Almayer and Willems, the only two white men on the east coast, Kayerts and Carlier become more like "accomplices" than companions, whose conversation degenerates into "snarls." Where is the hallowed sustaining racial cohesion advertised in the dominant imperial fictions? In Ballantyne's stories, for example, the heroes go out to remote, frozen Hudson's Bay stations and cheerfully endure the solitude, with the support of a jolly companion or two, to do their part in the civilizing work, and they return to that sustaining Mother Country absolutely intact, unshaken in their resolve, and untouched by any mere "wilderness." But no such ideals, no matter how subscribed to, serve to sustain these two.

Another comparable outpost that stands in marked contrast to this one is that of the missionary Mr. McKenzie that Quatermain visits near Mt. Kenya in *Allan Quatermain*. As remote as the Belgian outpost on the Kassai, McKenzie's mission station is a genuine European establishment:

a sudden bend in the river brought us in sight of a substantial-looking European house with a verandah round it, splendidly situated upon a hill...

Mr. McKenzie, his wife, and little blond daughter, all dressed in "ordinary English-looking clothes," greet the adventurers and take them up the roadway, lined with orange trees "positively laden with golden fruit," through the garden. Quatermain is exuberant:

And what a garden it was! I have always loved a good garden, and I could have thrown up my hands for joy when I saw Mr. Mackenzie's. First there were rows upon rows of standard European fruit-trees... English vegetables, vegetables, trees, and flowers... strawberries and tomatoes (such tomatoes!), and melons and cucumbers, and, indeed, every sort of vegetable and fruit. (*AQ*, p. 34)

But of course it is not simply the tomatoes that give Quatermain such joy, but rather the ideals signified by such a flourishing, European garden. Never were vegetables invested with such patriotic pride, or made to bear such moral freight. "Ordinary" and "standard" normalize, and thus privilege, that which is European, and it is this norm, a specifically British one, that is being congratulated here for the ideals of purpose, determination, vision, and industry it bespeaks. McKenzie seems to have been equally successful with the mission natives who maintain the extensive gardens with docility and apparent contentment and live in "neat mushroom-shaped huts." It is to McKenzie's credit, Haggard's fiction concludes, that he has thus replicated his home in Scotland and has indeed succeeded in importing spiritual, nutritional, and aesthetic enlightenment to one of the dark places of the earth.

In contrast, Kayerts and Carlier, supposedly fellow workers in the field, although admittedly faced with a more hostile, challenging geography in the Congo, are incapable even of starting the vegetable garden they had been instructed to plant. And the contrast of their surroundings provides a moral dimension not lost on readers who have been instructed in the century's great subject of Them and Us in Africa through adventure fiction and travel writing.

Besides the storehouse and Makola's hut, there was only one large building in the cleared ground of the station. It was built neatly of reeds, with a verandah on all the four sides. There were three rooms in it. The one in the middle was the living-room, and had two rough tables and a few stools in it. The other two were the bedrooms for the white men. Each had a bedstead and a mosquito net for all furniture. The plank floor was littered with the belongings of the white men; open half-empty boxes, torn wearing apparel, old boots; all the things dirty, and all the things broken, that accumulate mysteriously round untidy men. (p. 87)

That it was built "neatly" – although by Kayerts and Carlier's predecessor, now an inhabitant of the only other "dwelling place" here, the nearby mounded grave marked by a tall cross – and included a verandah, are the only points of similarity; the comparison ends there. This station, unlike McKenzie's, bespeaks none of the generic values, only slovenliness, passivity, and lack of discipline. Unlike those heroes constructed by the discourse, Kayerts and Carlier have a moral vacuousness which renders them susceptible to corruption from within and the wilderness without. Conrad's narrator makes a disturbing pronouncement, an elaboration of a similar observation made about Willems:

Few men realize that their life, the very essence of their character, their capabilities and their audacities, are only the expression of their belief in the safety of their surroundings. The courage, the composure, the confidence; the emotions and principles; every great and every insignificant thought belongs not to the individual but to the crowd: to the crowd that believes blindly in the irresistible force of its institutions and of its morals, in the power of its police and of its opinion. (p. 89)

How dispiriting it must be to discover that one's ideals are not one's own but have been constructed and sustained by a society and its discourse in whose absence that essence of self dissolves. The heroic self of travel and adventure narratives had been made of hardier, more stable, more pluckish stuff. Thus undermined is the sacred, monolithic nature of the Imperial resolve, seen as it is here, belonging only "to the crowd."

Equally subversive is the refusal to grant the white man his generic invincibility in the face of the wilderness. Kayerts' and Carlier's vulnerability to solitude and strangeness reminds us of Willems'; it will become Kurtz's also:

the contact with pure unmitigated savagery, with primitive nature and primitive man, brings sudden and profound trouble into the heart. To the sentiment of being alone of one's kind, to the clear perception of the loneliness of one's thoughts, of one's sensations-to the negation of the habitual, which is safe, there is added the affirmation of the unusual, which is dangerous; a suggestion of things vague, uncontrollable, and repulsive, whose discomposing intrusion excites the imagination and tries the civilized nerves of the foolish and the wise alike. (p. 89)

Unlike the genre's adventure heroes before them, they will fail to emerge from the wilderness intact, their resolve untouched. But civilization itself is made to bear some of the responsibility for their fatal unravelling, for it is found to be rather fragile, after all, a thin veneer that covers an essential hollowness, easily broken down. That civilization corrupts and imprisons and is therefore unworthy of export, subverts the imperial justification. Even though at first Kayerts and Carlier were "resolved to settle down comfortably to their new life," it proved "an impossible task" for them. But "to grapple effectually with even purely material problems requires more serenity of mind and more lofty courage than people generally imagine" (pp. 90–91), the narrator explains. Reversing the Darwinian formula assumed by the dominant imperial discourse, the white men, products of a disabling civilization, one that "had taken care of [them], forbidding them all independent thought, all initiative, all departure from routine," are not fit – "no two beings could have been more unfitted for such a struggle" (p. 91), the narrator observes – rather, they are inferior to the natives who are in charge here, to Gobila's spiritual resources and to Makola's efficiency and trading abilities.

Although in many ways the roles are effectively reversed – it is the natives who manage here, and the white men who effect disaster rather than "progress" at this outpost, who can barely feed themselves and who finally cannot even manage to survive – in their view of the Other they do resemble their counterparts in travel and adventure narratives, a view that affords them a sense of easy superiority. They too are products of European idealism and they have discovered in addition to the old newspapers some "wrecks of novels" lying about. In "the centre of Africa they made acquaintance of Richelieu and of d'Artagnan, of Hawk's Eye and of Father Goriot, and of many other people" (p. 94), all versions of heroism which encourage Kayerts and Carlier to define themselves as racially different from, and superior to, the Other who surround them. Thus our "pilgrims" see the natives as objects apart from them, outside their heroized European experience, and therefore incomprehensible, physical beings to be judged as animals:

They were naked, glossy black, ornamented with snowy shells and glistening brass wire, perfect of limb. They made an uncouth babbling noise when they spoke, moved in a stately manner, and sent quick, wild glances out of their startled, never-resting eyes... (p. 92)

As it does to Ballantyne's or Henty's heroes, the Other appears and disappears as an undifferentiated mass, seemingly from nowhere "out of the void at times," on foot or in canoes containing "men with spears in their hands." Kayerts and Carlier would look on at such scenes from a distance or watch Makola dealing with such unaccountable intruders who spoke an incomprehensible "gibberish," confiding to one another with smug superiority that some of "the herd" were fine physical specimens but generally the brutes were offensive, noisy and repellently "aromatic." In fact even in insisting upon "Makola," Kayerts and Carlier render the man who calls himself Price less powerful; denying him his name serves to neutralize him, a tactic they find helpful in dealing with a native so threateningly atypical. But in fact their attempts to do so are characteristically illusory and ineffectual. They have no more control over Makola than they do over anything else at this outpost. The forest is impenetrable to them, the languages spoken around them incomprehensible, and the life they are supposed to conquer is absolutely out of their reach. Even the fish consistently evade Carlier's line and the one hippo he finally manages to shoot floats downstream, also out of their reach, to Gobila's now hostile village. In remarkable contrast, the able and self-reliant generic adventure heroes domesticated and controlled their environment in ways unthinkable to Kayerts and Carlier.

Ironically juxtaposed with our necessarily unheroic view of them is their view of themselves. Like Conrad's first two novels, *Almayer's Folly* and *An Outcast of the Islands*, this fiction concerns what "we" do not know; their self-knowledge is as inadequate as was Almayer's or Willems'. The image of this outpost's resident white men reading themselves in the romanticized intrigues and adventures of Richelieu and d'Artagnan, in Hawkeye's adventures among the American Indian Other, and in the heroic altruism of Balzac's Père Goriot reminds us of those two other white men at an African outpost consuming the discourse that mirrors and justifies their presence, engraved and reproduced on the front pages of *The Graphic* and in the minds of its readers. The ex-soldier Carlier must see himself in d'Artagnan's exploits, no matter how unwarranted the reflection appears to us, and Kayerts, another loving father who like Almayer is willing to give up much for the well-being of his beloved daughter, must perceive his own self-sacrifices in those of Father Goriot. He must have found in Balzac's novel a soul-mate, for like that protagonist who lives in squalor so that his daughters can live with social advantages and luxuries, Kayerts sees himself as making similar sacrifices.

At the end of two months Kayerts often would say, "If it was not for my Melie, you wouldn't catch me here." Melie was his daughter. He had thrown up his post in the Administration of the Telegraphs, though he had been for seventeen years perfectly happy there, to earn a dowry for his girl. (p. 91)[2]

The depiction of Conrad's pilgrims of progress here is ironic and as far from the heroic portraits painted in the novels and the newspapers as possible. Consuming the twin fictions of novels and newspapers,

Kayerts and Carlier envisage themselves as heroic white men bringing about a glorious future – a vision juxtaposed with their actual doings. But they are not only victims of the fictions they consume – Conrad had originally entitled the story "A Victim of Progress" – but also perpetrators, and the consequences are fatal. Literacy is indeed as powerful and dangerous as the guns carried into the outpost by the natives from the coast. Haggard's Quatermain was right to fear certain of the effects of the white man's progress, such as gunpowder, universal suffrage, and daily newspapers, all of which he felt had brought "many evils in their train" (*AQ*, p. 218). He objects to these as potentially destructive instruments of Liberal thought; nonetheless, the yoking of guns and literacy is appropriate, for, as this fiction shows, the consequences of gunpowder and of fictions that create the crowd's blind beliefs and shape their ideal conceptions can be equally fatal.

Kayerts and Carlier prove active consumers of the fictions. As the empty slogans of the newspaper articles are read by them as Truth, so these fictional characters become more real to them than their own desolate lives. Absorbed in their fictions, carrying on "interminable and silly discussions about plots and personages... as if they had been living friends," Conrad's two pioneers do nothing to avert the actual disaster at hand. "They discounted [the characters'] virtues, suspected their motives, decried their successes; were scandalized at their duplicity or were doubtful about their courage" (p. 94). The irony of their safely distanced and sanctimoniously superior but sympathetic scrutiny of these fictional characters becomes apparent as the consequences of their passivity and ineptitude begin to take shape.

Engaged by their fictions, they do nothing to interfere with Makola's handling of the tribe from the coast. When they at first realize what has happened, that Makola has traded the company's ten station men, natives from another region, for ivory, and that the coastal tribe has also killed some of Gobila's men and burned some of his villages in the bargain, Kayerts and Carlier are indignant. But the second part of "Outpost" deals with their attempts to rationalize, evade, deny, and then finally accept and condone, the inescapable fact that they are both indeed slave traders, a fact difficult to reconcile with the prescribed ideals of the imperial endeavor. This fiction offers a new, perverted reading of the wisdom provided by *Peter Simple* that "private feelings must always be sacrificed for the public service." Such a belief belongs to a world elsewhere, a realm hard to recall at this point. And the destruction thus permitted and countenanced by the two "pioneers of trade and progress" will effect their own de-moralization as well. Cut off now from Gobila's friendship and generosity, confronted with their own ineptness, and finally disillusioned of any notion that they "manage" anything here, their moral unravelling is inevitable. Unlike Natty Bumppo or Allan Quatermain whose ideals thrive in the wilderness and remain untainted there, these two are undone by the distance from their accustomed, "civilized" life. They felt

something from within them was gone, something that worked for their safety, and had kept the wilderness from interfering with their hearts. The images of home; the memory of people like them, of men that thought and felt as they used to think and feel, receded into distances made indistinct by the glare of unclouded sunshine... (p. 107)

The heroic cohesion of the white man in the tropics is undermined here, a subversion prefigured by Willems and Almayer, "the only white men on the east coast." Driven into a most unheroic rage over some disputed sugar, and Carlier's admission that they are both "slavedealers," Kayerts shoots Carlier and then, utterly undone when he realizes he has killed an unarmed man, hangs himself. Once again, the subject is the white man's ignorance and the mischief that ignorance effects. They and those intended recipients of civilized enlightenment are victimized by the fictions they consume, the ones that shape their desires and forge their ideal self image. And as with Kurtz, the moral decline will be marked finally by the utter rejection of the fine words and inherited heroic ideals of the imperial rhetoric. Anticipating Kurtz's infamous expletive "Exterminate all the brutes!" Carlier too will voice his unmasked belief, born of the failure of his idealized self-conception, that "before the country could be made habitable," "all the niggers" would have to be exterminated (p. 108).

But rather than the natives, it is the intruders, the bearers of truth and light, who are exterminated here, as the grim symmetry of this story emphasizes. Pointed out to us in the first paragraph, along with other items of descriptive interest, is the grave and its tall cross under which the first white chief of the station now sleeps. Thus the failure of the promised "progress" is marked at the outset and marked again in the conclusion. When the company's steamer finally does return, several months later, Kayerts and Carlier have proven conclusively their unsuitability to carry out the civilizing work of Progress.

The Managing Director of the Great Civilizing Company (since we know that civilization follows trade) landed first, and incontinently lost sight of the steamer. The fog down by the river was exceedingly dense; above, at the station, the bell rang unceasing and brazen...

Climbing up the steep bank, he comes upon Kayerts:

And even he, the man of varied and startling experience, was somewhat discomposed by the manner of this finding. He stood and fumbled in his pockets (for a knife) while he faced Kayerts, who was hanging by a leather strap from the cross. He had evidently climbed the grave, which was high and narrow, and after tying the end of the strap to the arm, had swung himself off. His toes were only a couple of inches above the ground; his arms hung stiffly down; he seemed to be standing rigidly at attention, but with one purple cheek playfully posed on the shoulder. And, irreverently, he was putting out a swollen tongue at his Managing Director. (p. 117)

Ironically, this short story about a failed imperial endeavor first appeared in a periodical issue that contained articles that constructed the very idealism Conrad's fiction pronounces untenable. The context itself reenacts the story's narration. Cunninghame Graham, for one, noticed the irony of the title and wrote to Conrad a "commendation," in reply to which Conrad "hail[ed] back lustily" (Watts, *Letters*, p. 46), thus initiating a life-long correspondence and friendship. Kipling's "Slaves of the Lamp" – in which Stalky and Co. defend Empire in a ruthless, but approved of, manner – occupied the spot in the previous two issues of *Cosmopolis* devoted to Conrad's story in the June and July issues, and Watts observes that it was probably the contrast between the two that first inspired Graham to write Conrad (Watts, *Letters*, p. 20). But to most readers, the piece seemed more a gloomy aberration than an ironic subversion. It was certainly out of step with the patriotic concern of the moment, the sixtieth year of Queen Victoria's reign. In these Jubilee issues, then, "Outpost" was a voice in the wilderness, for the discourse that surrounded Conrad's fiction demonstrated a kind of blind belief in the invincible and benevolent force of civilization's progressive, enlightened institutions and moral outlook. Such invincibility was exactly Conrad's target.

A piece that could easily be subtitled "Our Colonial Expansion," accompanied the first installment of "Outpost," the one in which

Kayerts and Carlier discover the novels and newspapers. In this article, actually entitled "The Reign of Queen Victoria," Sir Richard Temple argues that he cannot separate "the greatness of Her Majesty" from "that of her world-wide Dominion," the growth of the empire itself. (*Cosmopolis*, 18 [June 1897]: 621). It goes on to explain that "the expansion of the Empire, its material development, its progress in all matters that are demonstrable by statistics" distinguishes the Victorian era. "This advance is not, moreover, confined to people, places, and things. It extends to the mental and moral qualities of man, and to his social condition," and "the results of this burgeoning empire," the writer argues, "have been both physically and morally improving." Moreover all these results, statistically measurable, have been part of a divine plan; they "have been due to the grace and favour of Almighty God" (p. 626). Sounding as high-minded as the pieces Kayerts and Carlier read and are inspired by, the actual article echoes the fictional one in speaking of Victorian England's "emissaries of light":

Mindful of their responsibilities towards the heathen over whom they hold sway or with whom they have influence, they have equipped and sent forth at great cost religious Missions, which are working among all dark or coloured races without any exception. The Victorian era, with all its secular magnificence, has yet been the one when self-sacrificing zeal, when pious care in organisation, has most been shown in the cause of Foreign Missions. (p. 626)

That we can recognize Kayerts and Carlier nowhere in this description can be explained only in part by the fact that they are not, in fact, English. They are so vaguely Belgian, and the endeavor is spoken of as so generally European, that it is difficult to make too special a case for the Victorian endeavor. For example, when we are told that the Managing Director heads up the "great Civilizing Company" because "we know that civilization follows trade," there is nothing to restrict this irony to the Belgian cause. The language of one discourse is indistinguishable from that of the others.

And in the July issue that contained the second installment of "Outpost," the installment in which the station men get sold into slavery and Gobila's people are killed and villages burned, the civilizing work of empire is extolled in another article, "The Globe and the Island."

The Jubilee celebration, however, was more, much more, than homage to the Queen's person. The British nation rejoiced as much over its own triumphs as over the virtues and the happy lot of its Sovereign. It seemed deliberately to determine to regard its vast power, its colonising success, its vital unity, its world wide territory, and to glory in them...Britain is imperialistic now...The "Little Englander" has wisely decided to efface himself. The political party which should talk of reducing the navy or snubbing the Colonies would have a short shrift. We are Imperialists first, and Liberals or Tories afterwards. (p. 81)

This construction of the imperial subject and of the imperial-colonial relationship is familiar. But one of the ironies implicit in the juxtaposition of Conrad's fiction with these articles is that they often notice and deplore the cruelty of other imperialists while England's motives appear transparent. For example, one writer criticizes the Spanish commanders in their imperial outposts: "The sufferings of the presentation of the Cubans, intensified by the always severe and frequently extremely brutal methods of the Spanish military commanders" (pp. 85–86). The barbarism of Spanish imperialism was one of Henty's favorite targets also, but in neither discourse is anything mentioned about the equally devastating effect of other European occupations, Belgian or British, causing as much mischief through such atrocities as those reflected in this fiction and in some of the public disclosures of the day (Mahood, *Colonial Encounter*, p. 7f), through inefficiency, ignorance and a perverted self-image fed by the discourse contemporary, among other things.

Conrad had temporarily abandoned the writing of *The Rescue* – the first of many such interruptions – in order to write "Outpost," which he completed in three weeks. He spoke of it in a letter to Garnett:

this story is *meant* for you. I am pleased with it. That's why you shall get it. I am sure You will understand the reason and meaning of every detail, the meaning of them reading novels and the meaning of *Carlier not* being armed. (Karl, *Letters*, I, p. 292)

And moreover, it was to be an artistic response to complaints about the diffuseness of his first two novels. Conrad admits to his publisher Fisher Unwin that he has sent it to Edward Garnett because "it refers (in its execution) to a certain discussion we had on matters of art and I should like to know whether I have succeeded in achieving my purpose – my artistic purpose" (Karl, *Letters*, I, p. 294).

But "Outpost" was a moral response as well. In the same letter to Unwin, he remarks:

It is a story of the Congo. There is no love interest in it and no woman – only incidentally. The exact locality is not mentioned. All the bitterness of those days, all my puzzled wonder as to the meaning of all I saw – all my indignation at masquerading philanthropy – have been with me again, while I wrote. (Karl, *Letters*, I, p. 294)

Thus it is the idea of pretence that is subversive here, of a purported philanthropy that merely "masquerades," not the heroic ideals themselves. For Conrad did express a belief in the heroic age, now past, and in the possibilities of heroic achievement. But as he saw for himself, the "progress" occurring in empire's outposts failed to resemble the heroic dreams of the past. In "The Heroic Age," written for the 1905 Trafalgar Day issue of *The Standard* – Henty's newspaper – and finally collected as the last chapter of *The Mirror of the Sea*, Conrad praises Nelson's heroism. But more marked is the nostalgia that colors this piece, the sense that such possibilities are over. As he admitted in "Geography and Some explorers,"

the geography which I had discovered for myself was the geography of open spaces and wide horizons built up on men's devoted work in the open air, the geography still militant but already conscious of its approaching end with the death of the last great explorer. (*Last Essays*, p. 12)

He writes here and elsewhere out of the nostalgic conviction that he is at the tail end of a tradition of "devoted work in the open air," a tradition he honors. His writing repeatedly objects to the appropriation of that tradition by the empire builders, who then fit it out in their rhetoric for their purposes, and who, more dangerously, come to believe the constructed fiction themselves. It resents the masquerade, disguising motives of personal gain with false or illusory high-mindedness. And the criticism focuses less on imperialistic Europe's desires to colonize undeveloped countries, than on the destruction its blunders and greed in fact effected in the name of enlightened benevolence.

Moreover, the words that construct the subject are no longer to be trusted. As the endeavor is corrupted so is the discourse that constructs it. Consumed as absolute truths, those words are dangerous fictions. Of Kayerts' and Carlier's absorption in their discussions of novels, Conrad writes:

They believed their words. Everybody shows a respectful deference to certain sounds that he and his fellows can make. But about feelings people really know nothing. We talk with indignation or enthusiasm; we talk about oppression, cruelty, crime, devotion, self-sacrifice, virtue, and we know nothing real beyond the words. Nobody knows what suffering or sacrifice mean except, perhaps the victims of the mysterious purpose of these illusions. (p. 106)

Like other modernists – Fitzgerald and Hemingway come readily to mind – Conrad acknowledges the distance between words and the truths they purport to represent, and thus necessarily distrusts leaning too heavily on any verbal construction as absolute truth. The Marlow of "Heart of Darkness," aware of such yawning gaps, will reject those words beyond which he can only know uncertain, slippery abstractions, the fine words and slogans. To read words as anything other than suggestions and approximations is a crucial mistake, one committed repeatedly, and usually fatally, by so many of Conrad's characters.

That subjects get constructed and ideals shaped by entities as insubstantial as words, Conrad himself was well aware, for his desires were also created and shaped by long acquaintance with this discourse and the ideals it espoused. But his going to Africa and experiencing the distance between the words and the reality that lies beyond those words, revealed the utter inadvisability of consuming fictions as truths. Between the place he actually found himself in and the real incompetence and lunacy he encountered on his trip up the Congo, and that other Africa, that site of Livingstone's endeavors he had read about with admiration, was an incredible gap; nowhere on that journey could he find the Africa he had read about, only the debris of disillusion. "An Outpost of Progress," then, tells the story of that disillusion, a telling that effectively counters the fictions constructed so persuasively by the dominant discourse of the day.

# CHAPTER 9

# The African fictions (II): "Heart of Darkness"

In contemporary reviews of *Youth* (1902), most readers responded primarily to the title story in that volume, preferring it to the other two, "Heart of Darkness" and "The End of the Tether." John Masefield, who would become England's Poet Laureate in 1930, found that "Youth" was not only the best of the three but "the best thing Mr. Conrad has done." He found the narrative of "Heart of Darkness" "most unconvincing," for it was "not vigorous, direct, effective, like that of Mr. Kipling," nor was it "clear and fresh like that of Stevenson" (Sherry (ed.), *Conrad*, p. 142). Again, as was the case with Conrad's earlier fictions, the standard against which this work was measured, one that spoke of exotic adventures in the nation's imperial outposts, was the adventure fiction of the day. On those terms, "Youth" was the favorite and, judged by familiar standards, very satisfying. But if the book had been published as Conrad had first hoped, as a trilogy of Marlow stories, readers might have seen that "Youth" was meant to sound the note which "Heart of Darkness" and "Jim" answered. Remembering Conrad's hope for *Three Tales of Land and Sea*, a volume that he regretfully abandoned, argues for reading the two remaining Marlow stories in *Youth*, not independently of one another, but in each others' company as dialogic voices arguing for a more complex vision of adventure than the monologic tellings of contemporary adventure fiction had heretofore admitted.

In a letter to William Blackwood, written in 1902, Conrad wrote that he had made "Youth" "out of the material of a boys' story" (Karl, *Letters*, II, p. 417). And it was recognizable as such, from the depiction of youthful pluck and idealism to the generic opening which argued a special case for England in its by now commonplace connection between the English adventure hero and the sea: "This could have occurred nowhere but in England where men and sea interpenetrate" (*Youth*, p. 3). And the racial privileging being celebrated here is a note that is sustained throughout the story. The young Marlow, definitely "one of us," admires the tenacity, discipline, and courage of his men on board the "Judea." He idealizes them as having "the right stuff," and can credit their discipline and courage only to:

> something in them, something inborn and subtle and everlasting. I don't say positively that the crew of a French or German merchant man wouldn't have done it, but I doubt whether it would have been done in the same way. There was a completeness in it, something solid like a principle, and masterful like an instinct – a disclosure of something secret – of that hidden something, that gift of good or evil that makes racial difference, that shapes the fate of nations. (p. 28)

As familiar to readers of adventure fiction as the racial privileging is the wide-eyed enthusiasm of the young Marlow. He could easily be bound on a Robert Ballantyne adventure so ready is he to embrace adventure wherever he can find it and be charmed by whatever presents itself. Although the "Judea" is described by the older, narrating Marlow as "all rust, dust, grime – soot aloft, dirt on deck," the old ship he is about to embark on appears to the young narrated Marlow to be as romantic as "a ruined cottage." The coat of arms remaining on the bow just under the ship's name – "a lot of scrollwork, with the gilt off" – and the accompanying slogan, "Do or Die," appeal to the young, adventure-seeking Marlow similarly: "it took my fancy immensely. There was a touch of romance in it, something that made me love the old thing – something that appealed to my youth!" (p. 5). It not only takes his fancy, he embraces it as a "creed" in just such a spirit as similarly high-minded G. A. Henty lads might have done.

At the height of the "Judea's" adversities, he thinks triumphantly, "By Jove! this is the deuce of an adventure – something you read about" (p. 12). His language here marks him as adventure fiction's ideal reader; his generic, unqualified exclamations are indistinguishable from those of the innumerable Neds and Jacks whose "right stuff" young Marlow has learned to subscribe to. And apparently, his ideas of heroism and of its requisite creeds have been shaped also by romanticized travel memoirs. Awaiting the "Judea's" readiness for sea – a period of interminable delays – he takes up *Sartor Resartus*. While the captain's wife at the same moment is retailoring or "overhauling" Marlow's clothes, he attempts Carlyle, not under-standing much of it at the time. That he has learned something from Carlyle will become apparent by "Heart of Darkness" where Marlow's outlook more overtly resembles a Carlylean view of life and commitment to work, but at the moment another book attracts young Marlow more immediately. In Frederick Burnaby's *Ride to Khiva*, he finds the soldier more of "a man" than the philosopher (p. 17). We remember *The Coral Island*'s hero recommending the reading of travel books to his young friends for the truths they could furnish, but there is no indication here that the young Marlow prefers Burnaby's book to Carlyle's because it is more factual. It simply celebrates a kind of heroism he has learned to project for himself. It is in search of such adventure, then that he takes himself off to London, at a moment when the possibilities for heroic action temporarily elude him on the disabled, docked "Judea," and comes back having spent three months pay on "a complete set of Byron's works and a new railway rug" (p. 16).

And these fictions seem to have constructed for him not only his ideals of heroic aspirations and conduct, that is, of "us," but also of the exotic Other. The East he is so anxious to reach is a name imaged already for him by the countless, seductive fictions he has read: "Bankok! Magic name, blessed name. Mesopotamia wasn't a patch on it...Java, another blessed name – like Bankok, you know" (p. 36). As Edward Said reminds us, it was Byron among many others, who contributed to building the Orientalist discourse that Marlow appears to have so readily consumed (*Orientalism*, p. 99). This was hardly an innocent encounter, then, for the East had been preceded and supplanted by its numerous legends. In words that will be echoed by the initial narrator of "Heart of Darkness," Marlow remembers:

And I thought of men of old who, centuries ago, went that road in ships that sailed no better, to the land of palms, and spices, and yellow sands, and of brown nations ruled by kings more cruel than Nero the Roman, and more splendid than Solomon the Jew. (p. 18)

As Chinua Achebe has noted, the European view of the Other has never been innocent, and young Marlow's is no exception.[1] Indeed, we see what we have been prepared to see. Thus, when Marlow finally arrives at Java's shores, what he sees is, predictably, "the East of the ancient navigators, so old, so mysterious, resplendent and sombre, living and unchanged, full of danger and promise." And when he notices the people gathered around, he looks upon them as undistinguishable Other and sees only "brown, bronze, yellow faces, the black eyes, the glitter, the colour of an Eastern crowd" (*Youth*, p. 40).

But this "exulting like a conqueror" is undercut by the sound not of the expected welcoming Eastern voices but of startling Western curses, oaths, in English, being hurled at him in the dark by the captain of a steamer, intended actually for the native caretaker ... not for "one of us." If contemporaries had not been so prepared to read "Youth" as conventional adventure fiction, they might have noticed the possibilities for ironic readings of young Marlow's heroic ideals and idealized conceptions, for his view of himself and his endeavor can often, in fact, be seen as at odds with our view. The inevitable blind spots that blurred the European's vision of the exotic Other operated similarly on readers who consumed the fiction as generic and therefore as a straightforward romance. Desiring a life of action, young Marlow's adventures are constantly delayed. The elusiveness of the adventure dooms him actually to a good deal of inactivity and rather mundane occupations. He makes a heroic vessel of what appears to us a leaky old wreck, and conceives his voyage in her as something out of a romantic traveller's tale, going ahead against all odds, do or die, a kind of sea version of Burnaby's ride. He appears in the grip of an ideal fueled by slogans and books that in a less romantic light seems short-sightedness and even destructive folly rather than heroic action. His enthusiasm even admits of humorous possibilities, for at one point he jumps into the burning hold, to show everyone else "how easily it could be done" only to be fished out "with a chain hook tied to a broom handle" (p. 21). While he shares Henty's lads' pluck, never did a Ned's or a Jack's deeds end so ignominiously; young Marlow's "right stuff" is more of a liability than an asset. He risks death readily enough, his own and that of many men, but for what? His idealized view of the endeavor contrasts with our own, for the "Judea" is actually fraught with rather unheroic disasters and delays and is bent on nothing more glorious than delivering a shipment of soggy coal to Bankok. "Do or Die" becomes an empty slogan when clung to so tenaciously. When romantic idealism endangers lives so foolishly, it appears a dangerous illusion indeed.

That this ironic view of young Marlow's heroism is justified, can be seen when viewed in the context Conrad intended. Although he opens his 1917 Preface to *Youth* with the disclaimer, "The three stories in this volume lay no claim to unity of artistic purpose," as already mentioned, Conrad had thought at one point that the three Marlow stories would make up a volume after their separate serial publications. He was working on all of them during the same period of time (June 1898–February 1899) and at one point was even submitting manuscript pages of "Heart of Darkness" and "Jim" to *Blackwood's* simultaneously. The latter, of course, grew well beyond a "sketch" to be serialized in two installments, and "End of the Tether" was written instead. But the original conception differed from that eventual fact. In a letter to David Meldrum, *Blackwood's* literary advisor, Conrad told him that "Jim" had not "been planned to stand alone. 'H of D' was meant in my mind as a foil, and 'Youth' was supposed to give the note" (Blackburn, (ed.), *Conrad Letters*, p. 94). The "note" "Youth" gives is thus answered in *Lord Jim*; both feature young, idealistic adventure seekers whose ideas of heroism have been shaped by various fictions. While young Marlow's reading – Burnaby to Byron – provides a sometimes comical contrast to his actual adventures, Jim's rowing off to Patusan armed only with an unloaded revolver, "a half-crown complete Shakespeare," and two other small books in dark covers (p. 237) strikes a more somber note, for all are equally ineffectual means of dealing with the actual events towards which Jim is rowing. A proven consumer and misreader of fiction, Jim reads Shakespeare to "cheer up" and takes his ideas of heroic conduct from the idealized protagonists of "light holiday reading," of which, perhaps, the two other volumes are examples. Jim answers the note struck in "Youth," for he too is the young Conway boy bent on adventure – both embrace the creed of "Do or Die" and both are "one of us"; but at the crucial moment, Jim fails to be the death-defying, decisive adventure hero of fiction and spends the rest of his life compensating for that perceived failure. "Heart of Darkness" provides a foil to those heroic ideals of the dominant fiction, embraced by the young Marlow and by Jim. While Jim plays out a possible fate of the young Marlow, "Heart of Darkness" rehearses another, and in doing so, expresses a distanced skepticism of the professed heroic ideals in Marlow who has learned to distrust and reject the generic definitions of heroism; in Kurtz, who also sets out "equipped with some ideals," we get still another possible trajectory of a course mapped out by a dangerously illusory idealism. Thus "Heart of Darkness" provides an alternate, darker version, a sinister sequence to "Youth," a foil to its essential hopefulness.

The few reviewers who said anything about "Heart of Darkness" either objected, as did Masefield, to its failure to resemble Kipling or Stevenson, or dismissed it as "extravagant" and "indulgent"; for example, a reviewer for *The Times Literary Supplement* wrote that the effect of the final scene "is reached by an indulgence in the picturesque horror of the villain, his work and his surroundings, which is pitiless in its insistence, and quite extravagant according to the canons of art" (Sherry, *Conrad*, p. 136). Finding what they were prepared to find, many read it as adventure fiction *manqué*, and thus pronounced the "extravagance" and "indulgence" bad form. Speaking of "Heart of Darkness," Paul Zweig observes in *The Adventurer* that the adventure story which had been "trimmed to a swift, bouyant genre" by such writers as Kipling and Stevenson, was now bogged down in gloomy "atmospherics," any action obscured by "an elaboration of imagery and extreme emotions" (p. 270). Contemporary readers objected to these shifts, the assumption remaining that Conrad's fiction wanted to resemble that of Kipling and Stevenson.

But that it could be read as adventure fiction, albeit failed, points out the powerful pervasiveness of the genre constraints within which this fiction was read as well as the ways in which it resembled that genre. Todorov also notes that resemblances between "Heart of Darkness" and the contemporary adventure story did exist, but only superficially in the title, the familiar frame and the setting. In significant ways, the fiction resisted genre requirements. That so little actually happens and that suspense is discouraged by early fore-warnings worked against reader expectation. Most ungeneric of all was the way in which the fiction underscored the truth that knowledge – "ours," in this case – is illusory and even inaccessible (see Todorov, "Knowledge in the Void"). But adventure served imperialism; an "adventurous spirit" precluded subversion, and like young Marlow, readers saw what they were prepared to see. Therefore, those reviewers who noted "Heart of Darkness," and its political content, assured their readers it posed no threat to imperial aims. A reviewer for the *Manchester Guardian* wrote "It must not be supposed that Mr. Conrad makes attack upon colonization, expansion, even upon Imperialism. In no one is the essence of the adventurous spirit more instinctive" (Sherry (ed.), *Conrad*, p. 135). Conrad himself in a letter to his Tory publisher, William Blackwood, defended it as "not gloomy," remembering the attacks levelled against his earlier works, especially *Almayer*, *Outcast*, and "Outpost." He went on to argue that simply describing "the criminality of inefficiency and pure selfishness when tackling the civilizing work in Africa is a justifiable idea. The subject is of our time" (Blackburn (ed.), *Conrad Letters*, p. 36), although he admitted that Blackwood might not find its subject appropriate for this number, the 1,000th number of *Blackwood's* – or *Maga*, as it was affectionately referred to by the initiated – where the story's first installment initially ran. Conrad knew it would strike a different note from the accompanying articles that would, and did, celebrate the traditional imperial ideas of Blackwood's very august publication.

But no one, as we have seen, seemed to have noticed. In fact, the context probably served to encourage generic expectations and predispose readers to read the story within the tradition being celebrated by the other articles in *Maga*, and not against it. The exception was Edward Garnett's review, written for *Academy and Literature* in 1902, in which he not only claimed "Heart of Darkness" as "the high-water mark of the author's talent" (Sherry (ed.), *Conrad*, p. 133) but also saw clearly the story's subversion. He saw it  as "a page torn from the life of the Dark Continent – a page which has been hitherto carefully blurred and kept away from European eyes" (Sherry (ed.), *Conrad*, p. 133). His metaphor is revealing, implying as it does that history, a text inscribed by writers, is a fallible, human endeavor subject to various distortions, not the monolithic, monologic narrative it was often assumed to be. Garnett argued that Conrad's particular focus effected an unblurring, a revelation of that which had remained concealed, and was therefore a new, subversive telling. More recent condemnations of Conrad's lack of subversion qualify but do not invalidate Garnett's insights. Achebe refers to Conrad as a "purveyor of comforting [racist] myths" ("An Image of Africa," p. 784), and Terry Eagleton argues that like any other conservative of his day, Conrad questioned merely the bourgeois materialism and commercialism into which imperialism usually degenerated rather than imperialism itself (*Criticism and Ideology*, p. 135). Garnett knew what Ford had noticed, that Conrad's allegiances were admittedly conservative, even feudal and aristocratic, and that his interest was in stability, not in revolution (Ford, *Conrad*, pp. 61, 77). Nonetheless, Garnett asserted, Conrad was intent on unmasking the benevolent pretensions of the essentially commercial endeavor, and subverting the genre that had constructed the subject as such was an effective means of doing so. "Taken from life," Garnett argued for the realism of this "impression of the conquest by the European whites of a certain portion of Africa, an impression in particular of the civilising methods of a certain great European Trading Company face to face with the 'nigger.'" Of all his contemporaries, Garnett alone writes that Conrad's interest is in the effect on

the white man's *morale*, when he is let loose from European restraint, and planted down in the tropics as an 'emissary of light' armed to the teeth, to make trade profits out of the 'subject races'... the isolation of the unnerved, degenerating whites staring all day and every day at the Heart of Darkness which is alike meaningless and threatening to their own creed and conceptions of life, the helpless bewilderment of the unhappy savages in the grasp of their flabby and rapacious conquerors (Sherry (ed.), *Conrad*, pp. 132–3).

And a few years later in an appreciation of *Nostromo*, Garnett repeated his understanding that in "Heart of Darkness" Conrad was taking the measure of "the imbecility, the cruelty, and the rapacity of the white man in the Dark Continent," by depicting the effects of such treatment on the white man himself, concerning himself largely with the "sapping" of his morale, "body, mind, and soul" (*Friday Nights*, p. 96).

Insightful as Garnett's remarks were, they all focused on Kurtz, the "emissary of light," rather than on Marlow. And of course, the story of the moral disintegration of Kurtz, our white man in the tropics whom all of Europe has helped to produce, was subversion enough. Although Kurtz, as the central "degenerate white" figure here, has been prefigured by an assortment of others within Conrad's earlier fiction, he is a far more complex version of Carlier and Kayerts, and a more significant one than Almayer or Willems. Unlike his former embodiments, he comes out to Africa for idealistic motives in addition to those of personal gain; initially, at least, Kurtz is bent on a civilizing mission. He is no ex-petty official on the fringes of power, come out only to mend his fortunes, but the enlightened product of European idealism, well educated, multi-talented, at the center of power, and on the way up. These forerunners in the earlier fiction and the other emissaries of light in "Heart of Darkness" inform our reading of Kurtz, "hollow men" all: those cynical opportunists, the "pilgrims," the station manager who endures as well as he does because he has no entrails and no scruples, and the members of the Eldorado Exploring Expedition who hide knowingly behind the slogans of the "cause." For as repugnant as Kurtz's degeneration is, both to us and to Marlow, it is finally preferable to the utter cynicism and sham being perpetrated by the others; and in making Kurtz his "choice of nightmares," Marlow aligns himself against that pretense officially endorsed by all the workers for the "cause" around him. The moral ideas Kurtz comes out "equipped" with – much as former adventurers were furnished with the requisite clothing and supplies for the wilderness – will prove as insubstantial as clothing and will "fly off at the first good shake" (p. 97), but that he does subscribe to principles that are so earnestly held and as easily exploded, principles purported by the discourse to be at the very center of the imperial project, solid and fixed, is the greater subversion here. It is just Kurtz's complexity, which allows us to view ideals as both potentially ennobling principles and as dangerous illusions, and his representativeness, that seriously dismantle the myth of empire.

"Heart of Darkness," as it narrates the degeneration of a failed idealist contrasts with both Lord Jim and with "Youth," but finally this is not only the story of Kurtz. In a letter to Blackwood justifying his method, admittedly "long in development," Conrad argues that the story must be viewed from the standpoint of the final scene, "where the interview of the man and the girl locks in – as it were – the whole 30,000 words of narrative description into one suggestive view of a whole phase of life and makes of that story something quite on another plane than an anecdote of a man who went mad in the Centre of Africa" (Karl, Letters, II, p. 417). Here Conrad seems to be defending his story against facile comparisons with similar ones that abounded in the popular press of the day. Like Todorov, Richard Ruppel notices the ways in which "Heart of Darkness" appears to belong to the tradition of exotic imperial tales so popular in the 1890s. At the same time, as Ruppel demonstrates, it provides a critique of that tradition and its imperialist assumptions. Ruppel argues that the similarities between "Heart of Darkness" and several Cutcliffe Hyne stories of 1897–99 are not coincidental, detailing one in particular – "the Transfer" – whose similarities include the frame narrator, the participating narrator on board a ship telling of his journey into the Belgian Congo and of the atrocities he witnessed there in search of an ivory trader "gone Fantee."[2] But in refusing to narrate only the "decivilizing" of another white man in the tropics, "Heart of Darkness" is an aberration. By focusing on Marlow, Conrad's fiction, considered next to others contemporary with it, registered a criticism of imperialism unavailable elsewhere.

Marlow is read by Garnett and other contemporaries as a kind of neutral narrator, a conventional storyteller much like the ones familiar to readers in the 1890s – albeit an unsuccessful one, most readers complained. No one could possibly take so long or use such literary language to relate a story to actual listeners, "hardly the sort of thing a raconteur would say across the walnuts," as Masefield wrote (Sherry (ed.), *Conrad*, p. 142). Only recently have readers paid much attention to the frame of either "Youth" or "Heart of Darkness," as told by anyone other than a neutral storyteller. Contemporary readers overlooked it, because of their predisposition, already discussed, and perhaps because they were the intended listeners – The Lawyer, The Accountant, and The Director – and to notice the frame and Marlow's role in it would be to hear the criticism and recognize the implications of that criticism for them-selves. In fact, one of the movements from "Youth" to "Heart" is towards a well-developed sense of audience.[3] Conrad claimed to have written the first as "a feat of memory," and while it gave him the chance to recall and relive for himself the experience of youthful adventure in all its novelty and glamour, his purpose in writing "Heart" was to impress that experience, and what it had come to mean to him, upon "the minds and bosoms" of his audience (*Youth*, p. xi). Thus, for contemporary readers, Marlow was either invisible or he was unrealistic and overly "precious."[4] In fact, his use in both narratives serves to underscore the ways in which "Heart of Darkness" works in dialogue with "Youth." The older Marlow comes to question the possibilities of the idealistic adventure he once celebrated, and moves to implicate his listeners as complicit in its demise.

To claim that it is Marlow who "controls our response to the events" in both "Youth" and "Heart of Darkness," and that it is "this voice rather than the specific events themselves that remains in our memory" (Graver, *Short Fiction*, p. 71) is characteristic of a more modern view, even though the origins and purposes of Marlow have been argued at great length.¶ Conrad himself introduced Marlow in the preface to "Youth" as his constant companion: "He haunts my hours of solitude, when, in silence, we lay our heads together in great comfort and harmony...I don't think that either of us would care much to survive the other" (p. x). Although the language here sounds like that used to describe the relationship between the narrator of "The Secret Sharer" and his alter ego who at night shared the narrator's "bed-place," and thus suggests little critical distance, Marlow is not so much Conrad's spokesman as a strategic innovation that served his purposes in disrupting the generic adventure story and its essentially dangerous monolithic illusions. His use increases the dialogic possibilities and allows the story to be the site of struggle between disparate languages and outlooks. As Mikhail Bakhtin observed, that very dialogic quality ensures that no one voice necessarily emerges the absolute victor, and is itself a subversion in this discourse that had always sought to champion the imperial subject (Bakhtin, *Dialogic Imagination*, pp. 315–320). And of course this external dialogue within the fiction expresses Conrad's own irresolution. The issues were complex, and his allegiances were mixed, but perpetuating the dialogue challenged the simplistic assumptions of the genre. Interestingly, that which Leavis had noted as a stylistic flaw, the "adjectival insistence" which he complained served to "muffle" rather than "magnify" (Leavis, *The Great Tradition*, p. 177), is also attacked by modern readings, such as Eagleton's, as ideological evasions. No mere stylistic problem, the murky impressionism of the modernist aesthetic equivocated, Eagleton argues. "The restlessly allusive suggestions which leave its meanings multiple and ambiguous and unachieved" work to avoid confrontation (*Criticism and Ideology*, p. 136). Achebe, too, refuses to dismiss the vagueness as a stylistic flaw, but rather sees it as an evasion of a more direct denouncement of racism and imperialism ("An Image of Africa," p. 784). Those same "gloomy atmospherics" that first disqualified "Heart of Darkness," for many readers, from the adventure tradition, were then seen to mar its art and thus qualify its entrance into the Great Tradition; most recently, those "atmospherics," once resented as unnecessary intrusions, have been read as moral evasions. Neither intrusive nor evasive in its "adjectival insistence" and in its disparate voices, the fiction's multiple meanings dramatize the complexities here, in the events themselves and in Marlow's changing responses to them, and finally make of the simplistic adventure story a profound moral tale.

Although the first-person participating narrator was a familiar device of adventure fiction, it had always served the writers' celebratory intentions and had never been used to question the events narrated; however, in "Heart of Darkness," Marlow's combative and challenging relationship to the frame he occupies and the events he narrates works to dislodge the myth kept in place by the dominant fiction. Older than magazine formulas, the convention of an intimate, informing relationship between the teller and his tale served Conrad's purpose well for the changes he rings on it. One shift is that here there are two central white men, Kurtz and Marlow, the observed and the observer. The white man's actions could remain "deeds of glory" as long as he was their chronicler, but now Marlow, as participant and as onlooker, presents new possibilities for subversive tellings. Another shift is that he is as opposed to his audience here as he is one of them, and the insights his experiences have afforded him confront and challenge his listeners' assumptions and 'complacent "civilized" views of life rather than condone them. Analogous to the uneasy relationship between Marlow and his listeners is the one between Marlow and his fellow workers within the fiction itself. The manager's murderous counterplot, discussed by Watts in *The Deceptive Text* – one that Marlow becomes dimly aware of – reveals a most ungeneric lack of cooperation between the white men in empire's outposts. Specifically, this dialogue made possible by Conrad's use of Marlow unveils the struggle that Eagleton points to at the center of "Heart of Darkness," between the idealism that had always described Europe's imperialist endeavor and its intensified commercial efforts made more pressing towards the end of the century by European economic depression, thus exposing "the discrepancy between its Romantic ideals and sordid material practice" (*Criticism and Ideology*, p. 134). In fact, one of the "unblurrings" here is the revelation that imperialism is enabled by an idealism that is and must remain ignorant of what imperialism actually means in practice.[6]

The awareness is Marlow's, but only imperfectly. Taking the hint from one of Conrad's letters that "Heart of Darkness" was, among other things, a study of racial difference, Edward Said sees Marlow as "Conrad's own version of the 'homme moyen Anglais'" (*Joseph Conrad*, p. 147). Marlow responds to his experience in the Congo much as his listeners, or readers, might have done, and in fact did.[7] Like many European travellers in the Congo of the 1890s, factual or fictional, Marlow resists analyzing the implications of what he sees – that the accountant's "admirable" starched collars necessitated forced labor or that the basic assumption underlying Kurtz's "eloquent" and "high-strung" report, i.e., suppressing "savage" customs, was, in fact, extremely problematic.

Furthermore, his knowledge is incomplete and his discourse is characterized by elipses, gaps, uncertainties. There are even some things he tells us, he did not want to know. Knowledge is not only inaccessible; it does not bear looking into too closely. Thus, in most ungeneric fashion, the fiction chronicles what the white man does not/will not know and what he does not do. After all, Marlow does not turn around once he witnesses the extent of colonial brutality his work, in fact, serves. He does not write the newspapers, nor demand an inquiry. Instead, he contributes to the darkness by suppressing the truth that even he has had to acknowledge, passing up the opportunities that do present themselves, and only relinquishing the report without the dark postscript that would have revealed so much. His lie to the Intended is, in a sense, the least of his deceptions, but it represents his refusal to enlighten those domestic guardians of the beliefs that enabled imperial practices to continue and thrive.

Rather, Marlow tries to defend himself – representative *homme moyen anglais*, that he is – against the disquieting realization borne in on him, that we are all capable of all things, by going to work and turning "his back on the station" and its fantastic charades and pretences. He sticks to the "redeeming facts of life" such as rivets, or snags in the river, or the smell of mud. No wonder an old book he finds, *An Inquiry into some Points of Seamanship*, is such a welcome discovery to him; its voice speaks simply of "chains and purchases," and its "singleness of intention, an honest concern for the right way of going to work" has a reality and purposeful substance not to be found elsewhere around him. And yet this work, too, which Marlow turns to as a source of restraint and self-knowledge, can be a kind of snare and even, ironically, forestall self-knowledge. Marlow's voice of civilized reason, "the speech that cannot be silenced," he assures his listeners, by the "wild and passionate uproar" and the "fiendish row" on shore and his allegiance to work and its demanding details offer him a comforting hold on reality, he believes. We are made to see, however, that these are comforting illusions. He turns, unquestioningly, to work that is, after all, a central subject of this narrative's inquiry. Clearly we are to see Marlow's understanding and his responses as limited; as Mahood remarks, there was undoubtedly good seamanship involved in the Middle Passage too (22). Certainly Conrad questions Marlow's blind devotion to efficiency and considers it as harmful as any of the other shrine-worshipping going on here – the natives to Kurtz or the pilgrims to ivory (see Hay, *Political Novels*, chapter 4).

In many ways, then, Marlow seems representative of those listeners aboard the "Nellie." But again it is the contrast with "Youth" that in focusing our attention on Marlow and the frame, dramatizes the widening distance between Marlow and his shipboard audience. It is that dialogue between the two that intensifies the criticism inherent in "Heart of Darkness." Throughout our reading, we are aware that for every similarity that unites narrator and audience, several differences divide them. No longer the friendly companion of "Youth," whose refrain of "Pass the bottle" marks him as one with the others around the table, this Marlow seems older, and far more skeptical of those slogans he had once embraced so readily. Marlow sets himself apart from the others, and views the events he narrates with an increasing discomfort and repugnance that distances him from the endeavor rather than celebrates it. The subsequent irritability he gives way to is just what the doctor warns him against ("Du Calme" is the futile medical advice) and it keeps erupting in the narrative also. In the opening pages, the anonymous narrator carefully describes this apartness. Sitting cross-legged against the mizzen-mast, Marlow "had sunken cheeks, a yellow complexion, a straight back, an ascetic aspect, and with his arms dropped, the palms of hands outwards, resembled an idol" (p. 7). A kind of "oriental" calm envelops him, distancing him from the others who are variously occupied, securing the "Nellie" and preparing to wait for the tide to turn. He appears to be a static figure in the story he narrates, ostensibly describing the calamitous effects of the wilderness on Kurtz, his progress and decline, while he, Marlow, holds closely to the surface of things and refuses to "go ashore." But that he has not returned home unaffected can be marked in his apartness from this group of which he was once a member.

Unlike his listeners, Marlow still "follow[s] the sea," and unlike even other seamen of "his class," he wanders when ashore in a most unseaman-like manner. Marlow is not even a typical story-teller, the narrator insists, for "to him the meaning of an episode was not inside like a kernel but outside, enveloping the tale which brought it out only as a glow brings out a haze" (p. 9). The speaker finds the method unusual but apparently appropriate to Marlow's oddly "inconclusive" tales. Of course, that a listener could find this tale absolutely "inconclusive" and not hear in it an unequivocal condemnation of imperial practices characterizes the speaker as undiscerning, and as blind to the actuality of imperial misdeeds as Marlow himself had been at first. After this catalogue of differences, we are not surprised by the non-conciliatory, challenging tone Marlow often takes with his listeners. The gap between them has widened considerably, presumably because of the insights afforded him by the story he is about to narrate. Unlike the generic adventure heroes, he has been changed forever by his adventures, and these changes and their attendant realizations so distance him from his audience that they can only be represented in an indirect, impressionistic telling; rather than a direct light, the enveloping "glow that brings out a haze" is the only illumination possible here.

And those listeners, while ostensibly the same four men are presented rather differently in "Heart of Darkness." Those five companions who had sat around the table, sharing the convivial bottle in a lighted room, presumably, have here been reduced to disembodied sighs and grunts and by the darkness that falls over them all. Also, in "Youth," the narrator notes that all five of them had begun life in the merchant service. When the narrator of "Heart of Darkness" observes that "Between us there was, as I have already said, somewhere, the bond of the sea" (p. 6), the "somewhere" of course is in "Youth." In that earlier story, the listeners included "a director of companies" who had been "a 'Conway' boy," an accountant who "had served four years at sea," a lawyer, "a fine crusted Tory, High Churchman, the best of old fellows, the soul of honour" who "had been chief officer in the P. & O. service in the good old days when mail-boats were square-rigged at least on two masts, and used to come down the China Sea before a fair monsoon with stun'sails set alow and aloft" (p. 3). But these same companions, so affectionately and nostalgically described in "Youth," become in "Heart of Darkness" simply "The Director of Companies," "The Lawyer – still "the best of old fellows" – and "The Accountant," now capitalized and frozen into their professions as though they did not exist outside of them. And, in a way, they do not. Conrad's insistence on their professional identities can be better understood in the light of a remark he made in an article entitled "Books" written for the *Speaker* in 1905. There he spoke of "men's ideas and prejudices, which are by no means the outcome of malevolence, but depend on their education, their social status, even their professions" (*Notes on*

*Life and Letters*, p. 9). Our ideals are shaped, the remark implies; how we are disposed to view such situations as will be described here depends largely on what we have been taught, what we have read, what class we belong to, and what we do for a living. Marlow's listeners, like Conrad's imagined readers, are so securely anchored by their civilized lives that Marlow doubts they can see with their own eyes what he is telling them of imperial misdeeds.

But what marks Marlow's distance from the prevailing attitudes and generic depiction most obviously is his insight that there is something odd and unnatural about Europeans being in Africa in the first place.[8] The invasion is a "fantastic" one he keeps reminding his listeners. In contrast to the European presence in Africa that he first encounters in make-shift coastal stations and a French man-of-war firing into the bush, "the voice of the surf... was something natural, that had its reason, that had a meaning." And as "natural and true as the surf along their coast" were the Africans themselves he glimpsed in their boats. "They wanted no excuse for being there," unlike the intrusion he is a part of (p. 61). Presenting the case from the point of view of the invaded also underlines the oddness of this invasion. Thus he explains the solitude of the land he had tramped through overland: "Well, if a lot of mysterious niggers armed with all kinds of fearful weapons suddenly took to travelling on the road between Deal and Gravesend, catching the yokels right and left to carry heavy loads for them, I fancy every farm and cottage thereabouts would get empty very soon" (p. 70). Posed this way, especially to these listeners, familiar as they are with those very roads, such an invasion should appear not only anomalous but extremely objectionable. While Marlow's racial epithets mark the extent to which he too has been shaped by education, class and profession, it is his apprehension of the unnaturalness of Europeans landing in Africa and assuming control that sets him apart from his listeners on the "Nellie." The "emptying" itself has dark and euphemistic suggestions; Marlow implies either a kind of forced "pacification" here or again the naturalness and appropriateness of the natives' response – clearing out. In either case his awareness is atypical.

No longer, so transforming has been the experience he narrates, is Marlow really one of them, as his frequent interruptions will remind us all. Marlow, who must defend himself against his listeners' occasional grunts of "absurd," and groans of disapproval and disbelief, exceeds the distance Haggard's Allan Quatermain sometimes creates between himself and his audience who also, he feels, cannot understand. But here the gulf has widened. While Quatermain often despairs of ever making his readers see the strange landscapes of jungle and veldt, or the fierce attractiveness of a Zulu war dance, or the thrill of an assemblage of Masai warriors, Marlow asks more of his listeners. His task is not only to make them see that exotic wilderness without, but the darkness within, a darkness about which the generic discourse has heretofore remained silent, but one to which Marlow and his listeners are all susceptible, he insists. He asks them to understand their own relationship to the imperial endeavor and their own complicity, as he has come to at least half perceive his own, in the events he is narrating. Not only have they all been shaped by their professions but also these men are institutionalized representatives of the civilization in the name of which this conquest – the "cause" – is being carried out, certainly beneficiaries of British imperialism. But Marlow's attempts to implicate them directly draw the sharpest complaints. When he suggests that their endeavors, as grand and meaningful as they might seem to all of them, are merely insignificant and illusory "monkey tricks" that afford an absorbing and comforting surface activity, a voice "growl[s]" out of the darkness that has fallen over the "Nellie," "Try to be civil, Marlow" (p. 94). In a sense, Marlow offers them a kind of fellowship, but one which they find repugnant and unacceptable.

But in suggesting that "civilization" is exactly the term that needs redefinition, Marlow challenges the very assumption of the discourse that other first-person narrators of adventure fiction had sought to stabilize; his narration unfolds its failure. By unveiling the much heralded promise of civilization as mere pretense, he exposes the fine words as simply pretty fictions. The celebrated "cause," worthy of export in whose name progress has been promised, reveals itself here as an easily penetrated veneer. That "progress," presumably railroads, schools, medical and agricultural improvements, has not arrived in this imperial outpost is evident to Marlow from the beginning in the abandoned boiler "wallowing in the grass" and in the "undersized railway truck lying there on its back with its wheels in the air" (p. 63). No light is being conferred on this imperial outpost. And the discrepancy between pronounced ideals and the actual practices is everywhere apparent. Only the brutality of colonial adventurism is present here, while to other whites – the accountant's annoyance with the dying man whose groans interfere with his work of recording the legal fictions of imperial usurpation, for example – and, more dramatically, whites to blacks. Those fallacious legalities and accounts maintained in "apple-pie order," whereby natives become "the enemy," and the Grove of Death where those brutalized natives withdraw to die, evidence a rapacious kind of "progress" indeed. These observations work on Marlow and contribute to the revulsion he feels, increasingly, for the others. Some of his first impressions of colonial brutality are gathered during his over-land trek to the middle station:

Once a white man in an unbuttoned uniform, camping on the path with an armed escort of lank Zanzibaris, very hospitable and festive – not to say drunk. Was looking after the upkeep of the road, he declared. Can't say I saw any road or any upkeep, unless the body of a middle-aged negro, with a bullet-hole in the forehead upon which I absolutely stumbled three miles farther on may be considered as a permanent improvement. I had a white companion too, not a bad chap, but rather too fleshy... I couldn't help asking him once what he meant by coming there at all. 'To make money, of course. What do you think?' he said scornfully. Then he got fever and had to be carried in a hammock slung under a pole. As he weighed sixteen stone I had no end of rows with the carriers. They jibbed, ran away, sneaked off with their loads in the night – quite a mutiny. So, one evening I made a speech in English with gestures, not one of which was lost to the sixty pairs of eyes before me, and the next morning I started the hammock off in front all right... (pp. 71, 72)

Marlow's responses reflect ironically on the white man's "progress." He describes here one of many flabby colonials – dishevelled, and drunken and ineffectual – who appears to license murder. And the white companion in no way accords with our expectations of the white man in the tropics. No emissary of light, he admits money as his only motive. Disease-prone and grotesquely overweight, it is his unheroic physical unfitness that goes far toward explaining the carrier's "mutiny." The scheming, strawless brick-maker, the manager whose only complaint about Kurtz's barbarism is that it "lacked method" and was therefore ineffectual, the absurd faithless pilgrims, "bewitched" by ivory, back-biting and contriving for "percentages," each epitomizes the contradictions between the ideal and the actual at the heart of the whole philanthropic pretence. And the closer Marlow approaches the Inner Station, the thinner the façade of philanthropic concern. Intended primarily for the home audience, generally feminized here, the "pretty fictions" become more sparse, and the endeavor reveals itself as nothing more subtle than a bank robbery or a horse theft.

Nor is there any substance, Marlow discovers, in civilization's promise to fortify its emissaries of light with sustaining ideals. Under the impact of the wilderness and its solitude, all the moral ideas knit into them by their education, upbringing, professions, books, and newspapers come unravelled, and are revealed as empty, insubstantial "fine words." And while Marlow's willingness to read the forest as "moral wilderness" reveals the ways in which current racist thinking has shaped him, we are also made to see, as Jeremy Hawthorn notes, that idealism must fail, not because of Africa's inherent savagery, but because of its conjunction with imperialism, for it offered only the enabling lie that could not be sustained in practice (*Conrad*, p. 160f). Kurtz's dedicated work for the International Society for the Suppression of Savage Customs leads irrevocably to his final dark conviction that what is really needed is to "Exterminate all the brutes!" The actual business of "suppressing" is not so far from "exterminating," after all, distinguished only by masquerading, incantatory words. Part of Marlow's complicated response to Kurtz – a repugnance for his deeds that followed his lack of restraint and an impatience with his excessive egotism – is a kind of loyalty. At least, as none of the other hollow men does here, Kurtz finally recognizes, with horror, the enormity of his own lack of restraint, his capabilities and behavior, and this illumination transforms him into a moral being for Marlow, and for us. The pretence of the others, their blatant cynicism, and their refusal to recognize any wrong-doing, contrast with Kurtz's admission and make Kurtz Marlow's "choice of nightmares."

For all of Marlow's evasions, he cannot escape unscathed. Coming to see, albeit tentatively, that he too is complicit in contributing to the pretence and allowing the masquerade to continue irrevocably changes him and compels him to unburden himself, if not to journalists or officials, then to others. Like another ancient mariner before him, he seeks a captive audience, but this one rejects his attempts to implicate them. From the moment he sets out, he confides that he feels his position is fraught with moral ambiguities and that he feels like an "impostor," especially when his aunt proudly insists that he is one of them, "an emissary of light, something like a lower sort of apostle," "'weaning those ignorant millions from their horrid ways'" (p. 59). As the would-be brickmaker of the Central Station tries to make Marlow understand his position – "did I see it?" – and be his confidant, so Marlow appeals to his audience. "Do you see [Kurtz]? do you see the story? do you see anything?" (p. 82) Failing to disabuse the brickmaker of his notions about Marlow's supposed influence in Europe, Marlow feels "in an instant as much of a pretence as the rest of the bewitched pilgrims." While narrating his conversation with this "papier-mâché Mephistopheles," he anticipates the lie he is finally drawn into, comparing the moral stink it engenders to the rotten stench of death. When the Russian extracts a promise from him to protect Kurtz's "reputation," and he is thus driven to champion Kurtz – who is, finally, his choice of nightmares over the others – he feels compromised in doing so. Refusing to destroy the fiancée's illusions about Kurtz and his work, the great "cause," and neglecting to turn over to the journalist Kurtz's complete report, dark postscript and all, he thus perpetuates the masquerade. This omission is marked by a despair that the truth will ever be permitted to surface in a society that avoids self-scrutiny as successfully as do the inhabitants of this fictive world, but it also makes him a party to the very pretence his telling has been bent on unveiling, and he seeks to share that burden with his listeners. All are complicit, his addressing these men implies, lawyers, accountants, directors, all. Conrad's own personal guilt and shame, effectively discussed by many of his biographers and critics, inform Marlow's narration too. Said, for example, speaks of the shame Conrad felt "in common with all men for allowing personal ideals to be corrupted" (*Joseph Conrad*, p. 98), and makes a convincing case for Conrad's presence in such characters as Bunter ("The Black Mate") and Kayerts and Carlier ("Outpost of Progress"). The same guilt and shame can be felt in his depiction of Marlow here. As inscribed subject, Conrad expressed views constructed by the discourse of the day. It was his willingness to question them – albeit not always steadily – that engages us.

And the disparate voices that characterize this struggle are not only those of Marlow and his designated listeners throughout the narrative. The frame is initially the site of a dialogic struggle between the anonymous narrator's musings and Marlow's more sombre pronouncements. The dialogue serves to make important distinctions that distance this story from the monolithic representations of the adventure/travel tradition and prevent it from being an easily consumed fiction. It is this fifth, unnamed listener, not Marlow, who at the beginning of the story speaks of London as the "greatest" town and of the Thames as the "venerable" stream and recalls the great men who have sailed on it, Englishmen all:

It had known and served all the men of whom the nation is proud, from Sir Francis Drake to Sir John Franklin, knights all, titled and untitled – the great knights-errant of the sea. It had borne all the ships whose names are like jewels flashing in the night of time, from the *Golden Hind* returning with her round flanks full of treasure, to be visited by the Queen's Highness and thus pass out of the gigantic tale, to the *Erebus* and *Terror*, bound on other conquests – and that never returned. It had known the ships and the men. They had sailed from Deptford, from Greenwich, from Erith – the adventurers and the settlers; kings' ships and ships of men on 'Change; Captains, Admirals, the dark 'interlopers' of the Eastern trade, and the commissioned 'Generals' of East India fleets. Hunters for gold or pursuers of fame they all had gone out on that stream, bearing the sword, and often the torch, messengers of the might within the land, bearers of a spark from the sacred fire. What greatness had not floated on the ebb of that river into the mystery of an unknown earth? ... the dreams of men, the seed of commonwealths, the germs of empires. (p. 8)

Here is the old equation, apparently unquestioned, between adventure and a benevolent imperialism, for even those "messengers" of might who bore swords also bore "a spark from the sacred fire." There is nothing here to tell us that those dreams, and seed and germs, should not be nourished; sanctioned as they are, their growth and development can only mean enlightened and welcome progress within this formula. Elsewhere we have heard Conrad speak approvingly of national greatness, of potential and realized heroism, and this particular hymn of praise echoes his own youthful admiration of Cook, Franklin, McClintock, and Livingstone described in "Geography and Some Explorers." Eagleton argues that while Conrad denounces "crudely unidealistic forms of imperialism," he is "ideologically constrained to discover in the British variant a saving 'idea'" (*Criticism and Ideology*, p. 135). And it is true, as Eagleton goes on to point out, that England, for Conrad the Polish emigré, was a special case, "the only barrier to the pressure of infernal doctrines born in continental back-slum," as Conrad himself professed in an 1885 letter to a Polish friend (Karl, *Letters*, 1, p. 16).[9] However, another effect of the "racial" quality Conrad calls attention to (referred to above by Said) is the internationalization of this enterprise. All Europe made Kurtz, and all represented here are responsible, from the Belgian company owners and managers, to the German Kurtz, the young Russian son of an archpriest, the Swedish captain, the French gunboat officers and crew, and the English Marlow. This eulogy to the bearers of the sacred spark is voiced, after all, by an unnamed narrator, and his voice is quickly countered by Marlow's. It is a view that is not allowed to dominate but permitted to stand only in opposition to another.

Marlow, apparently overhearing that first narrator's thoughts as though they were spoken, responds. He remembers that before Franklin and other such torch-bearing knights, England too had been one of the "dark" places of the earth:

> I was thinking of very old times, when the Romans first came here, nineteen hundred years ago – the other day.... Light came out of the river since – you say Knights? Yes, but it is like a running blaze on a plain, like a flash of lightning in the clouds. We live in the flicker – may it last as long as the old earth keeps rolling! But darkness was here yesterday. (p. 49)

Even Marlow's admiration for the British imperial endeavor – the red places on the map of Africa hanging in the Company's office mark sites of "real work," he observes – is not absolute but a choice of nightmares, to be preferred, for example, to the purple patches where "the jolly pioneers of progress drink the jolly lager-beer" (p. 13). But he understands that the great blank space on the map, which had provided such pleasure to his youthful imagination, has now been made dark with European discovery and desire; exactly how dark he has yet to learn. Nowhere does Marlow, or Conrad, seem to question seriously such idealistic imperial aims as originally espoused by Kurtz – "Each station should be like a beacon on the road towards better things, a centre for trade of course but also for humanising, improving, instructing" (p. 34) – just their reality. Rather it is the morally bankrupt Manager's cynical "Conceive you – that ass!" that Conrad, along with Marlow, moves to distance himself from. The ground occupied by the kind of heroism Conrad believed made any such progress possible is in contention here. While not wanting to relinquish that ground entirely and cherishing the ideals of such heroism, he shared the more skeptical views held by Stephen Crane and other contemporaries about its actual, effective presence. The dialogue between the Marlow of "Heart of Darkness" who rejects his aunt's idealized newspaper rhetoric and that younger one who had thrilled to "Do or Die" and had been compelled to suicidal heroism under its banner externalizes this conflict, without necessarily resolving it.

Marlow goes on to draw uncomfortable parallels between aboriginal Englishmen and their Roman conquerors and other native peoples and their present day European colonizers. And the comparison performs an unmasking of imperial endeavors generally. Any distinction between those knights and other Englishmen after them and more brazen conquerors is made extremely questionable by Marlow's presentation of a hypothetical Roman:

Imagine the feelings of a commander ... put in charge of one of these craft the legionaries – a wonderful lot of handy men they must have been too – used to build ... Imagine him here – the very end of the world, a sea the colour of lead, a sky the colour of smoke, a kind of ship about as rigid as a concertina – and going up this river with stores, or orders, or what you like. Sandbanks, marshes, forests, savages, precious little to eat for a civilized man, nothing but Thames water to drink. No Falernian wine here, no going ashore. Here and there a military camp lost in a wilderness like a needle in a bundle of hay – cold, fog, tempests, disease, exile, and death – death skulking in the air, in the water, in the bush. They must have been dying like flies here. Oh yes – he did it. Did it very well too, no doubt, and without thinking much about it either, except afterwards to brag of what he had gone through in this time, perhaps. They were men enough to face the darkness. And perhaps he was cheered by keeping his eye on a chance of promotion to the fleet at Ravenna, by and by, if he had good friends in Rome and survived the awful climate. (pp. 49, 50)

Marlow, the civilized sea captain going up a savage river, also survives to tell of what he has gone through. And the job up the Congo the Englishman signs on for sounds very much like the work of the Roman conqueror. But Marlow's telling, as we have seen, is more a confession than a boast; while scorning the philanthropic pretense, he also must admit his own complicity in it. While the point of this protracted sketch might ostensibly be to distance the Roman "squeeze" from Britain's "real work," the conqueror from the colonist, it in fact suggests similarities. The distinctions keep collapsing.

And his companion sketch of a second hypothetical Roman works similarly:

Or think of a decent young citizen in a toga – perhaps too much dice, you know – coming out here in the train of some prefect, or tax-gatherer, or trader even – to mend his fortunes. Land in a swamp, march through the woods, and in some inland post feel the savagery. The utter savagery had closed round him – all that mysterious life of the wilderness that stirs in the forest, in the jungles, in the hearts of wild men. There's no initiation either into such mysteries. He has to live in the midst of the incomprehensible which is also detestable. And it has a fascination too, that goes to work upon him. The fascination of the abomination – you know. Imagine the growing regrets, the longing to escape, the powerless disgust, the surrender – the hate. (p. 50)

If the first portrait suggests Marlow, this one reminds us of Kurtz; although he has come out in the service of ideals he subscribes to as well as to improve his finances, the fates of the two are similar. The presumed superiority of their civilized notions and ideals will fail them, and both will be overwhelmed by "the horror," by "disgust," "surrender" and "hate." Intending to distinguish the old Roman conqueror from "our" present colonist, Marlow succeeds in pointing out the similarities. The fiction moves dialogically to collapse the distinctions between various imperial endeavors.

Although the voice that praises such "bearers of the spark from the sacred fire" as John Franklin is superseded in the ensuing dialogues, it probably struck a familiar note to contemporary readers. In fact, part of the outward familiarity of "Heart of Darkness" to those readers, and that which kept them from reading it subversively, might be accounted for by its resemblance to other narratives in the subgenre of Rescue adventure.[10] Part of the reason it seemed to fit comfortably in that celebratory 1899 issue of *Maga* between a poem by Andrew Lang that venerated *Blackwood's* and its old, conservative tradition, and an article by an M.P. deploring the destructive effects of the Indian Mutiny, is that "Heart of Darkness" also narrates a rescue, an attempt to retrieve "one of us." The story of John Franklin and his attempted rescue by McClintock had been of great interest to the European reading public and to Conrad himself (Conrad, *Last Essays*, p. 11). Thus "Heart of Darkness" appeared to belong to a genre that had asserted a traditional heroism. Although Kurtz was a fictional, rather than an international figure, all of Europe had created him. But here the ground has shifted considerably. Franklin was, in fact, dead long before McClintock arrived, and Livingstone – that other prototypical giant whose shadow hovers over this narrative – actually refused to be rescued by Stanley, perhaps recognizing the American newspaper stunt for what it was.[11] Both rescue attempts were hazardous and costly, and Marlow thinks of his mission to save Kurtz in equally dangerous terms. It is as fraught with dangers, he reflects, as the rescue of "an enchanted princess" (p. 106). The move to make Kurtz a kind of passive, feminine object deserves more attention, but it does serve to connect him with the European women of the tale, the domestic custodians of an illusory idealism; it also serves to mark the distance from other, contemporary heroic rescue narratives. Most importantly, neither Franklin nor Livingstone needed rescuing from a failure of self restraint, a crumbling of resolve, an extinction of ideals; Kurtz, unlike either of them, needs to be saved from himself, and, clearly, for the company – nothing altruistic here – rather than for himself.

That the story takes this form suggests Conrad's regret. Measuring this rescue of Kurtz against that former one of Franklin marks the distance travelled from his youthful dreams of pure adventure and reflects Conrad's awareness that the possibilities for heroism such as Franklin's, McClintock's, and Livingstone's have diminished. All that remains of adventure here is the young Russian harlequin, blinded by a dangerous idolotry for Kurtz and an unquestioning consumption of his "truths," on the one hand, and on the other the unheroic, morally bankrupt and doomed Eldorado Expedition. Years later he was to write of the disparity that overwhelmed him, as it did Marlow, between his idealized expectations, created in large part by the travel writing and contemporary journals of discovery, and the disappointing reality of his first trip to Africa:

A great melancholy descended on me. Yes, this was the very spot. But there was no shadowy friend to stand by my side in the night of the enormous wilderness, no great haunting memory, but only the unholy recollection of a prosaic newspaper "stunt" and the distasteful knowledge of the vilest scramble for loot that ever disfigured the history of human conscience and geographical exploration. What an end to the idealized realities of a boy's daydreams! (*Last Essays*, p. 17)

And here he notes the contrast between his veneration for Livingstone, whom he has just described in this passage, and his disgust at Stanley's "newspaper stunt" that has cheapened and diminished the great man's intents. Livingstone, the last of the "militant geographers," could have been the African presence that would have ennobled Conrad's coming there, could have been the "shadowy friend," the "haunting memory" effaced by Stanley's stunt and by Conrad's own realization, seeing the Congo first hand, that in fact the professions of philanthropy that were taken up in the wake of such explorers as Livingstone were simply masquerades and served to disguise "the vilest scramble for loot…" (*Last Essays*, p. 17). Conrad used the adventure story and shaped his materials out of it, as he told his publisher (Blackburn (ed.), *Conrad's Letters*, p. 154), but in so doing subverted the conventional assumptions of that genre and demythologized the imperial subject as constructed by the adventure and travel writing of the day.

# Coda

While using the genre of adventure fiction to subvert certain major assumptions of the imperial subject as it had been constructed by the travel writing and the adventure fiction of the day, Conrad certainly did not challenge all of the myths central to that subject, as this study has shown. For example, he never seriously questioned the sexist and racist biases of the discourse. While Watt observes that Conrad subverts a stereotype of the exotic romance – "the notion that woman is the sublimely passive creature of Victorian convention" – in his depiction of, for example, Nina's aggressiveness (Watt, *Conrad*, p. 46), it is also true that the portrayals construct stereotypes of their own and that Conrad creates few, if any, living women.

Although a few individualized characters emerge from the Malayan fiction – Babalatchi, for one – Conrad's Africans are stereotypically, if sympathetically, depicted. And while Jeffrey Meyers finds that Marlow, and presumably Conrad, "commit[s] himself – emotionally and compassionately – to the Africans he encounters" (p. 60) in "Heart of Darkness," Achebe's charges of racism have great validity. Achebe contends that in "Heart of Darkness" Conrad depicts the Africans generally as speechless brutes, engaged in "mindless frenzy," and that he does so mainly in such dehumanized terms as "limbs or rolling eyes," and that the idea that "they" might claim a distant kinship with "us" repulses both Marlow and Conrad ("An Image of Africa," pp. 784–785). JanMohamed, in partial refutation of Achebe's argument notes that, after all, "Africans are an incidental part, and not the main objects of representation, in the novella" ("The Economy of Manichean Allegory," p. 71) – which is, in fact, very much to Achebe's point, that Africa for the colonial is simply a "setting and backdrop which eliminates the African as human factor" ("An Image of Africa," p. 788). In any case, Conrad's depiction of "them" reinscribes much of the racial

193

stereotyping essential to this fiction. While "they" are certainly not Haggard's fearsome warriors in either of Conrad's African fictions but rather victims of colonial intrusion and brutality, Conrad does nothing to disrupt the inevitable connection between "primitive," "intuitive," and "passionate."

However, in the various ways which this study has discussed, Conrad does work towards a de-construction, a dismantling, of the imperial myth as formulated by this fiction traditionally. Although in private letters, he admits an acceptance of British expansionism and a belief that Britain had indeed some attributes worth exporting, his fiction, in fact, depicts the European as a bungling or destructive intruder.[1] Lingard's incursions, while at least partially well intended, create more trouble than they solve and only add to the native rivalries and disputes. In Conrad's fiction, the white men in Africa – having come out for material gain – often succeed but only at the expense of the native. It is the European presence, we are made to feel here, that is responsible for the displacement and disruption of native peoples. In "An Outpost of Progress," neither Henry Price nor his wife are native to the district. The station men also have come from "a very distant part of the land" to serve "the cause of progress." Their displacement is made to explain their unhappiness – they miss their homeland, their families, familiar food – and their vulnerability to the native slavers from the coast. The Zanzibaris of "Heart of Darkness" whom Marlow meets, the lone mail carrier who travels between the coast and the station, the fireman and helmsman aboard Marlow's Congo steamer all have been subject to the displacing effects of imperialism, and all have been conscripted in the name of progress. However, no progress is to be seen; at least this fiction shows us none. Thus Conrad effectively challenges the heroic depiction of the white man in the tropics and exposes the imperial project as destructive.

From the vantage point of the 1990s, we might see Conrad's contributions to the demythologizing of imperialism as rather modest. We who have witnessed, from up close or afar, the brutal and chaotic aftermath of European expansionism in Africa and Asia, might find it difficult to credit earlier arguments for imperial expansion, or to admit the sincerity of its proponents who argued from other than economic necessity. But contemporary pronouncements were made with a force that was convincingly real; that they might constitute, in fact, a self-serving mythology was difficult to discern. Therefore, any move to oppose that hegemonic thinking, to see the subject anew in different terms than those already operating in the discourse of the day was remarkable. While he was certainly no revolutionary, then, Conrad's contribution to the disruption of the imperial subject as traditionally formulated was crucial.

In fact Conrad's subversion was a significant part of a larger shift underway at the time, all the more remarkable for the force of the dominant fiction it opposed. Although this willingness to view the imperial project in disinterested ways was reflected in the work of a growing number of writers, in its unpopularity and low visibility, it constituted something of an underground movement. Edward Garnett, the manuscript reader for Conrad's first publisher, Fisher Unwin, must have seen in Conrad's early work, which he welcomed and encouraged, uncommon ideas that resonated with his own. Since at least 1898, Garnett had hoped to start a new series – the Over-Seas Library – one which would make "no pretence at Imperial drum-beating, or putting English before Colonial opinion." It would aim, instead, "at getting the atmosphere and outlook of the new peoples recorded, if such is possible" (Karl, *Letters*, II, n. 61). Interested in writing about other lands, he meant to "challeng[e] – while exploit-ing – Kipling's readership" (Watts, *Deceptive Text*, p. 86). In various letters and reviews, he lauded W. H. Hudson's *The Purple Land* (1885) and his *Green Mansions* (1904), Olive Schreiner's *The Story of an African Farm* (1883), Mary Kingsley's *West African Studies* (1898), C. M. Doughty's *Arabia Deserta* (1888), and the travel sketches of Cunninghame Graham; he admired their ability to speak con-vincingly of other lands without any "spread-eagleism," and it was often his admiring articles about these works that won them any significant readership at all.[2] In May of 1898, while writing "Youth," and while engaged with the whole project as he then envisioned it of "Youth," "Heart of Darkness" and "Jim" making up a volume, Conrad had applauded Garnett's idea of a colonial series and his intention to include Graham's travel writing in the first volume (*Letters from Joseph Conrad*, p. 137). Garnett had proposed to Graham that his travel sketches and stories make up a first volume of the series, "an avowedly experimental series illustrating the life of English-speakers overseas" (Watts, *Deceptive Text*, pp. 169–171). Unfortu-nately, the experiment failed after a few volumes, but the awareness it expressed became more general.

While Garnett, and Conrad, were careful to distinguish Conrad's work from that of the early Robert Louis Stevenson, Garnett recognized that Stevenson's later fiction was attempting the same thing his Over-Seas Library aimed at. In a 1901 article, "The Contemporary Critic," he again argued for a kind of writing that recorded with accuracy, without imperial drum-beating, life in other lands. He spoke here of modern life's "fecundity, diversity, and complexity" that was reflected in a contemporary literature he commended for evincing a

sympathetic curiosity and keen inquiry as to the thousands of roads life is going. Wherever the civilized man places his foot, in whatsoever spot of the globe he finds his habitation, there is contemporary literature speedily recording *him*, and so adding to the old world's realization of its new life. (Garnett, *Friday Nights*, p. 364)

And here he instances, "Stevenson in the South Seas; Pierre Loti in Indo-China; Stephen Crane in Mexico; Joseph Conrad in Malaya; Henry Lawson in Australia" among others, as engaged in this commendable project.

In his *Travels with a Donkey*, Stevenson wrote that he had "been after an adventure all my life, a pure dispassionate adventure, such as befell early and heroic voyagers," and thus expressed an admiration familiar to Conrad also. And like Conrad's early fiction, Stevenson's late South Seas novels and stories, written from Samoa, challenged the possibility of such longed-for, dispassionate adventure, and recorded the dissolution of the dream of pure adventure. He too came to question the basic tenets of the literary genre that had traditionally promoted European expansionism, and he did so in a manner that undermined "the ethos of imperial England" (Menikoff, *Stevenson*, p. 98). In his South Seas fiction, "we" might be white-clad, but not necessarily the implacable forces for good depicted in Ballantyne or Henty. Even Haggard's heroes are exemplary in their way; after all, they have left behind them in England such dubious benefits as steam, telegraph and the penny post and have the good sense to see the problems intrinsic in such emblems of progress, and the work these heroes set about doing is applauded as responsible and constructive. In all the adventure fiction previous to Stevenson's, contact with the English has benefited the native; wrongs in this discourse have been righted by English power and know-how. White travellers from Masterman Ready to the boy heroes of Ballantyne and Henty have abolished the African slave trade, brought fire to the

benighted Patagonian Indians, restored native women to their
rightful husbands, and wrested usurpers from kingships not rightfully
theirs. Some of the heroes were even credentialed, like Haggard's
Captain Good of the Royal Navy who, along with those upstanding
members of the gentry, Quatermain and Curtis, restored the kingship
to Umslopagas and stayed on, selflessly, to improve native conditions.
They all represented the best England had to offer.

But in Stevenson's island fiction, there are no heroes, and thus the
subversion is closer to Conrad's. "We" are less than admirable; in
fact, opportunistic rascals and flotsam in various states of degeneration, having come out from England for various nefarious purposes,
abound in this fiction, and bring only disaster and disease to the
native population. That the British Empire had allowed to its
outposts the likes of Randall ( *The Beach of Falesá*, 1892), a sea-captain
"gone native," now drink-besotted and fly-covered, or Huish, (*Ebb
Tide*, 1893-4) the despicable cockney forerunner of Donkin, had not
previously been recorded in this discourse and certainly countered
the images in the popular press of the colonial endeavor. Rather than
promulgating stereotypes of the white man in the tropics, Stevenson
wanted to correct them, especially since he could see for himself they
no longer existed, if indeed they ever did. Another "romancer"
turned "realist," Stevenson meant to disabuse a misinformed home
audience through his "grimly realistic" "tough yarns" (Stevenson,
*Vailima Letters*, 1, p. 175). But while Haggard was criticized by some
for opposing Victorian sensibilities, Stevenson's *Beach* was actually
censored and was never printed, until recently, exactly as he wrote it.
Although the professed objection was its coarse language and sexual
explicitness, it was the amoral opportunism of the white traders in
Falesá and the unscrupulousness of European expansion generally
that was the more subversive revelation.[3] But finally, while *Almayer's
Folly* seems to take up in certain ways where *The Beach of Falesá* leaves
off, Conrad's criticism extends beyond Stevenson's. Both see the
native as the victim of imperial intrusions, but Stevenson's fiction
depicts an innocent, even romanticized, native whose paradise has
been lost by unscrupulous European intruders, a subversive but
somewhat simplified view that Conrad's fiction does not permit.
Imperial intrusions in Conrad's modernist texts enact a complex
reality in which the intruder is associated with a cause of purported
benevolence and is often a failed idealist himself, a kind of victim of
his own desires that have been shaped in complicated ways, and the

native, while indeed subjugated, even brutalized, is often not innocent and rarely romanticized.

Garnett must have realized that Stevenson's late fiction, while attempting the honest scrutiny that engaged Conrad, Crane, Schreiner, and Hudson, was creating an audience in many ways for Conrad's early novels that more openly spearheaded the generic subversion and more significantly demanded a new view of the imperial subject. With all these writers a shift had been initiated away from a monologic account of heroic action executed decisively by admirable Englishmen in imperial outposts, towards new, more complex and subversive tellings. That shift made possible the particular criticisms of such later British writers as Forster, Greene, Cary, and Waugh in whose colonial fictions the white men were ineffectual anti-heroes, complicit in but also victims of destructive colonial situations. Recent colonial fictions by white authors continue to record the complex consequences of the imperial venture and the far-reaching entanglements for both colonial and colonized alike. André Brink, Doris Lessing, Paul Scott, and Jean Rhys, are a few of those observers, some colonial sons and daughters themselves, whose many tellings proliferate the conversation Conrad so significantly contributed to and shaped. Like the work of recent Nobel Prize recipient, Nadine Gordimer, theirs has helped to break the silence long imposed on the Other.

Although she was a reader of adventure fiction – she is reported to have liked *King Solomon's Mines* in particular – Jean Rhys must have taken a sardonic interest in that fiction and its vision of benevolent, respected white men, the "rightful lords of all." As an uneducated, disinherited colonial daughter, she found the imperial promise to be empty, and her work marks a crucial departure from earlier colonial fictions. In the island world of *Wide Sargasso Sea* (1966), only colonialism's fallout is evident. Lords of nothing, "we" are "marooned," stigmatized and victimized in this imperial outpost, her fiction convincingly argues through the depiction of the Mason family's dissolution. But we would never recognize the place, Jamaica, if all we knew of it was what we had read in Victorian adventure fiction. That same setting had been quite differently depicted, as a place of gracious colonial life, exquisite balls, and genteel life in Marryat's fiction, for example. Ford's and Conrad's most successful collaboration, *Romance*, also posited a romantic, even glamorous West Indian setting, where bold British adventurers engaged with pirates and successfully overcame the various forces of evil ranged against them.[4] That it was primarily Ford's story, that it was written in a somewhat tongue-in-cheek manner and frequently discounted by Conrad notwithstanding, its existence be-speaks some ambivalence on Conrad's part, a nostalgia for a heroic past, and a regret that such adventure is over. But with Rhys's fiction, the possibility that such heroic adventure ever occurred becomes problematic, thus marking an important departure from the earlier subversions. The intermarriage, abandonment, isolation, exploitation, insanity, and suicide that characterize what remains of English life here in Spanish Town is meant to describe the Jamaica of 1839. Written as a kind of female counter-tale to Rochester's story in *Jane Eyre*, narrating the events of his life in Jamaica, but from Bertha's point of view predominantly, it confers speech and motive upon the madwoman in the attic, and at the same time corrects the Victorian telling of the imperial venture in a way that irrevocably transforms that subject for us.

In his *Predicament of Culture*, James Clifford speaks of the ways in which the independence movements of the mid-twentieth century contributed to

a new situation, one in which the "objects" of observation would begin to write back. The Western gaze would be met and scattered. Since 1950 Asians, Africans, Arab orientals, Pacific islanders, and Native Americans have in a variety of ways asserted their independence from Western cultural and political hegemony and established a new multivocal field of inter-cultural discourse. (p. 256)

Indeed, the abundant writings of the formerly colonized have repositioned and continue to richly inform this discourse. A thoroughly developed discussion of the particular contribution to these literatures Conrad's fiction makes is, obviously, beyond the scope of this study. But a brief mention of a few contemporary African writers, in particular, I believe will help to better contextualize Conrad's place in this discourse. Chinua Achebe, Bessie Head, Amos Tutuola, Ngugi wa Thiong'o, and Buchi Emecheta are only a few of the African writers now familiar to western audiences. But as early as 1930, Solomon Plaatje's *Mhudi* had broken the silence. By historicizing the Mfecane – the dispersal of British and Boer incursions into southern Africa of the area's various ethnic groups – *Mhudi* writes back at an imperial discourse by demythologyzing the fable of "primitive man's" timelessness. Outside intrusions and iron-age expansion explain these wars of wandering, not timeless carnage and bestiality (also see Davidson, *Africa in History*, pp. 232ff.). By dramatizing the Boer's religious hypocrisy, racism, and opportunistic treachery, by denouncing the devastating effects of the "fantastic invasion" generally, and by depicting the "inarticulate savage," so strangely silent under western eyes, as movingly eloquent, Plaatje effectively retells the story.

Similarly, Chinua Achebé's *Things Fall Apart* (1958) scattered the Western gaze by disturbing the hegemonic depiction of pre-colonial Africa as a place of squalor and anarchy, a place of darkness it was the white man's burden to illuminate. Here the "bush" is home to a group of Ibo, a multitudinous people whose complex social organization, religious beliefs, government practices and law intricately structure and give meaning to their lives, thus refuting all those travellers and writers who had complained that Africans had no religion, no government, no culture. Again by insisting on the actual historical moment in the late nineteenth-century when English missionaries first came to Nigeria – along with their colonial administrators and soldiers – and viewing this invasion from the point of view of the many Ibo individuals we have come to know throughout *Things Fall Apart*, the novel effectively Others the European and decenters his monologic discourse. Having just ordered the Ibo protagonist's execution, the District Commissioner, at novel's end, muses over the book he will write, *The Pacification of the Primitive Tribes of the Lower Niger*. But of course the novel itself exposes just how deaf to alternative voices the D.C.'s imperial discourse is, and its "difference" provides an ironic rejoinder to every (by now familiar) assumption underlying his contentment at bringing civilization to Africa (see Brantlinger, *Rule of Darkness*, chapter 10). Rather, the Ibo, and we, see that things, indeed, have fallen apart. In the context of post-colonial African writing, Achebe's novel makes the former colonial discourse – Hanning Speke's reading of Africa, for example – untenable.

A similar Kurtz-like colonial administrator gone out to Africa, a devout believer in *Pax Brittania*, reduced to exclamations of "Eliminate the vermin!" is depicted in *A Grain of Wheat* (1967). By situating his novel a few days before Independence, Kenyan writer Ngugi wa Thiong'o provides a historical context for Mau Mau, referred to elsewhere by Ngugi as The Kenya Land and Freedom Army (Ngugi,

*Decolonising the Mind*, p. 24). *A Grain of Wheat* images Mau Mau members as fighters for freedom against British oppression and reveals the historic roots of the disorders they were involved in, "the population transfers, the policies of 'reserve,' of gerrymandering, and of forced production, the negation of indigenous legal systems and religions, and, ultimately, the denial of the validity of indigenous cultures," as JanMohamed chronicles the devastation of colonialism (*Manichean Aesthetics*, pp. 2–3). Historicizing the agitation for Independence repositions the discussion and provides a clearer understanding of oppression, past and present. Here Ngugi strips away the euphemistic intentions of that familiar image of imperial discourse – that of the Imperial mother protecting her grateful colonial children – to expose, in the name of that "protection" the villages burned, the curfews enforced, and the "enemies" imprisoned.

That Conrad's work contributed significantly to the "writing back" of decolonization is attested to by such writers as Ngugi himself whose writing has been compared to that of Conrad. He notes the importance to him as a writer, of *Nostromo* – his "favorite" – in its multiple points of view, its disrupted chronology and delayed information (Ngugi, *Decolonising the Mind*, p. 76). According to University of Zambia Lecturer Ponnuthurai Sarvan, some have found traces of *Lord Jim* in Ngugi's *A Grain of Wheat*, while he himself undertakes a close analysis of the ways in which *Under Western Eyes* informs Ngugi's novel. Sarvan attributes Conrad's influence on formerly colonized, particularly African writers, to two causes in particular. In the first place, Sarvan contends, these writers must have recognized in Conrad their own disillusionment following Independence, specifically "his opinion that revolutions are often betrayed by success, and that power and materialism erode ideals and principles" (Sarvan, "African Eyes," p. 153). He notes also that "Conrad is an inspiration to the African writer who ventures to express himself through a foreign linguistic medium," in Conrad's case, his third language. Rather than granting him membership in Leavis's Great Tradition, they claim Conrad as a fellow polyglot and exile, writing from the margins.

Even though Ngugi has been writing in Kikuyu since 1980, his first works were in English, as have been the works of many African writers who have chosen not to write in their native language, among them Chinua Achebe, Wole Soyinka, and Peter Nazareth. Nazareth, an Ugandan writer, claims to have been put on to Conrad by Ngugi. The Polish exile writing in English began "to make sense" to the Goan Ugandan reading at Leeds University. He describes himself at the time as being in the midst of a "breakdown" occasioned by Ugandan Independence the year before, "a psychic dissolution of the fixed world I had known and taken for granted." He claims that it was Conrad and Frantz Fanon, neither of whom had "made sense" to him formerly, who now helped him break apart [his] old perception of the world and to re-educate [him]self almost from scratch ("Out of Darkness," p. 173). In Nazareth's opinion, Conrad disturbed the "glass dome" colonialism had imposed over the colonial world. To Nazareth's thinking, Conrad broke up that "monolithic worldview" and made the language which had been imposed and had carried that monolithic worldview "less inevitable, more tentative" (p. 174).

Countering Achebe's and Wilson Harris's charges of racism in Conrad, Nazareth instead points out Conrad's essentially subversive quality and, in fact, the irony of his inclusion in the colonial curricula.

There was censorship in the colonial world: no Marx or Lenin. But there was Conrad, sneaking through as a member of Leavis's Great Tradition, actually undermining that tradition. Jane Austen's characters in *Mansfield Park* could live a luxurious life while the patriarch left for the colonies; Conrad actually takes us to the colonies to show us what happened there when the patriarch or his agents arrived and how his wealth at home came from brutal colonial action. Conrad was therefore a mental liberator: not only for those blinded at home but also for those who were to come later, the colonized elite wearing the eyes of Europe. (p. 178)

Interestingly, over eighty years later, Nazareth notices the same subversion at work in Conrad's fiction that Garnett had written about, and does so in similar terms. Both notice, and in Conrad's own image of "making us see," that he had effected an "unblurring." The shift Nazareth makes here is in understanding the importance of restoring clearsightedness not just to the metropolitan audience, but more urgently to those colonized who themselves had consumed the monolithic view of the dominant discourse.

Such also is the concern of Homi Bhabha who writes of the scatterings that become gatherings in the nations of others, and focuses particularly on the problems inherent in narrating those nations. He too sees that the project must be a disruptive and dialogic one, to expose the enterprise as other than monologic (see "DissemiNation"). He points to such disruptions as Houston Baker's reading of the Harlem Renaissance, one that employs and extends the metaphor of writers as warriors engaged in "radical maroonage." Such acts of resistance and subversion are required in dismantling the stereotypes constructed by the imperial discourse, stereotypes especially difficult to dislodge because "interiorized," as Eagleton observes. Such a destruction constitutes the necessary first step of decolonization (Deane, *Nationalism*, p. 10).[5]

But it was Conrad's early fiction, whose many voices undermined the monologic telling, that anticipated and enabled this transformation. Although initially slow-selling and mis-read by many as adventure fiction *manqué*, it nonetheless came to occasion new views of the imperial subject. A reformulation, it subverted generic expectations and disturbed the hegemonic construction in place, convincingly insisting that the exotic, as a category constructed by the dominant colonial discourse, no longer served imperial purposes.

# Notes

## I CONSTRUCTING THE IMPERIAL SUBJECT

1 John Gordan discusses the extent to which Conrad borrowed from Brooke, noting that although Conrad never directly mentioned him, the English Rajah's influence was apparent, especially in *Lord Jim*. Gordan is not only a rich source of information about Brooke but also convincingly illustrates that Jim's experiences in Patusan closely follow Brooke's in Sarawak. (Gordan, *Joseph Conrad*, pp. 64–73). The major difference remains that Brooke left Sarawak in far better condition than Jim left Patusan, thus marking a diminishment in imperial accomplishments. C. T. Watts, writing six years after Gordan, argues, on the basis of more recent evidence, for additional influences of Brookiana on Conrad (p. 209). See below, chapter 5.

The writing of Alfred Russel Wallace, who so nearly anticipated Darwin, comprised Conrad's "favorite bedside" reading, according to Richard Curle. In an article that takes Curle's observation as a starting place, Florence Clemens demonstrates the extent of Conrad's debt to Wallace by comparing passages from Wallace with passages from Conrad's various Malaysian fictions. Quoting Curle, Clemens writes "[*The Malay Archipelago*] was [Conrad's] favorite bedside companion. He had an intense admiration for those pioneer explorers – 'profoundly inspired men' as he called them – who have left us a record of their work; and of Wallace, above all, he never ceased to speak in terms of enthusiasm. Even in conversation he would amplify some remark by observing, 'Wallace says so-and-so,' and *The Malay Archipelago* had been his intimate friend for many years" (Clemens, "Bedside Book," p. 305).

2 Alan Moorehead has recently concurred that the European imports of "doctors, priests, administrators and policemen," constituted a "fatal impact" upon the peoples of the South Pacific. "If they had been left undisturbed they might have gone on forever without [those "gifts"], and at the time of Cook's arrival they were probably happier than they were ever to be again" (Moorehead, *Fatal Impact*, p. 3).

3 These writers did well to maintain their "informational," eye-witness reportorial stance, for the problem of incredulity had been a real one, apparently, for returning travellers. James Bruce's reports from Abys-

sinia were often met with disbelief. Boswell writes that when Dr. Johnson spoke with Bruce on the subject of his "extraordinary travels," Johnson "had not listened to him with that full confidence, without which there is little satisfaction in the society of travellers" (James Boswell's *Life of Johnson*, p. 606). Mungo Park, according to H. C. Adams in his *The Wonder Book of Travellers' Tales*, told Sir Walter Scott that he would not publish the facts of his adventures he had just related to Scott, facts Scott found "far more striking and interesting than any which [Park] had published," for fear they would not be believed. (Adams, *Wonder Book*, p. 128). And even Cook, who had also worked for veracity through a factual, unadorned presentation, was subject to disbelief and even parody. Again, according to Adams, *The Surprising Adventures of Baron Munchausen* (1785) lampooned Cook and some of his reported adventures – i.e. "The stoppage of the leak," and "The wonderful bird's nest" – along with satirizing Bruce and several other celebrated travellers' accounts. The current of disbelief attested to by such reports and parodies presented a real problem to subsequent travellers and provided them with a powerful motive to appear credible and objective; their writing had to defend itself against such disbelief in order to gain the support needed for continued exploration/colonization.

## 2 ADVENTURE FICTION

1 The enemies of public libraries, that is, free libraries supported by public rates, in the 1870s, 80s, and 90s often compared those public libraries to public houses; the one was declared to be as great a cause of wasted lives as the other (Altick, *Common Reader*, pp. 232–233). See Louis James, *Fiction for the Working Man* for the availability and variety of working-class fiction.

2 The story that Rhodes was in the audience that day at Oxford in 1870 and upon hearing Ruskin's call to duty set off for South Africa with fire in his eyes is such an irresistible one that it survives in spite of the fact that he had already returned to Kimberly when Ruskin delivered this lecture, the first in his Slade professorship at Oxford. Rhodes had been at Oxford earlier and returned in 1873. Although he was not present for the lecture, however much we would like him to have been, the lecture was written, published and much discussed.

3 The creator of that eternal youth, Peter Pan, attests in his Introduction to the 1913 edition of *The Coral Island* to his admiration for Ballantyne: "[He] was for long my man, and I used to study a column in *The Spectator* about 'forthcoming books,' waiting for his next as for the pit door to open." And the excitement generated by Ballantyne's adventures survived, for Barrie, into adulthood. He goes on to recall his anticipation of meeting, at his "solemn London club...a learned American who had vowed that he would show me how to make a fire as Jack made it in *The Coral Island*. We adjourned to the library (where we knew we were not

likely to be disturbed), and there from concealed places about his person, he produced Jack's implements... in half a minute my friend had made fire, at which we lit our cigars and smoked to the memory of Ballantyne and *The Coral Island*" (*CI*, pp. vi–viii).

4 These cited examples are from copies in my possession; see bibliography.

5 Jeffrey Meyers' study, *Fiction and the Colonial Experience*, considers the colonial novels of Greene, along with those of Conrad, Kipling, Forster, and Cary as comprising one of two distinct "streams"; the other, he claims, is made up of the adventure fiction of Haggard, Henty, Buchan, and the early Kipling, among others. As I argue throughout, it is Conrad's fiction in large part that causes the initial divergence, but the streams are intimately related, nonetheless. Greene, in his *Journey Without Maps*, follows consciously in both Haggard's and Conrad's steps. Early in that work, he speaks of the attractions that motivated his trip to Africa, the willingness "to suffer some discomfort for the chance of finding – there are a thousand names for it, King Solomon's Mines, the 'heart of darkness'..." (p. 19). Towards the conclusion, he remarks again: "The need, of course, has always been felt, to go back and begin again. Mungo Park, Livingstone, Stanley, Rimbaud, Conrad represented only another method to Freud's, a more costly, less easy method, calling for physical as well as mental strength. The writers Rimbaud and Conrad were conscious of this purpose, but one is not certain how far the explorers knew the nature of the fascination which worked on them in the dirt, the disease, the barbarity and the familiarity of Africa" (p. 248). Behind Greene's trip to Africa is Conrad's, but behind Conrad – for Greene, as for so many other readers – is African travel writing and the adventure fiction of Haggard.

### 3 THEM AND US

1 Edward Said examines at some length the quality of Kim's attractiveness for contemporary readers surrounded as they were by fictional Judes, in particular, whose every desire was doomed. How compelling, then, must have appeared Kim's world, so optimistic, full of possibilities and success, available – the point is clear – only to the racially privileged chamaleon Kim. (*Kim*, pp. 37–43).

2 Impatience with the complexities of democratic morality can be seen in Kingsley's championing of Sir James Brooke who, although he had just been knighted in 1848, was also being censured in the House of Commons for his "inhumane treatment of the Dyaks" in suppressing piracy in the Malayan archipelago and civil strife in Sarawak (Uffelman, *Kingsley*, p. 24). Kingsley wrote to Brooke in sympathy and was moved similarly to dedicate to the Rajah his current work, *Westward Ho!* Both the occasion for the book, the Crimean War, and Brooke's censure were examples, for Kingsley, of the home government's mismanagement, and of its utter lack of understanding of and support

for its forces in the field, those soldiers – among whom he would number Brooke – who were carrying on the actual, manly work of empire. In a letter Brooke wrote back to Kingsley in 1859, ten years after his initial successes in Sarawak, he echoes Kingsley's own dissatisfactions with the inefficiencies of the present government:

> My life is pretty well at its dregs, and I shall be glad indeed to pass the few remaining months or years in quiet, and free from the anxieties which must beset the post I have occupied, but which of late years have been increased tenfold, owing to the course or rather no course pursued by the Government. It is a sad but true experience, that everything has succeeded with the natives, and everything has failed with the English in Borneo. (*Westward Ho!*, p. 221)

Brooke's vow made twenty years earlier – "Fortune and life I give freely, and if I fail in the attempt, I shall not have lived wholly in vain" – envisioned native resistance as the source of possible failure, rather than government bungling. That irony, if true, is very much to Kingsley's point.

3 Although the slave trade within the British empire had been outlawed in 1807, the abolition of slavery already in those colonies was the work of the Abolition Society many years later. Under their leadership's influence in Parliament, a law was passed in 1833 freeing all slaves in British colonies after a one to seven year period of enforced apprenticeship and with compensation to their owners, £37 10s per slave (Thomson, *England in the Nineteenth Century*, p. 89; Bourne, *Palmerston*, pp. 623). Oliver speaks of Marryat's unsuccessful attempt to stand for Parliament in the Reform interest in 1833; voters found his stand on the slavery issue less than satisfactory. Oliver instances the time "when attacked on the slavery question, which affected his family's fortunes in the West Indies, [Marryat] parried the thrust by saying: 'When I look to the factory and find infants working in penury and misery for seventeen hours a day, how can I pass by such a scene and think of the black slave?'" (pp. 88, 89). This evasiveness seems to have cost him the election, but he had already made his position clear the year before in *Newton Forster*, a novel that depicted well-cared for, happy slaves on a Barbadian slave plantation. As Brantlinger's discussion of that novel reveals, it constituted an elaborate argument against the slave trade and for the continuation of slavery (*Rule of Darkness*, p. 6of).

4 Nerlich suggests that the naturalizing assumption here "that people are born masters or slaves" had been at work at least since Hobbes' *The Leviathan* (1651) and Bernard de Mandeville's *Fable of the Bees* (1714). Again, as he argues throughout, adventure validated exploitation and made natural the domination of the strong over the weak (Nerlick, *Ideology*, pp. 206–208).

5 Writing here a few years before mid-century, Ballantyne anticipates the great interest in cannibalism Victorian writers increasingly took after 1850. Although writing about Africa, Jablow and Hammond's obser-

vations pertain to British imperial efforts world-wide: "In the imperial
period writers were far more addicted to tales of cannibalism than the
Africans ever were to cannibalism." They report on Stanley's "zealous
horror of anthropophagy" which led him to repeat "every tale of
cannibal tribes that he heard in addition to creating quite a number of
his own." Winwood Reade [a populizer of travel accounts in Africa]
"sprinkled cannibals about West Africa rather like raisins in a cake" (p.
94). Such an insistence in the discourse on "their" savagery, according
to Brantlinger, helped justify "our" civilizing endeavors, i.e. intrusion
and conquest ("Victorians and Africans," p. 184).

6 Andrew Lang was originally among those who agreed with Tylor. But
his thinking underwent changes during the century's last decades. For
one thing, he read *West African Studies* (1899) by Mary Kingsley
(Charles' niece), and was impressed with her conclusion that "The final
object of all human desire is a knowledge of the nature of God" (p. 95).
As will Lang in his *Magic and Religion* (1901), she refutes Tylor's basic
assumptions: "Although a Darwinian to the core, I doubt if evolution in
a neat and tidy perpendicular line, with Fetish at the bottom and
Christianity at the top, represents the true state of things. It seems to me
– I have no authority to fortify my position with, so it is only me – that
things are otherwise in this matter" (p. 101).

7 Adventure fiction, in fact, worked to dislodge early and mid-Victorian
complacency toward the imperial project, which, especially in Africa,
was highly controversial. In the 40s, Rajah James Brooke's argument for
settlement in Borneo as opposed to coastal West Africa, "the white
man's grave," was a powerfully convincing one to many Victorians.
And Lady Jane Franklin's view, a decade later, that exploration in
Africa's interior was ill-advised was shared by many.

8 This passage goes on to privilege the adventurer especially in contrast
with those other prominent figures of the day, Haggard's targets, the
financier and the politician:

> "Adventurer" – he who goes out to meet what ever may come. Well, that is
> what we all do in the world one way or another, and, speaking for myself, I am
> proud of the title, because it implies a brave heart and a trust in Providence.
> Besides, when many and many a noted Croesus, at whose feet the people
> worship, and many and many a time-serving and word-coining politician are
> forgotten, the names of those grand-hearted old adventurers who have made
> England what she is, will be remembered and taught with love and pride to little
> children whose unshaped spirits yet slumber in the womb of centuries to be.
> (p. 81)

Such opportunism, even English, does not distinguish "one of us,"
Haggard implies. In his opposing disinterested adventure to other, more
self-serving endeavors, he echoes R. L. Stevenson and anticipates
Conrad.

9 Is Haggard remembering Speke's account of his initial reception at the
court of Mtésa, King of Uganda? That Speke chose not to sit on the

ground or prostrate himself in the customary way amazed all present and terrified those who were concerned for his well-being. But, as he relates:

I had made up my mind never to sit upon the ground as the natives and Arabs are obliged to do, nor to make my obeisance in any other manner than is customary in England... I felt that if I did not stand up for my social position at once, I should be treated with contempt during the remainder of my visit, and thus lose the vantageground I had assumed of appearing rather as a prince than a trader...

And of course, Mtésa recognized Speke's superiority and consented to his bringing with him and sitting upon his own iron stool. His "point gained," Speke "rejoic[ed] in [his] victory" (*Journal*, p. 283).

10 Haggard was not alone in heeding the warning of Gobineau and others against miscegenation. In his four volume work *Essai sur l'Inégalité des Races Humains* (1853–55), Joseph-Arthur, Comte de Gobineau – himself an embattled royalist – wrote that Aryan societies would flourish as long as they remained pure, and that civilizations would weaken and fall through racial mixing. This quasi-scientific thinking was the common property of many late nineteenth-century Europeans. Tragically, the thinking survived and flourished in Hitler's Germany, and also in South Africa. The Immorality Act of 1927, prohibiting "ancestral mingling" or "carnal intercourse between European and African" was one of apartheid's first laws. It was amended in 1950 to prohibit "carnal intercourse between White and any non-White." In 1957 the penalty was increased to seven years imprisonment.

### 4 THE SHIFT TOWARD SUBVERSION

1 In 1892, Coventry Patmore, author of *The Angel in the House*, a long poem that celebrated married love, wrote Henley objecting to the "peculiar and... uneconomical allusions to sex" he found in Henley's poetry and in the articles Henley chose to include in the *Observer*, and that since his own wife and daughters were "only decent Englishwomen," he felt it necessary to exclude the *Observer* from their home at Lymington. Henley replied that he was sorry "the N.O. is no longer to be read *chez vous*," but also "sorry for Lymington this week. For Greenwood (once more with us) [was] in his best form, and Blank and Dash and Three Stars and the others [were] 'equal to themselves!!'" (Buckley, *William Ernest Henley*, p. 156). Although Henley prided himself on his anti-Grundy forthrightness, and indeed offended the Victorian sensibilities of Patmore and others, some readers found him timid and conventional. In a consolatory letter to Cunninghame Graham, Conrad accuses Henley, now editor of the *New Review*, in July of 1898, of being "a horrible bourgeois" for refusing to publish Graham's *Aurora la Cujini: A Realistic Sketch in Seville*, a story about a legendary gypsy dancer. Whether it was the references to lesbianism, sweaty arm-pits and the aphrodisiac effects of blood which

had made it hard to find a publisher (Karl, *Letters*, II, n. 80), or some other objection that deterred Henley isn't clear. In any case, two months later in October of '98, Conrad wrote Henley a letter of gratitude for giving him his "chance" when he accepted "Nigger" for serial publication in his *New Review* (Karl, *Letters*, pp. 106–110). Conrad was a comparatively unknown writer at the time, to Henley, and Conrad's appreciation of Henley's encouragement of new talent is an acknowledgement of the courage that generally characterised Henley's editorial career.

2 It is Todd G. Willy's contention that "Henley's role in the shaping of [*The Nigger of the "Narcissus"*] was not at all limited to being admired from afar... and that actually the fiction "was consciously tailored by its author to meet the particular sensibilities of a single reader," Henley himself (Willy, "Conquest," p. 163). Disconcerted by cooling relations with his first publisher, T. Fisher Unwin, Conrad wrote Garnett that he would next try Henley. Conrad knew that Henley's response to his first two novels had been disapproving, at least of the few chapters he had been able to get through. So he was determined – according to Willy – to write as a member of the regatta of the "Commodore of the Victorian literatti." Thus he wrote an anti-sentimental tale of manly, "hairy-chested" action, and followed the formula of Henley's gunboats that "aimed their torpedoes" at sentimental, liberal reformers and "rose-water revolutionists" (Willy, "Conquest," p. 169). After Henley's acceptance of the story, Conrad steered "away from Henley's wake," but, as Willy points out, precisely how far, and how intentionally, remains a matter of contention (p. 179).

3 During the early years of the First World War, Haggard confided to his diary many such thoughts; he felt the war was beneficial and took some satisfaction in it as a fulfillment of his warnings:

In some ways I think the war is doing good in England. It is bringing the people, or some of them, face to face with elementary facts which hitherto it has been the fashion to ignore and pretend are non-existent. To take one very humble example. How often have I been vituperated by rose-water critics because I have written of fighting and tried to inculcate certain elementary lessons, such as that it is a man's duty to defend his country, and that only those who are prepared for war can protect themselves and such as are dear to them. 'Course! bloody! brutal! Uncivilised!' such has been the talk. (Haggard, *Private Diaries*, pp. 21–22)

4 Elsewhere also Haggard implies the degeneracy of the English civilian population by celebrating the magnificence of Zulu and of German military efficiency. In *Cetywayo and his White Neighbors* (1882) that he wrote upon his return from South Africa, he describes the Zulu military system as the "universal-service system of Germany brought to an absolute perfection, obtained by subordinating all the ties and duties of civil life to military ends" (p. 21). This book was presented as "a candid on-the-scene report of conditions at a significant time in South Africa's

history, an analysis of the forces operating to shape its future," but was largely disregarded by "Whitehall, where Haggard sought most of all to exert influence" (Cohen, *RK to RH*). Undoubtedly that inattention was due in large part to the anti-democratic impulse implicit within the book. Wendy Katz adds that the criticism became more overt after the Boer War, particularly in *Ayesha* (1905) and *Queen Sheba's Ring* (1910). In the first decade of the century, Katz remarks,

the perceived threats of degeneracy from within and invasion from without were intensified, due mainly to military humiliations suffered during the Boer War, German domination of South West Africa, German designs on Delagoa Bay on Africa's eastern coast, and a general strain on Anglo-German relations. Moreover, Haggard's sense of the degeneration of the race and its attendant lack of military consciousness made decadence a prime target for attack. (Katz, *Rider Haggard*, p. 46).

5 JanMohamed's observations about Isak Dinesen pertain here, for although Dinesen did not arrive in Africa until 1914, her responses sound rather like those of Haggard and his heroes. She and her friends, Denys Finch-Hatton and Berkeley Cole "set up an idyllic pantisocracy in the 'white' Highlands" of Kenya, according to JanMohamed. They enjoyed their roles as aristocrats – she was a baroness, after all – and saw themselves as feudal rulers in this African Eden. In rejecting industrialized civilization with its bourgeois commercial and mechanistic values, they chose to "exalt the freedom of the untamed." Like Haggard, her ire was reserved for the middle-class settlers, colonial bureaucrats and missionaries whose attempts to instill "respectability" in the natives she found objectionable. She dealt with her Gikuyu "squatters" unhampered by the more cumbersome democratic workings that would pertain at home, but she took her role as a responsible feudal ruler quite seriously – as their doctor, mother, father, provider, judge and coun-selor. As JanMohamed points out here in his very even-handed analysis of Dinesen's writings, generous and compassionate as she was toward the native, it was the colonial situation itself based as it was on a fundamental inequality that enabled her largesses. After all, in Kenya, as in South Africa, rich farming lands had been deemed "vacant" and claimed as "Crown property." Their lands, in effect confiscated, the Gikuyu were confined to "reserves," and the land was given to European, particularly English, investors and farmers. As a result, "for both the moderate-size farmer, such as Dinesen (6,000 acres) and the larger farmer, such as Lord Delamare (1 million acres), this meant the creation of a new feudal culture" (JanMohamed, *Manichean Aesthetics*, p. 57). Without quite acknowledging it, she benefited from the colonial situation with its manichean oppositions of "white and black, good and evil, salvation and damnation, civilization and savagery, superiority and inferiority, intelligence and emotion, self and other, subject and object" (*Manichean Aesthetics*, p. 4).

6 Sometimes Haggard takes aim at both targets at once, government

bungling and commercialism. Katz points to *Jess* (1887) as such a work that not only quite specifically attacks Gladstone's policy during the first Boer War, but also "opens fire upon English commercialism, the spirit-destroying force, for Haggard, in late nineteenth century England" (Katz, *Rider Haggard*, p. 53).

7 Anticipating Guerard's reading of Conrad's *Heart of Darkness* as "the journey within," Freud and Jung both read Haggard's fictional treks into Africa as voyages from the known into the unconscious, unknown self, beyond the frontiers of Victorian taboos and away from civilization and its discontents (Etherington, *Rider Haggard*, pp. 53, 54).

8 Patrick Brantlinger refers to Haggard's romances as "Imperial Gothic," fictions in which "the savage in us all under the civilized skin" is celebrated and industrialism is condemned. Another essentially subversive aspect of Haggard's gothicism, Brantlinger contends, is his interest in the occult – much of Haggard's writing today is catalogued in libraries and book stores as science fiction – thus marking another vein in his thinking that countered the prevailing scientific rationalism of progressive Victorian thought. (See Brantlinger, *Rule of Darkness*, chapter 8, "Imperial Gothic: Atavism and the Occult in the British Adventure Novel, 1880–1914").

## 5 TRAVEL WRITING AND ADVENTURE FICTION

1 Conrad frequently disparages "boys' adventure tales" as dangerous fictions. As early as 1896, he was defending his *Nigger of the 'Narcissus'* from possible accusations of "lack of incident." "The incomplete joy, the incomplete sorrow, the incomplete rascality or heroism – the incomplete suffering" is life, he argued in a letter to Garnett. Only in "a boy's book of adventures" do events occur otherwise (Karl, *Letters*, 1, p. 321). For Lord Jim, equipped for "the world of adventure" by "a course of light holiday literature," the ideals of heroism there espoused will prove fatal. But even the criticism often carries with it a sympathetic attachment. In Conrad's later story, "The Secret Sharer," the doppelgänger figure – another son of a country parson and Conway boy of whom so much was expected, another "one of us" who fell short of the heroic ideal – asks the captain to maroon him on the nearest island. The captain/narrator's protest, "Maroon you! We are not living in a boy's adventure tale" (*'Twixt Land and Sea Tales*, p. 131), reflects the ambivalence Conrad often reveals on the subject of idealized heroism, for indeed the captain does maroon him and saves them both in so doing.

2 Murray Pittock in his "Rider Haggard and *Heart of Darkness*" makes a compelling case for Haggard's influence on Conrad's writing, especially, discernable, Pittock claims, in "Heart of Darkness" and Haggard's *She*. In both fictions, the central character has "desire on a 'collosal scale'" and both inspire duty, even love. Both stories, Pittock continues, concern journeys into mysterious interiors via a river, in order to meet a

mysterious character in the heart of Africa. While this plot does describe
the archetypical hero's journey, the specifics here do resonate for readers
of Conrad.

3 John A. McClure's *Kipling and Conrad* (1981) focuses on the "colonial
struggles" central to both writers' fictions. While, he maintains, Conrad
is "against the whole [colonial] venture," and Kipling "is a strong
defender of the idea of colonial domination," both "elucidate the
painful contradictions of the colonialist's situation" (pp. 2–4).

4 The influence on Conrad of Cutcliffe Hyne in particular and the exotic
magazine fiction of the 1890's in general is the focus of Richard Ruppel's
"*Heart of Darkness* and the Popular Exotic Stories of the 1890's." In this
article he describes at some length a Hyne story remarkable for its
similarity to Conrad's later novella to show the ways in which Conrad's
fiction participated in the imperial discourse of the late nineteenth-
century, often through compliance but sometimes through opposition.

5 Reynold Humphries sees a further connection between Conrad and
Almayer. Both suffered similar identity problems, he claims; that is,
Conrad anglicized both his own name and Olmeijer's, and both forsook
their native languages, and identities, for English. That Almayer speaks
English rather than Malay or Arabic, the foreign languages available to
him, confirms his identification with "father" Lingard and thus with
imperial Britain, Humphries convincingly argues. But his contention
that Conrad submerged his former identity and Polish past similarly to
take on the language and the point of view of imperial Britain, is more
problematic. Of course, Conrad "chose" English for a multitude of
reasons, and his identification with imperial Britain was less complete
than Humphries argues, as I try to demonstrate throughout this study
(see Humphries, "Discourse," p. 128).

6 *ALMAYER'S FOLLY*

1 Peter Knox-Shaw contends that *An Outcast of the Islands* in particular, but
I would argue *Almayer's Folly* as well, refused to behave like other fictions
in the "desert island genre" that in other ways it superficially
resembled; in so doing he provides another clue to the early mis-reading
of Conrad's first fictions. He uses Ballantyne's *The Coral Island* as the
representative desert island fiction for its view of the Coral Island as
edenic, unfallen. The only problem with this paradise for Ballantyne, is,
of course, the natives themselves. "With such vehemence does Ballantyne denigrate his Melanesians (all his islanders are black), that every
intrusion into their preserve appears as an advance for the cause of
heaven," according to Knox-Shaw (*Explorer*, p. 121). And, as he shows,
every action the English heroes undertake is to restore that which is
"natural" – babies to their mothers, wives to their "rightful" husbands.
In Conrad's "desert-island" fiction, the "intruders" of course do
nothing of the kind. In the fallen world of Conrad's early fiction, no such

restoration of order is possible, Knox-Shaw maintains. In *An Outcast of the Islands*, in particular, he argues, Conrad "dismantles Providence," rather than portraying imperial outposts as edenic or the imperial intruders as providential (see Knox-Shaw, *Explorer*, chapter 6).

2 The century's three Reform Bills – of 1832, 1867 and 1884 – plus the Education Act of 1870 all served to steadily widen the franchise, effectively creating new and diverse readerships throughout the century. This growth can also be measured by the proliferation, already discussed, of periodical literature whose numbers multiplied increasingly towards the end of the century. In particular, the Reform Bill of 1884 had "enfranchized two million new voters in Great Britain and half a million in Ireland, bringing the total electorate to over four million" (Karl, *Letters*, I, p. 16). See also Amy Cruse's *The Victorians and Their Reading*, Louis James' *Fiction and the Working Man, 1830–1850*, and Margaret Dalziel's *Popular Fiction 100 Years Ago*.

3 As most readers today rightly contend, Conrad's writing appears to share the racist and ethnocentric qualities of most of his contemporaries. My argument throughout is that Conrad was one of the first writers of colonial discourse even to suggest that the formerly silenced had a voice or a point of view at all that could be, and needed to be, represented, oppositional as it might be. Prepared to identify with his host country, his British bias did not prevent him from challenging the assumptions underlying that country's dominant discourse nor from effectively beginning the work of dismantling the "naturalness" of the imperial endeavor.

4 We also can recognize in Conrad's Malay fiction the stereotyping of "the East" and of "the Arab" that, as Edward Said's study demonstrates, is written into the discourse of Orientalism. Here Conrad contributes to that constructed category, "the Orient," through his depiction of Abdullah, characteristically making his salaams, and Rashid, usually depicted pulling his neatly trimmed beard. However, Conrad's depiction of them as conniving, untrustworthy and self-serving are traits shared – to Almayer's thinking – by Almayer's other competitors, the Malays: "there was no mercy to be expected from Arab or Rajah; no rice to be got on credit in the times of scarcity from either" (p. 27). In fact, Adbullah's presence, with his substantial gowdowns and many clerks, seems more "natural" than that of the English or Dutch. It pre-dates and certainly survives Almayer's presence in Sambir.

## 7 AN OUTCAST OF THE ISLANDS

1 Related to this idea is the static view of the Other – timeless and unchanging – juxtaposed with the colonizer's dynamism and progressiveness achieved with the metaphor of time-travel, implied in Willems' susceptibility to the wilderness and made explicit in "Heart of Darkness." There Marlow imagines himself travelling back in time to

"the first ages of man," as he steams up the river into the heart of the continent. For Marlow, and Conrad, his relationship to that original, primitive condition is an uneasy one. Unlike Gauguin or Lawrence, Conrad did not think of such a journey as "going home." It might represent origins, but they are to be left behind. It constitutes a force to be resisted. Africa's heart – essence – is dark because it is so unevolved, so "original" and therefore uncivilized and threatening to the European. While much has gone wrong with present civilization – "an old bitch gone in the teeth," as Pound put it – going "back to nature," is suspect. That Conrad uses the "wilderness" to represent the tangled web of desire and corruptibility within, also indicates his sense of that external nature as demoralizing and poisonous.

## 8 "AN OUTPOST OF PROGRESS"

1 Stanley, himself a correspondent for the *New York Herald*, would go home and "report" on his travels in the *Herald* and in his books *How I Found Livingstone* (1872), *Through the Dark Continent* (1878), and *In Darkest Africa* (1890), all of which worked to justify the colonizing work, particularly King Leopold's, in Africa. The natives in this discourse are either intransigent savages who stupidly resist Europe's civilizing efforts, or commendably cooperative servants. (As Mannoni's discussion makes clear, Stanley's apprehension of the Other as either Caliban or Ariel is at least as old as Prospero; here it is just one more version of North America's "bad" and "good" Indians.) It was Stanley's task to go up the Congo in 1877 and procure the surrounding land for King Leopold. He did so by making "treaties" with over 400 native kings and chiefs by which they unknowingly surrendered their land. Like the "wedding certificate" in Stevenson's novel *The Beach at Falesá*, the writing concealed its treacherous intention and disguised the real project as enlightened benevolence, "masquerading philanthropy" indeed.

2 Mahood notes contemporary counterparts also, arguing that Conrad was remembering the events of 1890 through the events of 1895, specifically the Stokes affair. Charles Stokes was executed in the Eastern Congo in 1895, under orders of a State official, for supplying guns to an Afro-Arab slaver. Some felt justice had been done to a dangerous gunrunner. Others saw him "as an exemplary character who had been forced to abandon his vocation as a missionary in order to ensure the future of his eleven-year-old daughter (Mahood, *Colonial Encounter*, p. 9).

Mahood chronicles other disclosures of the 1890s that informed Conrad's remembering of 1890, for example that of Herbert Ward (a member of Stanley's Emin Pasha Relief Expedition). Ward revealed in 1890 that the Congo Free State – that all of Europe helped create, after all – was trading Africans for ivory, the very subject of the second installment of "An Outpost of Progress." That so few of these disclosures were seriously attended to, that the Jubilees, for example, took precedence over any of these reports, is pertinent to "Heart of Darkness" and its concern with the suppression of dangerous truths.

## 9 "HEART OF DARKNESS"

1 In an essay that argues forcefully for Conrad's own racism, Achebe's point is that travellers "with closed minds can tell us little except about themselves." Conrad was "blinkered" with "xenophobia," Achebe asserts, but "even those not blinkered ... can be astonishingly blind." As an example he cites Marco Polo who returned from China and wrote nothing about the flourishing art of printing, then unknown in Europe, or about the Great Wall. He somehow hadn't noticed either; presumably not in his experience, they were simply unavailable to him. "An Image of Africa: Racism in Conrad's *Heart of Darkness,*" *The Massachusetts Review*, 18 (1977), pp. 782–794. For the already constructed "East," see Said's *Orientalism.*

2 See also Pittock. Mahood also notices in "Heart of Darkness" the influence of contemporary tales of exotic adventure – among them works by Haggard – and notes in Conrad "a ninetyish zest for chilling our spines" (p. 29). She criticizes Conrad for being a victim of fiction himself, condemning the stereotypes he perpetuates here of an Africa already sensationalized by contemporary tales. His depiction of Africa as lacking social restraint is clearly derived from popular fiction, rather than fact, as she demonstrates. Nonetheless, she finds that the novel transcends these genre constraints and that it is a "forthright indictment of the colonialists' wanton disruption of African life" (p. 15).

3 In their study of the typescript and the holograph of "Heart of Darkness," Marion Michael and Wilkes Berry conclude that many of the changes, accidentals and substantives, worked to emphasize a conversational, story-telling quality and to underscore the relationship between the audience and the narrator.

4 The frequent preference for "The End of the Tether" to the other two stories might well have been a kind of attack on Marlow who narrates, within a frame narrator, both "Youth" and "Heart of Darkness," often referred to disapprovingly as "Mr. Conrad's convention." The *TLS* reviewer found "Tether" the best because it was "less clever and much less precious."

5 It was only in 1957, twelve years before Lawrence Graver's work, *Conrad's Short Fiction*, that A. J. Guerard felt compelled to correct what he felt had been an oversight or misreading until then: "it is time to recognize that the story is not primarily about Kurtz or about the brutality of Belgian officials but about Marlow its narrator" (p. 37).

6 For a close study of the ways in which "Heart of Darkness" narrates the failure of idealism, see Jeremy Hawthorn, *Narrative Technique and Ideological Commitment*, chapter 6.

7 As Hunt Hawkins' research makes clear and as Conrad's *Congo Diary*

reveals, Conrad saw colonial brutality on his trip up the Congo in 1890. What he witnessed – forced labor and inflicted violence – others did too, but few who returned to Europe reported what they had seen in King Leopold's "Free State." According to Hawkins, "even the missionaries, whose presence depended on Leopold's goodwill, hesitated to reveal what was going on" (p. 96). The few who spoke out about the atrocities – Roger Casement and George Washington Williams, for example – were the exceptions who proved the rule, and although their open letters and reports contributed to anti-Congo agitation carried on in the press between 1895 and 1897 especially, little came of those reports and agitation (see also John Hope Franklin).

8 Employing an extended analogy between the writer and the producer assembling his drama, Benita Parry illuminates the ways in which Conrad's "production" emphasizes the bizarre and unusual. She concludes that readers "acquainted with colonialism's doctrines and the official version of its aspiration and practice are thus invited to make new and conscious judgments of received assumptions and reported conditions because these have been transmuted as strange and astonishing" (p. 24).

9 Another issue that entangles Marlow here, and probably Conrad as well, is that of current alternatives to European incursion in Africa. Many conscientious "Little Englanders" who advocated non-intervention, for a variety of motives, found themselves often deeply conflicted over the question of withdrawal. Many expressed the opinion in the daily press that while intervention in the first place might have been a mistake, pulling out now would be disastrous. Thus the editor of *The Gentleman's Magazine* speaks of the "immediate resumption of cannibalistic orgies" if British forces were to withdraw from Kumassi and Benin. Nor can other European countries abandon ship at this point, the writer continues: "To the African the massacres, so revolting to a European, constitute the solemn discharge of a religious duty, and the only method by which they can be stamped out is by the sternest measures of repression, accompanied by the inculcation of more enlightened ideas. Withdraw English, French, or German rule, and the worst forms of sacrifice would become universal" (*The Gentleman's Magazine* (November, 1898): 518–519). Molly Mahood speaks at some length about the Benin affair of the previous year – 1897, the Jubilee year – and of the ways it was used to demonstrate "the need for the white man to assume the burden of colonial rule" (p. 30). She recognizes this acknowledgement of the burden in Marlow's affirmation that the earth is a place where we must "breathe dead hippo, so to speak, and not be contaminated..."

10 "Rescue," as a self-justifying intrusion in which "one os us" is saved from Africa's dark forces, was the operating motif in many factual accounts of current interest as well. Henry Morton Stanley, who had claimed the British public's attention in his "rescue" of David

Livingstone in late 1871, was asked to lead the Emin Pasha Relief Expedition. Mounted in 1886, this rescue effort occupied much public attention in the late 1880s and into the 90s. Rumors of disaster and of duplicity, letters from staff members, conflicting dispatches from Stanley, reports of Native treachery, the "rescue" proved newsworthy for some time. In large part, that rescue attempt was undertaken out of a national conscience made uneasy by its failure to save General Gordon in Khartoum, a victim of the same Mahdist uprisings that purportedly threatened Emin Pasha. The early vacillation of opinion over the necessity of committing British troops in the Sudan, followed by the rising tide of public sentiment in the spring, summer and fall of 1884 in favor of such a move, a desire stymied by Gladstone's government that was loathe to act decisively, until too late, the subsequent accusations, justifications, and regrets, all constituted a compelling conversation carried on in the pages of the popular press for years to come.

11 That Stanley's purported "rescue" of Livingstone was, in fact, an elaborate publicity maneuver for *The New York Herald*, is treated at length in Simmons' *Livingstone and Africa*, p. 140f.

## CODA

1 Fiction, it seems, allowed Conrad to tell truths that were perhaps unavailable to him in his various letter-writing modes. Ever aware of the rhetorical occasion, he modulated the subject, the tone, and the point of view accordingly. Thus he admitted in a letter written to a Polish friend, Mme. Angele Zagorska – and written in Polish – in December of 1899 that his feelings about the Boer war were extremely complex. Although he sympathized with a people who were fighting for their freedom, he wrote her, he doubted the Dutch – an essentially "despotic" people – understood the idea of liberty at all. He felt that actually liberty could "only be found under the English flag all over the world" (Karl, *Letters*, II, p. 230). The nationalistic sentiments here are entirely consonant with Polish thinking at the time. But at the same time, in a letter, already referred to in chapter 4, to his English friend, Ted Sanderson, he takes a more real-politic, practical stance in sharing his conviction that the war was creating, rather than solving, a situation that the country would tire of because of the "ruthless repression" that would necessarily accompany and follow it. "The *reasonable English ideals* (I am quoting Sir F. Milner's words) are not attained in that way. Their instruments are time and deep-seated convictions of the race, – the expansive force of its enterprise and its morality," and he goes on to take a strategic interest in the war, wishing he had a better map, and wondering how exactly Buller and Kitchener will proceed now (Karl, *Letters*, II, pp. 211, 212).

2 It was Garnett's laudatory article in the *Spectator* (1904) that was responsible for the success of *The Purple Land*'s second edition in 1904 after its initial publication twenty years earlier, when it received little

attention. Schreiner's novel, which beat no imperial drum, did not do nearly as well as that other, more exciting African fiction, *King Solomon's Mines*, that appeared two years later in 1885 (Cohen, *Rider Haggard*, p. 90).

Interestingly, with the advantage of almost ninety years hindsight, Patrick Brantlinger also sees Schreiner's voice as an alternative to the "spread-eaglism" of the day. He speaks of "the unsung heroes" of his book, *The Rule of Darkness*, as "those Victorian and Edwardian opponents of imperialism, such as Hobson, William Morris, and Olive Schreiner, who expressed a similar vision. They were always in the minority, though sometimes able to win local skirmishes" (p. 16).

3 The most objected-to passage, one on which the entire novel turns, concerned the "marriage contract" by which the white trader, Wiltshire, might possess a native girl, Uma. Based on his own experience in the Gilberts, Stevenson had noted that the women were all legitimately married. "It is true that the certificate of one, when she proudly showed it, proved to run thus, that she was 'married for one night,' and her gracious partner was at liberty to 'send her to hell' the next morning; but she was none the wiser or the worse for the dastardly trick" (Stevenson, *Letters and Miscellanies*, p. 289). His fictional certificate read similarly, but the editor of *The London Illustrated News*, Clement Shorter would not have it. As the editor of "a family newspaper" he felt it "his duty" to delete it (Menikoff, *Stevenson*, pp. 86, 87). Such "dastardly" behavior did not accord with either accepted Victorian modes of conduct or with the dominant version of English benevolence and heroism in the tropics.

4 Interestingly, it was Ford Madox Ford who wrote the very appreciative preface to Rhys' first publication, a volume of stories entitled *The Left Bank* (1927).

5 Achebe argues that, in fact, much African fiction now, bent on exposing and reversing stereotypes from within, is aimed primarily at African audiences. In his essay, "The Novelist as Teacher," he points to the sales figures for a few of his novels to prove that, indeed, the African writer is under no compulsion to write for foreign audiences. "Last year [1964] the pattern of sales of *Things Fall Apart* in the cheap paperback edition was as follows: about 800 copies in Britain; 20,000 in Nigeria; and about 2,500 in all other places. The same pattern was true also of *No Longer at Ease*" (*Hopes and Impediments*, p. 41).

Thus Sartre's understanding of Fanon's project, that while the writing of the colonized (and formerly colonized) meant to "talk back," its audience was not foreign. "Fanon has nothing in for you at all," Sartre tells his European audience. "…he speaks of you often, never to you…an ex-native, French-speaking, bends that language to new requirements, makes use of it, and speaks to the colonized only: 'Natives of all underdeveloped countries, unite!' (Fanon, *Wretched of the Earth*, p. 10).

# Bibliography

Achebe, Chinua. "An Image of Africa: Racism in Conrad's 'Heart of Darkness.'" *The Massachusetts Review*, 18 (1977): 782–794.
*Hopes and Impediments*. New York: Doubleday, 1989.

Adams, H. C. *The Wonder Book of Travellers' Tales*. New York: Liveright Publishing Corp., 1936.

Allen, William. "G. A. Henty." *Cornhill*, 1,082 (Winter 1974/75): 71–100.

Altick, Richard D. *The English Common Reader: A Social History of the Mass Reading Public 1800–1900*. Chicago: The University of Chicago Press, 1957.

Arendt, Hannah. *The Origins of Totalitarianism*. New York: Harcourt, Brace & World, Inc., 1966.

Arnold, Guy. *Held Fast for England: G. A. Henty, Imperialist Boys' Writer*. London: Hamish Hamilton, 1980.

Baines, Jocelyn. *Joseph Conrad: A Critical Biography*. New York: McGraw-Hill Book Company, 1960.

Bakhtin, Mikhail, M. *The Dialogic Imagination*. Austin: University of Texas Press, 1981.

Ballantyne, Robert Michael. *Black Ivory: A Tale of Adventure among the Slavers of East Africa*. 1873. Chicago: Afro-Am Press, 1969.
*The Coral Island*. 1857. Intro J. M. Barrie, London: James Nisbet and Co., Ltd., 1913.
*Hudson Bay or Everyday Life in the Wilds of North America*. 1848. London: Thomas Nelson and Sons, 1879.
*Martin Rattler*. London: Blackie and Son Ltd., 1858.
*Shifting Winds: A Story of the Sea*. New York & Chicago: Franklin Publishing Co., 1866.
*Snowflakes and Sunbeams; or, the Young Fur Traders*. 1856. London: Ward, Lock & Co. Ltd., 1901.
*Ungava: A Tale of Esquimau Land*. 1857. London: T. Nelson & Sons, 1895.

Barrow, John, ed. *Captain Cook's Voyages of Discovery*. London: J. M. Dent & Sons Ltd., 1906.

Beaglehole, J. C. *The Life of Captain James Cook*. Stanford: Stanford University Press, 1974.

Benjamin, Walter. *Illuminations*. 1955. New York: Schocken Books, 1969.

Bennett, George. *The Concept of Empire: Burke to Attlee, 1774–1947*. London:

Adam and Charles Black, 1953. Vol. 6 of *The British Political Tradition*. Ed. Alan Bullock and F. W. Deakin.

Bhabha, Homi, K., ed. *Nation and Narration*. London: Routledge, 1990.

Blackburn, William, ed. *Joseph Conrad: Letters to William Blackwood and David S. Meldrum*. Durham, North Carolina: Duke University Press, 1958.

Bolt, Christine. *Victorian Attitudes to Race*. London: Routledge & Kegan Paul, 1971.

Boswell, James. *Life of Johnson*. 1791. Oxford: Oxford University Press, 1953.

Bourne, Kenneth. *Palmerston: The Early Years, 1784–1841*. New York: Macmillan Publishing Co., Inc., 1982.

Brantlinger, Patrick. *Rule of Darkness: British Literature and Imperialism, 1830–1914*. Ithaca: Cornell University Press, 1988.

"Victorians and Africans: The Genealogy of the Myth of the Dark Continent." *Critical Inquiry*, 12 (Autumn 1985): 166–203.

Brooke, James. *Letter from Borneo with Notices of the County and Its Inhabitants*. London: L. & G. Seeley, 1842.

*Narrative of Events in Borneo and Celebes*. Ed. Capt. Rodney Mundy, R. N. London: J. Murray, 1848.

Buckley, Jerome Hamilton. *William Ernest Henley: A Study in the "Counter-Decadence" of the 'Nineties*. New York: Octagon Books, 1971.

Churchill, Winston S. *A Roving Commission*. New York: Charles Scribner's Sons, 1951.

Clemens, Florence. "Conrad's Favorite Bedside Book." *The South Atlantic Quarterly*, xxxviii, 3 (July 1939): 305–315.

Clifford, James. *The Predicament of Culture*. Cambridge, Mass.: Harvard University Press, 1988.

Cloete, Stuart. *African Portraits*. Cape Town: Constantin Publishers, 1969.

Cohen, Morton. *Rider Haggard*. London: Hutchinson & Co. Ltd., 1960.

Cohen, Morton, ed. *Rudyard Kipling to Rider Haggard: The Record of a Friendship*. London: Hutchinson & Co. Ltd., 1965.

Colvin, Sir Sidney. *Memories & Notes of Persons & Places, 1852–1912*. New York: Charles Scribner's Sons, 1922.

Conrad, Joseph. *Almayer's Folly*. 1895. New York: Doubleday, Page & Co., 1924.

*Congo Diary*. Ed. Zdzislaw Najder. New York: Doubleday, 1978.

*Conrad's Prefaces to his Works*, intro. Edward Garnett. 1937. New York: Haskell House Publishers Ltd., 1971.

*Last Essays*. New York: Doubleday & Page, 1926.

*Lord Jim: A Romance*. 1900. New York: Doubleday & Page, 1924.

*The Mirror of the Sea*. 1906. New York: Doubleday & Page, 1924.

*Notes on Life and Letters*. New York: Doubleday & Page, 1923.

*An Outcast of the Islands*. 1896. New York: Doubleday & Page, 1924.

*A Personal Record*. 1912. New York: Doubleday & Page, 1923.

*The Rescue*. 1920. New York: Doubleday & Page, 1924.

*The Shadow Line*. 1917. New York: Doubleday & Page, 1924.

*Tales of Hearsay.* New York: Doubleday & Page, 1925.

*Tales of Unrest.* 1898. New York: Doubleday & Doran, 1928.

*'Twixt land & Sea Tales.* 1912. London: J. M. Dent & Sons Ltd., 1923.

*Youth.* 1902. New York: Doubleday & Page, 1924.

Cruse, Amy. *The Victorians and Their Reading.* Boston: Houghton Mifflin Co., 1935.

Curtin, Philip. *The Image of Africa.* Madison, 1964.

Dalziel, Margaret. *Popular Fiction 100 Years Ago.* London: Cohen & West, 1957.

Dangerfield, George. *The Strange Death of Liberal England.* New York: Capricorn Books, 1935.

Dark, Sidney. *Robert Louis Stevenson.* New York: Haskell House Publishers, Ltd., 1971.

Davidson, Basil. *Africa in History.* New York: Macmillan, 1968.

Deane, Seamus, Ed. *Nationalism, Colonialism and Literature.* Minneapolis: University of Minnesota Press, 1990.

Derrida, Jacques. "Racism's Last Word." *Critical Inquiry,* 12 (Autumn 1985): 290–299.

Eagleton, Terry. *Criticism and Ideology.* London: NLB, Humanities Press, 1976.

*Exiles and Emigrés.* New York:Schocken Books, 1970.

Eigner, Edwin M. *Robert Louis Stevenson and Romantic Tradition.* Princeton, New Jersey: Princeton University Press, 1966.

Etherington, Norman. *Rider Haggard.* Boston: Twayne Publishers, 1984.

Fanon, Frantz. *The Wretched of the Earth.* Intro. Jean-Paul Sartre. New York: Grove Press, Inc., 1963.

Fernando, Lloyd. "Conrad's Eastern Expatriates: A New Version of his Outcasts." *PMLA,* 91, 1(January 1976): 78–90.

Fleishman, Avrom. *Conrad's Politics: Community and Anarchy in the Fiction of Joseph Conrad.* Baltimore: The Johns Hopkins University Press, 1967.

Flora, Joseph M. *William Ernest Henley.* New York: Twayne Publishers, Inc., 1970.

Ford, Ford Madox. *Joseph Conrad: A Personal Remembrance.* 1924. New York: Octagon Books, Inc., 1965.

*Portraits from Life.* Chicago: Henry Regnery Company, 1937.

Forster, E. M. *A Passage to India.* New York: Harcourt, Brace & World, Inc., 1924.

Foucault, Michel. *The Archaeology of Knowledge and the Discourse on Language.* Trans. A. M. Sheridan Smith. New York: Pantheon Books, 1972.

Franco, Jean. "The Limits of the Liberal Imagination: *One Hundred Years of Solitude* and *Nostromo.*" *Punto de Contacto/Point of Contact,* 1, 1(December 1975): 4–16.

Franklin, John Hope. *George Washington Williams: A Biography.* Chicago: The University of Chicago Press, 1985.

Frye, Northrup. *The Anatomy of Criticism.* New Jersey: Princeton University Press, 1957.

Fussell, Paul. *The Great War and Modern Memory*. London: Oxford University Press, 1975.

Gallagher, John. *The Decline, Revival and Fall of the British Empire*. Cambridge: Cambridge University Press, 1982.

Garnett, Edward. *Friday Nights: Literary Criticisms and Appreciations*. New York: Alfred A. Knopf, 1922.

Garnett, Edward, ed. *Letters from Joseph Conrad, 1895–1924*. Indianapolis: Bobbs-Merrill Co., 1928.

Gates, Henry Louis Jr. "Writing 'Race' and the Difference it Makes." *Critical Inquiry*, 12(Autumn 1985): 1–20.

Gide, André. *Travels in the Congo*. Berkeley: University of California Press, 1969.

Goonetilleke, D. C. R. A. *Joseph Conrad: Beyond Culture and Background*. London: Macmillan, 1990.

Gordan, John Dozier. *Joseph Conrad: The Making of a Novelist*. 1940. New York: Russell & Russell, Inc., 1963.

"The Rajah Brooke and Joseph Conrad." *Studies in Philology*, xxxv (October 1938): 613–34.

Graver, Lawrence. *Conrad's Short Fiction*. Berkeley: University of California Press, 1969.

Green, Martin. *Dreams of Adventure, Deeds of Empire*. New York: Basic Books, Inc., 1979.

Greene, Graham. *Journey without Maps*. 1936. Middlesex, England: Penguin Books, 1976.

*The Lost Childhood and Other Essays*. New York: The Viking Press, 1951.

Greenwood, Thomas. *Sunday School & Village Libraries*. 1892.

Guerard, Albert J. *Conrad the Novelist*. 1958. Cambridge, Massachusetts: Harvard University Press, 1965.

Haggard, H. Rider *Allan Quatermain*. 1887. Mattituck, New York: Ameron House, 1983.

*Cetywayo and his White Neighbors*. 1882. London: Kegan Paul, Trench, Trubner & Co., Ltd., 1896.

*The Days of My Life*. Ed. C. J. Longman. 2 vols. London: Longmans, 1926.

*King Solomon's Mines*. 1886. Barre, Massachusetts: Imprint Society, 1970.

*The Private Diaries of Sir H. Rider Haggard 1914–1925*. Ed. D. S. Higgins. New York:Stein and Day, 1980.

*She, A History of Adventure*. 1887. London: Collins, 1969.

"A Zulu War Dance." *Gentleman's Magazine*. (July–December, 1877): 94–107.

Hammond, Dorothy and Alta Jablow. *The Africa That Never Was*. New York: Twayne Publishers, Inc., 1970.

Harris, Wilson. "The Frontier on which *Heart of Darkness* Stands." *Heart of Darkness*. Ed. Robert Kimbrough. New York: W. W. Norton, 1988.

Hawkins, Hunt. "Conrad and Congolese Exploitation." *Conradiana* 13, 2 (1981): 94–100.

Hawthorn, Jeremy. *Joseph Conrad: Language and Fictional Self-Consciousness*. Lincoln, Nebraska: The University of Nebraska Press, 1979.

*Joseph Conrad: Narrative Technique and Ideological Commitment*. London: Edward Arnold, 1990.

Hay, Eloise Knapp. *The Political Novels of Joseph Conrad*. Chicago: The University of Chicago Press, 1963.

Heath, F. W., ed. *Churchill in his own Words: Years of Adventure*. New York: Capricorn Books, 1966.

Henty, G. A. *By Right of Conquest*. 1891. London: Latimer House Ltd., 1957.

*By Sheer Pluck, A Tale of the Ashanti War*. 1884. New York: A. L. Burt.

*On the Irrawaddy, A Story of the First Burmese War*. 1897. London: Blackie and Son, Ltd., 1912.

*Under Drake's Flag, A Tale of the Spanish Main*. 1883. New York: A. L. Burt Company.

*The Young Franc-Tireurs and Their Adventures in the Franco-Prussian War*. 1872. New York: A. L. Burt.

Herbert, T. Walter. *Marquesan Encounters: Melville and the Meaning of Civilization*. Cambridge, Massachusetts: Harvard University Press, 1980.

Hillier, Robert Irwin. *The South Seas Fiction of Robert Louis Stevenson*. Diss, University of New Hampshire, 1985. Ann Arbor: UMI, 1985. 8607458.

Hobson, J. A. *Imperialism: A Study*. London: George Allen & Unwin, Ltd., 1902.

Hogarth, Paul. *The Artist as Reporter*. London: Studio Vista, 1967.

Houghton, Walter E. *The Victorian Frame of Mind, 1830–1870*. New Haven: Yale University Press, 1957.

Humphries, Reynold. "The Discourse of Colonialism: Its Meaning & Relevance for Conrad's Fiction." *Conradiana*, 21, 2 (1989): 107–133.

James, Henry. *The Future of the Novel*. Ed. Leon Edel. New York: Vintage Books.

James, Louis. *Fiction for the Working Man, 1830–1850*. London: Oxford University Press, 1963.

JanMohamed, Abdul R. "The Economy of Manichean Allegory: The Function of Racial Difference in Colonialist Literature." *Critical Inquiry*, 12(Autumn 1985), 59–87.

*Manichean Aesthetics*. Amherst: University of Massachusetts Press, 1983.

Jeal, Tim. *Livingstone*. New York: G. P. Putnam's Sons, 1973.

Jean-Aubry, Gérard. *Joseph Conrad: Life and Letters*. 2 vols. New York: Doubleday, Page & Company, 1927, vol. 1.

*Manichean Aesthetics*. Amherst: University of Massachusetts Press, 1983.

Karl, Frederick R. and Laurence Davies, eds. *The Collected Letters of Joseph Conrad, 1861–1897*. Cambridge: Cambridge University Press, 1983. Vol. 2 (1983), vol. 2 (1986), vol. 3 (1988).

Katz, Wendy. *Rider Haggard and the Fiction of Empire*. Cambridge: Cambridge University Press, 1987.

Kay-Shuttleworth, James. *Sir James Kay-Shuttleworth on Popular Education*.

Ed. Trygue Tholfsen. New York: Teachers College Press, Columbia University, 1974.

Keppel, Henry. *Expedition to Borneo of H.M.S. Dido for the Suppression of Piracy: With Extracts from the Journal of James Brooke, Esq. of Sarawak (Now Agent for the British Government in Borneo).* 2 vols. London: Chapman and Hall, 1846.

Kiely, Robert. *Robert Louis Stevenson and the Fiction of Adventure.* Cambridge, Massachusetts: Harvard University Press, 1964.

Kingsley, Charles. *Westward Ho!* 1855. The Spencer Press.

Kingsley, F. E., ed. *Charles Kingsley: His Letters and Memories of his Life.* New York: Scribner, Armstrong & Company, 1877.

Kingsley, Mary. *West African Studies.* 1899. New York: Barnes & Noble, 1964.

Kipling, Rudyard. *Kim.* 1901. Intro. Edward W. Said, London: Penguin, 1987.

Knox-Shaw, Peter. *The Explorer in English Fiction.* London: Macmillan, 1987.

Lang, Andrew. *Essays in Little.* 1891. New York: AMS Press, Inc., 1968.

*Magic & Religion.* London: Longmans, Green, & Co., 1901.

Leavis, F. R. *The Great Tradition.* New York: New York University Press, 1969.

Ledyard, John. *A Journal of Captain Cook's Last Voyage.* 1783. Chicago: Quadrangle Books, 1963.

Lee, Robert F. *Conrad's Colonialism.* The Hague: Mouton, 1969.

Livingstone, David. *The Last Journals.* 1874. 2 vols. Westport, Connecticut: Greenwood Press, 1970.

*Livingstone's Private Journals, 1851–1853.* Berkeley: University of California Press, 1960.

*Missionary Travels and Researches in South Africa.*

Livingstone, David and Charles. *Narrative of an Expedition to the Zambesi and its Tributaries; and of the Discovery of the Lakes Shirwa and Nyassa, 1858–1864.* New York: Harper & Brothers, 1866.

Lucas, E. V. *The Colvins and their Friends.* New York: Charles Scribner's Sons, 1928.

McClintock, Captain Francis L., R.N. *The Voyage of the 'Fox' in the Arctic Seas: A Narrative of the Discovery of the Fate of Sir John Franklin and His Companions.* 1860. Rutland, Vermont: Charles E. Tuttle Company, 1972.

McClure, John A. *Kipling & Conrad: The Colonial Fiction.* Cambridge, Massachusetts: Harvard University Press, 1981.

Macmillan, Harold. *Winds of Change.* London: Macmillan, 1966.

Mahood, M. M. *The Colonial Encounter.* London: Rex Collings, 1977.

Maitland, A. *Speke.* London: Constable, 1971.

Mannoni, O. *Prospero and Caliban.* New York: Frederick A. Praeger, 1956.

Markham, Captain Albert Hastings, R.N., A.D.C. *Life of Sir John Franklin and the North-West Passage.* London: George Philip & Son, 1891.

Marra, John. *Journal of the Resolution's Voyage in 1771–1775.* 1775. New York: Da Capo Press, 1967.

Marryat, Frederick. *Masterman Ready.* 1841. London: George Routledge and Sons, Ltd.

*Mr. Midshipman Easy.* 1836. London: George Routledge and Sons, Ltd., 1896.

*Peter Simple.* 1834. London: George Routledge and Sons, Ltd., 1896.

Megaw, J. V. S., ed. *Employ'd as a Discoverer.* Sydney: Reed, 1971.

Menikoff, Barry. *Robert Louis Stevenson and 'The Beach of Falesá': A Study in Victorian Publishing.* Stanford, California: Stanford University Press, 1984.

Meyers, Jeffrey. *Fiction and the Colonial Experience.* New Jersey: Rowman and Littlefield, 1973.

Moorehead, Alan. *The Fatal Impact.* New York: Harper & Row, 1966.

Moser, Thomas. *Joseph Conrad: Achievement and Decline.* Hamden, Connecticut: Archon Books, 1966.

Michael, Marion and Wilkes Berry. "The Typescript of 'Heart of Darkness'." *Conradiana*, 12, 2 (1980): 147–154.

Morf, Gustav. *The Polish Heritage of Joseph Conrad.* 1930. New York: Haskell House, 1965.

Najder, Zdzislaw. *Joseph Conrad: A Chronicle.* New Jersey: Rutgers University Press, 1983.

Nazareth, Peter. "Out of Darkness: Conrad and Other Third World Writers." *Conradiana*, 14, 3 (1982): 173–187.

Nerlich, Michael. *Ideology of Adventure.* Vol. 1. Minneapolis: University of Minnesota Press, 1987.

Ngugi wa Thiong'o (James). *Decolonizing the Mind.* London: James Currey, 1986.

O'Neill, Kevin. *André Gide and the Roman D'Aventure.* Sidney: Sydney University Press, 1969.

Orwell, Sonia & Jan Angus, eds. *The Collected Essays of George Orwell.* 4 vols. New York: Harcourt, Brace & World, Inc, vol. 1.

Palmer, John A. *Joseph Conrad's Fiction: A Study in Literary Growth.* Ithaca, New York: Cornell University Press, 1968.

Pinsker, Sanford. *The Languages of Joseph Conrad.* Amsterdam: Rodopi N.V., 1978.

Pittock, Murray. "Rider Haggard & *Heart of Darkness.*" *Conradiana*, 19, 3 (1987): 206–208.

Poncins, Gontran de. *Kabloona.* New York: Reynal & Hitchcock, Inc., 1941.

Pratt, Mary Louise. "Scratches on the Face of the Country; or, What Mr. Barrow Saw in the Land of the Bushmen." *Critical Inquiry*, 12(Autumn 1985): 119–143.

Quale, Eric. *Ballantyne the Brave: A Victorian Writer and his Family.* London: Rupert Hart-Davis, 1967.

Rickman, John. *Journal of Captain Cook's Last Voyage to the Pacific Ocean.* 1781. New York: Da Capo Press, 1967.

Rotberg, Robert. *The Founder: Cecil Rhodes and the Pursuit of Power*. New York: Oxford University Press, 1988.

Ruppel, Richard. "*Heart of Darkness* and the Popular Exotic Stories of the 1890's" *Conradiana*, 21, 1 (1989): 3–14.

Ruskin, John. *The Works of John Ruskin*. Ed. E. T. Cook and Alexander Wedderburn. 39 vols. London: George Allen, 1905, vol. 20.

Said, Edward. "Intellectuals in the Post-Colonial World." *Salmagundi* (Spring-Summer 1986): 44–81.

*Joseph Conrad and the Fiction of Autobiography*. Cambridge, Mass.: Harvard University Press, 1966.

*Orientalism*. New York: Random House, 1978.

The Problem of Textuality: Two Exemplary Positions." *Critical Inquiry*, 4, 4 (Summer 1978): 673–714.

*The World, the Text, and the Critic*. Cambridge: Harvard University Press, 1983.

Salmon, Edward. *The Literature of the Empire*. New York: Henry Holt & Company, 1924. Vol. 7 of *The British Empire*, ed., Hugh Gunn, 12 vols.

Sarvan, Ponnuthurai. "Under African Eyes." *Joseph Conrad: Third World Perspectives*. Ed. Robert D. Hamner. Washington D.C.: Three Continents Press, 1990.

Schwarz, Daniel R. *Conrad: "Almayer's Folly" to "Under Western Eyes."* Ithaca, New York: Cornell University Press, 1980.

Sherry, Norman. *Conrad's Eastern World*. Cambridge: Cambridge University Press, 1966.

Sherry, Norman, ed. *Conrad: The Critical Heritage*. London: Routledge & Kegan Paul, 1973.

Simmons, Jack. *Livingstone & Africa*. London: English Universities Press Ltd., 1955.

Singh, D. S. Ranjit. *Brunei, 1839–1983*. Singapore: Oxford University Press, 1984.

Smith, Janet Adam, ed., *Henry James and Robert Louis Stevenson: A Record of Friendship & Criticism*. London: Rupert Hart-Davis, 1948.

Speke, Captain John. "The Discovery of the Victoria N'Yanza." October–November, 1859. *Travel, Adventure, and Sport from Blackwood's Magazine*. Edinburgh and London: William Blackwood and Sons.

*Journal of the Discovery of the Source of the Nile*. New York: Harper & Brothers, 1864.

*What Led to the Discovery of the Source of the Nile*. 1864. London: Frank Cass & Co., Ltd., 1967.

Stevenson, Robert Louis. *Treasure Island*. 1883. New York: Grosset & Dunlap, 1947.

*Letters to his Family and Friends*. Ed. Sidney Colvin. 2 vols. London: Methuen & Co., 1899.

*Letters & Miscellanies of Robert Louis Stevenson*. Vol. 19. New York: Charles Scribner's Sons, 1901.

228 Bibliography

*Vailima Letters.* Ed. Sidney Colvin. 1895. 2 vols. New York: Greenwood Press, 1969.

*The Works of Robert Louis Stevenson.* London: Chatto & Windus, 1912, vol. 18.

Street, Brian V. *The Savage in Literature: Representations of 'Primitive' Society in English Fiction 1858–1920.* London: Routledge & Kegan Paul, 1975.

Swearingen, Roger G. *The Prose Writings of Robert Louis Stevenson, A Guide.* Hamden, Connecticut: Archon Books, 1980.

Thomson, David. *England in the Nineteenth Century, 1815–1914.* Baltimore, Maryland: Penguin Books, 1950.

Thorburn, David. *Conrad's Romanticism.* New Haven: Yale University Press, 1974.

Todorov, Tzvetan. *The Conquest of America.* New York: Harper & Row, 1982.

"Knowledge in the Void: *Heart of Darkness.*" *Conradiana.* 21, 3 (1989): 161–172.

Torgovnick, Marianna. *Gone Primitive.* Chicago: University of Chicago Press, 1990.

Tylor, Edward B. *Primitive Culture.* 1871. London: J. Murry, 1929.

Uffelman, Larry K. *Charles Kingsley.* Boston: Twayne Publishers, 1979.

Wallace, Alfred Russel. *The Malay Archipelago.* New York: Harper & Brothers, 1869.

Warner, Oliver. *Captain Marryat: A Rediscovery.* London: Constable and Company, Ltd., 1953.

Watt, Ian. *Conrad in the Nineteenth Century.* Berkeley: University of California Press, 1979.

Watts, C. T. *The Deceptive Text.* Sussex: The Harvester Press, 1984.

*Joseph Conrad: A Literary Life.* New York: St. Martin's Press, 1989.

Watts, Cedric ed. *Joseph Conrad's Letters to R. B. Cunninghame Graham.* Cambridge: Cambridge University Press, 1969.

Wharton, Captain W. J. L., ed. *Captain Cook's Journal During his First Voyage Round the World Made in H. M. Bark "Endeavour."* 1768–71. London: Elliot Stock, 1893.

Willy, Todd G. "The Conquest of the Commodore: Conrad's Rigging of 'The Nigger' for the Henley Regatta." *Conradiana.* 17, 3 (1985): 163–182.

Young, Vernon. "Lingard's Folly: The Lost Subject." *Kenyon Review,* 15 (Autumn, 1953): 522–539.

Zweig, Paul. *The Adventurer.* New York: Basic Books, Inc., 1974.

# Index